MW01121937

Germany, Civilian Power and the New Europe

New Perspectives in German Studies

General Editors: Professor Michael Butler, Head of the Department of German Studies, University of Birmingham and Professor William Paterson, Director of the Institute of German Studies, University of Birmingham

Over the last twenty years the concept of German studies has undergone major transformation. The traditional mixture of language and literary studies, related very closely to the discipline as practised in German universities, has expanded to embrace history, politics, economics and cultural studies. The conventional boundaries between all these disciplines have become increasingly blurred, a process which has been accelerated markedly since German unification in 1989/90.

New Perspectives in German Studies, developed in conjunction with the Institute for German Studies at the University of Birmingham, has been designed to respond precisely to this trend of the interdisciplinary approach to the study of German and to cater for the growing interest in Germany in the context of European integration. The books in this series will focus on the modern period, from 1750 to the present day.

Titles include:

Michael Butler and Robert Evans (*editors*)
THE CHALLENGE OF GERMAN CULTURE
Essays Presented to Wilfried van der Will

Michael Butler, Malcolm Pender and Joy Charnley (*editors*)
THE MAKING OF MODERN SWITZERLAND 1848–1998

Wolf-Dieter Eberwein and Karl Kaiser (*editors*)
GERMANY'S NEW FOREIGN POLICY
Decision-Making in an Interdependent World

Jonathan Grix
THE ROLE OF THE MASSES IN THE COLLAPSE OF THE GDR

Henning Tewes
GERMANY, CIVILIAN POWER AND THE NEW EUROPE
Enlarging Nato and the European Union

Maiken Umbach
GERMAN FEDERALISM
Past, Present, Future

New Perspectives in German Studies
Series Standing Order ISBN 0–333–92430–4 hardcover
Series Standing Order ISBN 0–333–92434–7 paperback
(*outside North America only*)

You can receive future titles in this series as they are published by placing a standing order. Please contact your bookseller or, in case of difficulty, write to us at the address below with your name and address, the title of the series and the ISBN quoted above.

Customer Services Department, Macmillan Distribution Ltd, Houndmills, Basingstoke, Hampshire RG21 6XS, England

Germany, Civilian Power and the New Europe

Enlarging Nato and the European Union

Henning Tewes
Director, Konrad-Adenauer Foundation
Warsaw
Poland

First published 2002 by
PALGRAVE
Houndmills, Basingstoke, Hampshire RG21 6XS and
175 Fifth Avenue, New York, N. Y. 10010
Companies and representatives throughout the world

PALGRAVE is the new global academic imprint of
St. Martin's Press LLC Scholarly and Reference Division and
Palgrave Publishers Ltd (formerly Macmillan Press Ltd).

ISBN 0–333–96508–6

This book is printed on paper suitable for recycling and made from fully managed and sustained forest sources.

A catalogue record for this book is available from the British Library.

Library of Congress Cataloging-in-Publication Data
Tewes, Henning.
    Germany, civilian power and the new Europe : enlarging Nato and the European union / Henning Tewes.
       p. cm. — (New perspectives in German studies)
    Includes bibliographical references and index.
    ISBN 0–333–96508–6
       1. Germany—Foreign relations—Europe, Eastern. 2. Europe, Eastern—Foreign relations—Germany. 3. Security, International. 4. Europe, Eastern—Economic conditions—1989- 5. Germany—Economic policy—1990. 6. Post–communism—Europe, Central. 7. Post–communism—Europe, Eastern. 8. European Union—Europe, Central. 9. European Union—Europe, Eastern. 10. Civil–military relations. I. Title. II. Series.

DD290.3 .T49 2001
327.43—dc21
                                                          2001036093

10   9   8   7   6   5   4   3   2   1
11 10 09 08 07 06 05 04 03 02

Printed and bound in Great Britain by
Antony Rowe Ltd, Chippenham, Wiltshire

For my parents,
Dorothea and Dieter Tewes,
with love and gratitude

Contents

Preface

At different stages, the research for this thesis was funded by the Economic and Social Research Council, the Institute for German Studies at the University of Birmingham and the Richard Blackwell Scholarship Fund. I am grateful for their support. When researching in Germany I was generously supported by the Institut für Europäische Politik (then in Bonn), in particular by Barbara Lippert, Sven Graf Arnswald and Peter Becker. The Library and Press Archive of the Konrad Adenauer Foundation in Bonn proved tremendously resourceful, and in the persons of Frau Duffner, Frau Kübler and Frau Bestler tremendously helpful too. My sister Dörte was an unfailing reserve of emotional and organizational strength. No brother could wish for a better sister, no friend for a more spirited companion.

The research conducted in Poland was the most difficult part of the project. It enabled me to add East Central European perspectives to German and British ones, however, and to gain an angle on a set of events that were, for all intents and purposes, still ongoing at the time of writing. I am indebted to the Warsaw Office of the Konrad Adenauer Foundation for providing the necessary lightness of touch and organizational support. That I would return in a different function and with a different task was then not within the realms of my immediate imagination, and is something I have never regretted.

Since its creation in 1994 the Institute for German Studies at the University of Birmingham has assembled a group of magnificent experts on German politics. Talking 'shop' with Vladimir Handl, Adrian Hyde-Price, Charlie Jeffery, Kerry Longhurst, Penny Turnbull and Marcin Zaborowski was both encouragement and control, both carrot and stick, in crucial phases of this project.

I am grateful to Suzanne Nicholas, Tommy Jobbyselliat and Michael Dadgadlivbil Aylwin for checking my style and for attempting to cure me of the continental disease of using big words for small matters.

The main part of the thinking behind this book was done in Oxford, where, because of teaching duties and old friendships, I continued to live. I am grateful to Keble College for appointing me to a College Lectureship in Politics. It helped in so many ways. I apologize to Jonathan Lipkin for inflicting the entire manuscript upon him – repeatedly – and thank him for applying his ceaselessly inquisitive and entirely unforgiving intellect to it. My personal gratitude and academic respect extend to many of those who taught me and discussed with me the history and politics of postwar Europe: Ann Branch, Benjamin Cope, Marina Costa Lobo, Richard Crampton, Anne Deighton, James Forder, Piers Ludlow, Anand Menon, Gaëtane Nihoul, Nozomi Okuyama, Jane Rempel, Marco Veremis, Josefine Wallat and Jonathan Wright. The learning curve was steep.

Willie Paterson's contagious enthusiasm for life in general, and this project in particular, was a constant source of encouragement, and did much to imbue me with the energy needed to finish it on time. Peter Pulzer was the guardian and benefactor of this book from the very beginning. With his dry humour, acute intelligence and healthy scepticism, he ensured that the trees did not grow into the sky. Perhaps he taught me much more than I will ever know. It was an honour and a pleasure.

List of Abbreviations

BdV	Bund der Vertriebenen
CAP	Common Agricultural Policy
CDU	Christlich Demokratische Union
CFE Treaty	Conventional Forces in Europe Treaty
CSCE	Conference on Security and Cooperation in Europe
CSU	Christlich Soziale Union
DBV	Deutscher Bauernverband
DM	Deutsche Mark
DG	Directorate-General
DNVP	Deutschnationale Volkspartei
EBRD	European Bank for Reconstruction and Development
EC	European Community
ECSC	European Community for Coal and Steel
EDC	European Defence Community
EEC	European Economic Community
Efta	European Free Trade Area
EMS	European Monetary System
EMU	Economic and Monetary Union
ERM	Exchange Rate Mechanism
EU	European Union
FDI	Foreign Direct Investment
FDP	Freie Demokratische Partei
FRG	Federal Republic of Germany
GATT	General Agreement on Tariffs and Trade
GDP	Gross Domestic Product
GDR	German Democratic Republic
G7/G8	Group of Seven/Eight Summit of Leading Industrial States
IGC	Intergovernmental Conference
INF Treaty	Intermediate-range Nuclear Force Treaty
NACC	North Atlantic Cooperation Council
Nato	North Atlantic Treaty Organization
NSdAP	Nationalsozialistische deutsche Arbeiterpartei
OECD	Organization for Economic Cooperation and Development
OEEC	Organization for European Economic Cooperation
OSCE	Organization for Security and Cooperation in Europe

PDS	Partei des Demokratischen Sozialismus
Phare	Pologne et Hongrie: Actions pour la Reconversion Économique
QMV	Qualified Majority Voting
SPD	Sozialdemokratische Partei Deutschlands
START	Strategic Arms Reductions Treaty
WEU	Western European Union
WTO	World Trade Organization
UN	United Nations

Introduction

In 1990, the future of Europe's international politics hinged on two questions. One was how unification would affect the conduct of German foreign policy. The other was whether, and how, those institutions that had given security and prosperity to Western Europe during the Cold War would now do the same for the entire continent. The intersection of these questions is the topic of this book. It asks, quite plainly, what made Germany's policies towards its immediate eastern neighbours tick. It answers that German policies were driven by the motivations, and the inhibitions, of a Civilian Power.

When the Berlin Wall fell, Berlin became a city literally overnight. Germany became a unified country in less than a year. Whether Europe would also become one continent again, however, was less clear. The freedom for which the peoples of Eastern Europe had fought did not necessarily contain solutions for the unsettled international politics of East Central Europe. And for much of the period under discussion, the Western institutions that became increasingly attractive to the nascent East European democracies did not quite know how to handle their surge in popularity. When Vaclav Havel warned at the Nato headquarters in Brussels that 'an alliance of democratic states cannot close itself off from like-minded neighbouring states for ever', he was met with stunned silence. And when François Mitterrand said in Prague a few months later that an Eastern enlargement of the European Community (as it then was) would take *des dizaines des années*, he only gave voice to the widespread anxiety and disorientation that existed about the international politics of the western part of the continent.[1]

Considering the anxiety and disorientation that abounded immediately after German unification, the development of German policies towards East Central Europe was a successful and happy one. The bilateral treaties that Germany signed with each of its neighbouring countries established the basis for good neighbourliness and friendly cooperation. Although ghosts from the past continued to haunt Czech–German and Polish–German relations, there was clear and visible overall progress. Especially in those countries that had to deal with the legacies of occupation, expulsions and border changes, it was not uncommon to hear in the late 1990s that the quality of relations with Germany bordered on the miraculous. But above all, German policy towards East Central Europe was successful because it laid the foundations for the Western integration of these countries. When Poland, the Czech Republic and Hungary became members of Nato on 12 March 1999, many in Poland thought that this was the most important event in Polish history since the advent of Christianity in 966. At least for Poland, if not also for other East Central European countries, membership of Nato and the European Union was more than a foreign policy option. It was a civilizational choice. Western integration would help to ensure the most basic values of European culture: the rule of law, liberal democracy, security and prosperity. It was by no means clear in 1989/90 that Germany would become a promoter of these East Central European aims, nor indeed that it would be capable of investing the kind of political capital that was needed to attain them.

In the scholarly debate that ensued after 1990, opinions differed on how unification would affect German foreign policy. One set of observers hoped, or feared, that the removal of external constraints, in conjunction with Germany's geographical centrality in Europe, would render German foreign policy more independent and more assertive.[2] Other observers argued that the key influences on German foreign policy would be those that had affected the Federal Republic's foreign policy before 1990. Hence unified Germany, though expected to become more important, was expected to pursue its aims multilaterally, cooperatively and peacefully. On this line of reasoning, a contribution by the German political scientist Hanns Maull attracted considerable attention.

Maull claimed that Germany, just like Japan, constituted a new type of state, a 'Civilian Power'.[3] These new Civilian Powers, Maull argued, found it much easier to shed sovereignty to supranational institutions because of their postwar experience. They had also learnt, from their own experience, that the costs of military force were dangerously high and should be avoided if at all possible. Finally, Maull pointed out that the foreign policy of Civilian Powers was strongly tied to the values that governed their domestic politics.

Since the strong focus on nation states and military force was, in Maull's view, obsolescent, the Federal Republic's tradition of military reticence and multilateralism was a trend to be followed. In an international environment in which traditional forms of conducting foreign policy were undermined, Civilian Powers were ideally placed for dealing with new challenges. In contrast to those who argued that Germany's unification and its central position in Europe demanded a shedding of the Federal Republic's old foreign policy habits, Maull contended that Germany was, in fact, a prototype, which other states should emulate. We may add that the civilianization of international politics, at least in the 'OECD world', has been a general trend since the late 1940s. This trend was reinforced by the end of the Cold War, but did not originate from it. With the increasing significance of frameworks of cooperation and integration, like Nato, the OSCE, the European Union and the G7/ G8 summits, this civilianization is now functionally more intensive than it ever has been. With the democratization of Southern Europe, Latin America and Eastern Europe, it is also geographically more extensive. Since this is so, a rigid separation between Civilian Powers and other states is impossible. On the contrary, all states in the 'OECD world' pursue a more civilized foreign policy now than they once did. Our reference to Germany as a Civilian Power, therefore, is merely to suggest that Germany is particularly close to the ideal type.

Due to a lack of empirical material, the literature on German foreign policy published immediately after unification was, for the most part, either predictive or prescriptive. Few contributions contained analytical insights. This was also true for Maull's 'Civilian Power' argument. It implied that the decisive influences on German foreign policy were the establishment of democracy in the Federal Republic, and the patterns that characterized the Federal Republic's foreign policy: non-military conflict resolution, multilateralism and democratic values. But this claim was neither empirically illustrated nor theoretically developed. The fact that Maull views Germany's domestic institutions and historical experience as key sources of its foreign policy raises important theoretical questions which will be addressed in the first chapter of this book.

There are two reasons why German policies towards East Central Europe were chosen as a test case of the Civilian Power argument. First, as indicated above, the international politics of East Central Europe were significant for the international politics of Europe as a whole. In 1989/ 90, the beginning of the period under discussion here, the international politics of East Central Europe were far removed from the ideal of

Civilian Power: democracy as the domestic basis of Civilian Power was only nascent; military force was organized in an alliance that had been oppressive (and was now dissolving); voluntary multilateralism was virtually non-existent. But although the objective state of civilianization in East Central Europe was still feeble, its chances were better than they had been since 1945, and perhaps since the beginning of the century.

The second reason, related to this, was that the fate of civilianization in East Central Europe depended critically on Germany. Despite the legacy of the Federal Republic's Ostpolitik, or perhaps because of it, important bilateral problems remained to be solved. Some of these promised to be thorny. Next, in contrast to its policies vis-à-vis Western Europe, Germany was not constrained by multilateral commitments vis-à-vis its 'new' Eastern neighbours. Change in Germany's policy would therefore be more easily discernible here, since policies could not be based on already established patterns. German policies towards its Eastern neighbours, then, promised to be a prolific test case: the objective need for civilianization was large; Germany's room for manoeuvre was substantial.

It follows that the question about Germany's Civilian Power behaviour can be subdivided into two questions. The structural question relates to the overall scope of policies Germany *could* have pursued vis-à-vis its Eastern neighbours after 1990. It asks which conditions made *X* possible, that is, how it was *possible* that Germany acted as a Civilian Power in its policies towards East Central Europe. The answer is that the structural preconditions were the end of the Cold War and German unification. These structural preconditions explain indirectly what we are interested in, because they explain what was possible and what was not. What they do not explain, however, is the historical question at the heart of the book, namely why *X* happened rather than *Y*. Although German unification and the end of the Cold War illuminate the scope of possible German policies in post-Cold War Europe, they do not provide a direct explanation of why Germany responded to the forthcoming challenges as a Civilian Power rather than in any other way. Developing the argument originally put forward by Hanns Maull, we will argue that one can explain German foreign policy above all with reference to domestic institutions and historical experience. We will term these two factors Germany's 'foreign policy culture'. In the first chapter, the concept of foreign policy culture will be located in the current debate in international relations theory.

Maull's original argument had only defined civilianization as democratization, non-military conflict resolution and multilateralism. As indicated in the title of this book, these principles were applied more narrowly in the case of Germany and East Central Europe: they resulted in the Eastern enlargement of Nato and the European Union. In the same way that Western integration had laid the foundation for the civilianization of the Federal Republic's foreign policy in the 1950s, Western integration was now at the heart of Germany's Civilian Power policy vis-à-vis its Eastern neighbours. Germany's Civilian Power act was inherited and replicated.

The fact that, in the case of Germany and East Central Europe, civilianization was Western integration leads to two observations about the content of the following pages. First, Germany's Civilian Power act could not be a solo performance. Much of this book is therefore devoted to a discussion of how Germany gathered support for its Eastern policies from its Western partners. The discussion of EU enlargement will reveal, first, the intimate relationship between Germany and France and, secondly, the supreme significance of EMU for all other EU matters, including enlargement. In a similar vein, the discussion of Nato enlargement will illustrate the special weight commanded by the United States within Nato in general, and for the making of German security policy in particular.

Secondly, it points to a definitional issue related to terms involved in previous descriptions of Germany's policies towards the region: Ostpolitik. Since 1949, however, the countries at which Ostpolitik was directed were distinct for a specific system of political and economic government, and for their adherence to a military alliance. In addition Ostpolitik, to a large measure, was also always Deutschlandpolitik, that is, it was concerned with German unification. After 1989/90, circumstances changed considerably. The need for Deutschlandpolitik was obviated through unification. The coherent bloc of communist states disintegrated, both in domestic order and in alliance solidarity, into a number of relatively stable market democracies on the one hand, civil war on the other, and a number of countries in between these extremes. Finally, German policies towards East Central Europe now mirrored its policies to the West. Germany's Eastern policies, in other words, became far less affected by the legacy of Ostpolitik than by the legacy of Western integration.

While we will largely refer to the Western integration of East Central Europe not with reference to individual countries, but with reference to a particular group, significant differences between countries will emerge. Whereas Poland was by far the most important country in German thinking, and the only one with whom Germany entertained significant bilateral relations, German–Hungarian relations were more cordial but also less intensive than German–Czech relations. The dormant oblivion of German–Slovak relations, by contrast, illustrates that to a large extent civilianization was a demand-led strategy.

By about 1995 it had become common knowledge among observers of German foreign policy that being surrounded by stable democracies had become an absolute German priority. However, this was in fact a slow process, which only gathered momentum in 1993/94, and which in its initial conception did not include the enlargement of Nato. After 1993, however, the Western integration of East Central Europe emerged as a German priority. Indeed the clarity was such that the present discussion suggests the term *raison d'état*. According to this reasoning, the purpose of German foreign policy was to ensure security and prosperity in Germany. This was unattainable without security, stability and prosperity in East Central Europe. Stability and prosperity, in turn, were too large a task to be handled by Germany alone, and therefore East Central Europe's multilateral stabilization, which was in fact Western integration, became a key objective of German foreign policy. This illustrates that acting as a Civilian Power was in Germany's interest. In contrast to its usage by some observers, then, the term Civilian Power is not used here as referring to a state that has only ideals and no interests.[4] Instead, one of the purposes of this book is to find out why German policy makers defined their interests in the way they did. Although this book is no comparative study of Civilian Power, it is at least to some extent informed by the question as to why some states, like Japan and Germany, but also Holland and Sweden, should approximate to the Civilian Power ideal type more closely than others.

In Chapters 4 and 5, German policies within the enlargement of Nato and the EU are broken down into a number of particular roles Germany played. Even without following the theoretical claims made in the first chapter, one can follow the idea that the behaviour of states, just like that of individuals, can be conceptualized in terms of specific roles. Consider for instance how a woman in a family enacts the roles of wife, career woman, lover, mother, daughter and daughter-in-law. All of these are formed through a mixture of expectations from the environment and the beliefs of the particular woman in question. Although different roles are often in perfect harmony with one another, they might also be in conflict. Consider the difficulty of reconciling the role of a good wife with that of a successful career woman, for instance, or that of a good student with that of a good sportsman. Indeed, the saying that one 'cannot be all things to all people' is a more casual way of stating that one's social life has come to a role conflict that must be resolved. Conceptually speaking, much of the following discussion is built upon the assumption that states, like individuals, fulfil certain roles in their social conduct, and that we understand their behaviour better if we identify these roles.

Germany played six roles that were relevant for the Western integration of East Central Europe. As discussed in Chapter 4, Germany's roles regarding the enlargement of the European Union were as *integration deepener* and *integration widener*. Whereas the *integration deepener* role had characterized the Federal Republic's European policy since the 1950s, the role of the *integration widener*, pushing for rapid enlargement to East Central Europe at the expense of deepening, was new. Although Germany had also been a prime promoter of the enlargements in the 1970s and 1980s, its support did not weaken its resolve to pursue further deepening. In the 1990s, it was much more difficult to reconcile a rapid Eastern enlargement with the deepening of integration that had been decided at Maastricht. This role conflict testifies to Germany's basic dilemma after unification. On the one hand it had actual, long-standing commitments in the West. On the other hand, it had desirable, new commitments in the East. Its primary foreign policy orientation remained in the West. Yet the primary risks to its security and well-being lay in the East. These conflicting foreign policy priorities explain why much of what German policy makers did in the period under consideration was contradictory, and much of what they said was an attempt to conceal this contradiction.

The assertion that the roles Germany played were not evidently reconcilable is also illustrated by German policies within the enlargement of Nato. Three roles had characterized the Federal Republic's security policy: the *Atlanticist*, for which a close relationship with the United States was the basis of all policy; the *Gaullist*, which sought to weaken the West German–American security compact in favour of a genuinely West European one; and the *Muscovite*, proposing a loosening of Western ties in order to gain more room to manoeuvre vis-à-vis Moscow. Among these roles the *Atlanticist* had dominated ever since the late 1940s, and, as will be illustrated in Chapter 4, was reinforced through the modalities of German unification. After 1990, these traditional roles were complemented by a security concern for East Central Europe. This resulted in the emergence of a role that is here coined the *Warshaviste*.[5] In the event, the *Warshaviste* was the determining factor for Germany's promotion of Nato enlargement. The discussion in Chapter 4 will reveal that, in contrast to EU enlargement, Nato enlargement was hotly contested in Germany's foreign policy establishment, bringing to the fore the different role conceptions that affected policy, and opening up dividing lines between government and opposition, among the governing parties, and within the largest governing party, the CDU.

The reference to these roles indicates that this book is not primarily about Civilian Power, but instead uses the Civilian Power ideal type in order to help explain the mechanisms of German foreign policy. This reveals that although Germany did, by and large, adhere to Civilian Power principles, it did not do so at times because of the very contradictions intrinsic in Civilian Power itself. This manifested itself, first, in the fact that German policy makers were tripped up by the domestic institutions that were the very basis of Civilian Power – especially so with respect to EU enlargement, where domestic interests constrained German policy. It also manifested itself in the debate over Nato enlargement, where German policy makers were torn between the supposed benefits Nato enlargement would bring for stability and democracy in East Central Europe, and the possible injuries it would inflict on relations with Russia. Finally, it manifested itself in the fact that German policy makers were far more active in implementing their Civilian Power ethos vis-à-vis Germany's immediate Eastern neighbours than vis-à-vis South-eastern Europe or the Baltic states. While this does not disqualify the argument that Germany did, in a geographically limited and functionally intensive way, act like a Civilian Power, it adds a qualification by illustrating that even Civilian Powers have limited resources and special interests.

To have identified a role, in other words, is not the same as to explain policy. Though the roles Germany played gave its policies their specific direction, they cannot explain these policies in every detail. German leaders had a considerable degree of flexibility in the interpretation and application of the Civilian Power ideal type, and this included the assertion of more narrowly defined national interests.

In a nutshell, we will argue that the Federal Republic's beliefs and patterns of foreign policy making had become so engrained by 1990 that it was difficult to change the foreign policy of unified Germany in the way some people had hoped, and others had feared. Hence, the end of the Cold War and German unification explain German policies only indirectly. The key to understanding the foreign policy of unified Germany lies not in Germany's geographical situation but in the changes that West Germany underwent after 1945.

1
What Is Civilian Power?

Introduction

Hanns Maull's thinking on Civilian Power has undergone considerable change. Whereas it was largely prescriptive in its original form, it later became more narrowly focused on foreign policy analysis, working with the concepts of foreign policy culture and role theory that are also developed here.[1] Equally, whereas Maull at first proposed the Civilian Power approach as an argument about the distinctiveness of Germany and Japan, he later conceded that other states also have the potential to act like Civilian Powers. Common to both aspects of Maull's work is a theoretical assumption that is never explicitly discussed, namely that the nature of international politics makes *possible* the policies which Maull presents as *desirable*. The aim of this first chapter is therefore to discuss the theoretical assumptions on which Maull's argument rests.

The chapter will first outline the concept of Civilian Power as originally presented by Maull. It will then argue that the origins of the norms and values inherent in the Civilian Power approach can be traced back in part to the classical liberals of the late eighteenth and nineteenth centuries, and in part to the more socially oriented liberals of the late nineteenth and early twentieth centuries. This discussion will elucidate that Maull's version of liberal international theory is very different from the liberal theories of the 1970s and 1980s. The third part will link Civilian Power to those approaches in international relations theory to which it is akin, especially democratic peace theory and the study of security communities. It will borrow constructivist arguments in order to demonstrate that it is possible to institutionalize the norms of liberal international theory at the international level. The chapter will then discuss briefly a number of questions on the nature of power intrinsic to the Civilian Power concept.

In the second part, we will introduce the concepts of foreign policy culture and role theory which enable us to apply the Civilian Power concept to foreign policy analysis. A foreign policy culture is an explanatory tool used to trace the effect of culture and identity on the process of interest definition. It is a set of beliefs collectively held by foreign policy makers about the importance of particular issues for the conduct of foreign policy, in particular about the use of military force, multilateralism and the influence of society. Significantly, a foreign policy culture can change. How such change occurs is conceptualized with the use of role theory. Roles are defined as persistent patterns in a state's foreign policy behaviour. They are most decisively affected by a set of role conceptions held by a foreign policy elite. The sum of these role conceptions, which are specific to a country, makes up a foreign policy culture. This foreign policy culture is the prism through which other influences, internal and external, normative and material, have to pass before they affect policy.

The Civilian Power concept

The concept of Civilian Power, in particular in its application to German foreign policy, experienced a mixed reception. In line with the term 'civilian', it is often associated with the purely non-military conduct of foreign policy. This neglects the residual emphasis on military power that is integral to the concept, as much as its strong normative commitment. Other commentators have ascribed to the concept a purely economic orientation, similar to that of a trading state, the foreign policy of which is characterized by the pursuit of narrowly defined national economic interests.[2] Others still have taken it as a state that 'limits itself to do-goodism and cheque-book contributions to peace-keeping measures'.[3] None of these descriptions come very close to the original concept as put forward by Hanns Maull.

The starting point of Maull's analysis is the claim that interdependence between states and societies precipitates mutual vulnerabilities so that states are left incapable of guarding the security and prosperity of their societies unilaterally. The conclusions Maull draws from this analysis are twofold. First, classical realist concepts such as the autonomy of the nation state, the primacy of military security, balance-of-power politics and the notion of a narrowly defined 'national interest' can no longer account for the nature of international politics. They are thus neither adequate instruments for the conduct of foreign policy, nor suitable concepts for its study. Secondly, interdependence will result in the creation of models of governance that will affect the nature of the nation state. Although nation states will persist as important loci of decision making, they will do so as a middle layer in between forms of international governance on the one hand, and domestic and trans-national structures on the other. The Civilian Power approach, then, is the prescription of new forms of international governance geared toward an era in which nation states cannot unilaterally fulfil the tasks which once sustained their existence.

Civilian Power is about exerting influence. Its objective is the civilian-ization of the international environment, which means that through a process similar to the civilianization within nation states, the use of military force is tamed in order to guarantee the rule of law, prosperity and legitimate governance. Here, ends are inseparable from means. In order to tame violence, Civilian Power practises restraint in the use of military force; in order to build up international institutions, it favours collective action; in order to address non-military threats to security, it employs non-military foreign policy instruments. In this way, policy instruments are indistinguishable from policy objectives, and both re-volve around the core principles of collective or cooperative security and democratic values.

The concept of collective or cooperative security is of particular sig-nificance, because it links the Civilian Power concept to Norbert Elias's analysis of domestic civilization.[4] Elias observed that the monopoliza-tion of physical violence within nation states had led to 'pacified social spaces', which were maintained not only by governmental constraint, but also, in the process of civilization, by the increasing self-constraint of social actors.[5] The use of force, Maull argues, monopolized in domes-tic politics by the nation state, needs to be monopolized at the inter-national level by a regime of collective or cooperative security. Such a regime implies that 'the traditional central principles of international relations – sovereignty, self-help and non-interference – be replaced by a new central principle, namely the inadmissibility of any organized use of force either at home or abroad, except in self-defense against an aggressor'.[6]

This encroaches significantly on state sovereignty. States would have to accept surveillance of their domestic policies and, potentially, the violation of their territory through the stationing of multi-national troops. Yet only through such a security regime, Maull main-tains, can the costs of military force be combated. A collective or cooperative security regime would commit itself to the collective deterrence of an aggressor, and to the application of sanctions if deterrence alone did not suffice. However, Maull is clear about the *ultima ratio* of any arrangement of collective security, namely that to be credible it must deploy forces in certain cases and according to particular principles: 'based on a collective decision (rather than unilaterally) and confined strictly to purposes of effective peace-keeping, peace-making, deterrence, and defense against the aggressive use of force.'[7]

These principles are of particular relevance for the present discussion. First, they elucidate that the concept of Civilian Power does not refer to the exclusively non-military foreign policy with which it is often confused. Just as using armed police in order to stop a bank robbery is hardly the end of civil society, Civilian Power relies residually on the use of military force. It is not pacifist.[8] Secondly, the 'collective security regime' that Maull advocates does not have to be modelled on the United Nations. Although Civilian Powers favour such pure forms of collective security, they 'approve, in the face of the real problems and deficits of such systems, measures of co-operative security'.[9]

The second core principle inherent in Maull's Civilian Power concept is the notion of rights. This relies on the acknowledgement and pursuit of universally recognized values: above all, the spread of democracy and the recognition of human rights. In a sense, this points to a tension inherent in the Civilian Power concept, pertaining to the question of whether the pursuit of peace or the defence of democratic rights should take priority. As we have seen, the non-military conduct of foreign policy is an integral part of the concept. This may, but may also not be, reconcilable with the defence of human rights. In this respect the policy makers of a Civilian Power might face hard decisions and tough choices, and we will see in the discussion in Chapter 4, for instance, that the German debate over Nato enlargement was full of these.

The emphasis on rights gives the Civilian Power approach the character of an emancipatory project, which provides the most obvious link with the political philosophy from which it derives most of its insights and convictions – liberalism. It is to liberalism in its classical and social forms that the discussion will now turn in order to embed the concept of Civilian Power in its intellectual origins and to point out to what extent it differs from the approaches of liberal international theory that were prominent in the 1970s and 1980s.

Civilian Power and liberalism

Maull's emphasis on human rights and the rule of law in international affairs testifies to a classically liberal suspicion of state power. It is an acknowledgement that the state can be as detrimental to the well-being of individual human beings in international affairs as in domestic affairs, and that its power needs to be checked, limited and codified in the rule of law. Liberal international thinkers argued that foreign policy would be more peaceful if representative of, and responsible to, civil society – a claim that has more recently been developed into democratic peace theory, which we will discuss below. What we should stress at this juncture is that Civilian Power as well as democratic peace theory emanated from liberal thought, which in turn was grounded in the assertion of the rights of the individual. Liberalism as a political philosophy and liberal thought as an approach to the study of international relations are deeply linked.

In contrast to the emphasis on democratic values, the Civilian Power concept only follows classical liberalism in part when it comes to the postulate of *laissez-faire*. To the classical liberals, 'Government was conceived as a bad thing in itself, always oppressive to individuals, frequently unjust, nearly always expensive and inefficient.'[10] Although this was a principle originally developed with regard to domestic affairs, it increasingly developed into a doctrine of foreign policy. In particular, *laissez-faire* stressed the benefits of free trade and the principle of non-intervention. Almost all liberal thinkers from the late eighteenth century came to believe in the positive effects free trade would have on world peace.[11]

The liberal thinker with whom the doctrine of *laissez-faire* came to be associated most was Richard Cobden. This was true not only for the advocacy of free trade, but also for the other principle of *laissez-faire*, non-intervention. Cobden argued that any meddling in the affairs of other nations was financially costly, facilitated the imposition of imperialism and risked a greater war: 'The great rule of conduct for us in regard to foreign nations is, in extending our commercial relations, to have with them as little political connexion as possible.'[12]

While the doctrine of *laissez-faire* and the concept of Civilian Power share an emphasis on the benefits of markets, they are diametrically opposed with regard to the doctrine of non-intervention. Maull advocates explicitly the end to classical notions of sovereignty and non-intervention, and it is this aspect which is possibly the most radical of his proposals. 'In principle', he argues, 'Civilian Powers do not exclude at all an interference in the internal affairs of other states.'[13] Of course, Maull reiterates the necessity for such interference to be legitimated by international organizations and enacted by a collective security arrangement. Nevertheless, this is a long way from Cobden stating: 'I do not think I am responsible for seeing right and truth and justice carried out all over the world.'[14] Maull does.

The turning point in the history of liberalism arrived when liberal thinkers became increasingly convinced that the principle of *laissez-faire* was ill suited to the needs of a fully fledged industrial society. *Laissez-faire* had been an expression of the view that human interests were in natural harmony with one another, which meant that all state interference was superfluous, if not dangerous. Liberals now argued that human interests were often dissonant, and that state activity was needed to bring them back into harmony. The state thus became the agent of social transformation. Although this challenge to *laissez-faire* originated primarily from the dissatisfaction with its domestic effects, the new role for state activity was soon translated into the international sphere.

The views on international economics championed by the new liberals combined the liberal tradition of free trade with the assertion that free trade had to be accompanied by other measures of international economic government. What the new liberals of the late nineteenth and early twentieth centuries had diagnosed for the first time was the condition of interdependence. Leonard Woolf, for instance, succeeded in demonstrating not only to what extent interdependence could be beneficial, but to what extent it already existed through various functional arrangements, for instance in international telephone and postal agreements.[15] This led to two conclusions. First, international economic life had to be regulated. J. A. Hobson advocated 'international government' to fulfil this task, 'government' here referring to a loose framework of coordination rather than to any formal institutional structure.[16] Hobson maintained that this would reduce chance and uncertainty in the world economy, and encourage states to adhere to an 'open door' policy towards trade and investment. Secondly, war had become futile. Norman Angell, for instance, made plain that 'the security of wealth is due to other things than armaments'.[17]

The significance of the concept of international interdependence for Maull's Civilian Power approach can hardly be overestimated. It is from this diagnosis that Maull derives his views on the changed nature of international relations, on the costs of military force and on the inability of nation states to deal effectively with new challenges. Of course, in current international relations theory the concept of interdependence is most closely associated with Robert Keohane and Joseph Nye.[18] But it is important to remember that the diagnosis of interdependence was made first in the early twentieth century, at a time when the world was as yet quite unaware of the levels of economic interaction to which we are accustomed today, and of phenomena such as world or cold wars.

The new liberals' most radical proposal for international government was the creation of a collective security regime. The principle of non-intervention had been criticized by liberals ever since the 1870s, when William Gladstone had argued that mere balance-of-power thinking did not suffice as a legitimation for Britain's abstention from armed intervention in the Bulgarian crisis in 1876, calling instead for a set of moral criteria or a 'public law of nations.'[19] With Gladstone liberalism came to believe that there were universal principles that had to be defended, if necessary, by the use of military force. Liberalism had embraced the concept of a 'just war'. It is against this background that Maull can legitimize the potential use of force within a collective security regime. Since the Civilian Power concept, too, supports the norms of a 'public law of nations' it cannot afford the pacifism with which it is sometimes confused.

As the European powers stumbled into the First World War, liberals identified the old system of the balance of power as one of the main reasons for the slide into catastrophe. During the crisis of July 1914, there had not been a mechanism to slow down war preparations, and to arbitrate or adjudicate between the disputing factions. In 1916, J. A. Hobson came to note that to

> watchers of the present conflict it seems an intolerable thought that, after the fighting is done, we should once more return to a condition of 'armed peace' with jealous, distrustful, and revengeful Powers piling up armaments and plotting singly or in groups against their neighbours until Europe is plunged into another war more terrible, more bloody, and more costly than this.[20]

The way out of this quagmire called the 'balance of power' was seen in a collective security arrangement, which offered mechanisms of arbitration and adjudication that could prevent future war: the League of Nations. If such an arrangement limited state sovereignty, so be it. The horrors of the war had convinced the liberal thinkers of the interwar years that new mechanisms for the prevention of war had to be found. In this sense, the League of Nations prefigured Civilian Power.

It was of course through Woodrow Wilson that the liberal call for collective security made its most formidable impact. Wilson proposed the Fourteen Points that became the strongest normative input into the new era, and it was his leadership that led to the inception of the League of Nations. However, though liberals had been united in their call for a collective security arrangement and in their support for the League, the Versailles treaty and the actual establishment of the League divided them deeply. Many were disappointed that the losers of the war, most notably Germany and Russia, had not been granted membership in the League, and that the United States had not joined; in any case, the imposition of the Versailles treaty was seen to have cost Britain and France their moral credibility. Hobson deplored that the 'perversion of this great ideal of a League of Nations into a present instrument for autocratic and imperialistic government will rank in history as a treason to humanity as deplorable as the Peace Treaty with which it was so injuriously bound.'[21]

Maull does consider the danger that any system of collective security can be instrumentalized by the rich and powerful.[22] Yet the danger of abuse does not stop him from believing that the principle itself is right, and he clearly believes that a system of collective security offers the best prospects for a civilianized world order. Collective security is thus a concept that is neither unique to the Civilian Power approach nor untried in practical politics. We have already seen that Maull allows some leeway in the interpretation of collective security systems. The warning that these systems have 'real problems and deficits' testifies to the fact that the League of Nations as well as the United Nations for a number of reasons failed to prevent war.[23] In its call for 'cooperative security' arrangements, then, the Civilian Power concept shows that despite its liberal heritage it is a child of its times.

Civilian Power, social constructivism and the democratic peace

As liberals noted what was 'objectively' in a state's interest (peace, wealth), they expected states to achieve these interests through cooperation, that is, through international economic government and collective security arrangements. In other words, the functional need for cooperation was expected to invent its own solution. This reasoning leaves the analyst with a puzzle: if state cooperation is so obviously beneficial, why have states repeatedly acted contrary to it? As we have seen, the core assumptions of the Civilian Power approach were in place at the beginning of the century, some as early as two hundred years ago. None of them prevented the outbreak in the world of two hot wars and a cold one, not to mention innumerable smaller conflicts both between states and within them. In order to address these conceptual difficulties, let us briefly consider the different schools of international relations theory.

The above discussion has already indicated that this book is placed in the liberal tradition of international relations theory. The liberalism it subscribes to, however, is a particular one. In the diagram below, two dividing lines in international relations theory are identified, one between constructivism and rationalism, the other between systemic and non-systemic theories. The former dividing line is an epistemological one, that is to say it separates different theories according to their belief about how we attain knowledge. Rationalist theories assume that there exist objective laws according to which actors act and an objective world of facts that the scholar can discover. Actors' interests are definable in terms of these objective laws. Thus, for realists of all persuasions, state interests can be defined in terms of power and security; for Marxists, in terms of capital accumulation. Constructivist theories, on the other hand, assume that these interests are problematic, that they depend on social interaction, on cultural influences and on the identity of actors.

	Rationalism	**Constructivism**
Systemic	Neorealism Marxism	IR constructivism
Non-systemic	Realism Rationalist liberalism	Constructivist liberalism

The second dividing line, between systemic and non-systemic theories, is a methodological one, that is to say it separates approaches according to their preferred level of analysis. In rationalist theories, neorealism and Marxism are systemic theories because they explain state behaviour through the pressures of the international system of which states form part. Neorealists argue that the anarchical order of the international system requires states to strive for power and security; Marxists argue that the pressures of the international economy force states to accumulate capital. Correspondingly, constructivist systemic theories explain state identities primarily through interaction at the international level.

Non-systemic theories, on the other hand, focus more closely on individual actors. This is true for classical realism, which explains international politics through a quality common to all states, namely the quest for power. It is also true for what is here coined 'rationalist liberalism', which explains state policies through the rational quest for peace and wealth. Constructivist non-systemic theories, on the other hand, focus on the particular features of a state and the values and norms it adheres to, and try to deduct particular foreign policy patterns from these features.

In other words, liberal international thought is divided here into rationalist liberalism and constructivist liberalism. Whereas rationalist liberalism sees state interests as derivative of objective material factors, constructivist liberalism views state interests as affected by social interaction. This distinction places the Civilian Power concept in the school of constructivist liberalism. It is constructivist because it pays attention to the norms and values that affect how German policy makers define their interests; it is liberal because it explains foreign policy through the form of government, relations between state and society, and the importance of international organizations.

The key constructivist claim of interest here is the view that 'anarchy is what states make of it', in other words that the anarchical international system is not necessarily one of self-help, but can be one of collective security, depending on the degree to which states have succeeded in building collective identities.[24] This claim is linked to an argument put forward by Karl Deutsch, namely that a 'security community' is a community in which states share the conviction that they really can solve their disputes without the use of military force.[25] The prime example of such a security community, made possible through the formation of a collective identity, is Nato.[26]

The crucial point in the constructivist argument about state interaction is that interaction affects state interests and identities. Hence, interests are not just given by the apparently anarchical nature of the international system, but can change through interaction. Relations among states do not have to be marked by continuity, as neorealists claim, but may be marked by change. This does not mean that because of the formation of a collective identity, states are no longer guided by the pursuit of their interests. It merely means that how these interests are defined depends on the social context within which states act.

How does this constructivist argument sit with the Civilian Power argument? Maull shares the view that there exists a link between democratic domestic institutions and a peaceful conduct of foreign policy – later developed into the postulate that democracies do not go to war with one another.[27] Through democratization, Maull argues, the rules and structures governing the core of interdependence around the OECD countries can be expanded. Democratization is therefore an integral aspect of the civilianization of world politics. Yet, the Civilian Power also stretches beyond democratic peace theory. First, it assumes that democratic peace theory has overemphasized the significance of democracy for the issue of peace and war. Following Kant, the Civilian Power concept holds that democracy is a necessary but by no means sufficient condition for peace. The fact that states do not go to war with one another, even if cogently explained by democratic peace theory, tells us little about the way they conduct their relations. In some instances, this may be peaceful rivalry; in others, it may be close cooperation. In this respect, the Civilian Power approach is akin to the study of security communities. Especially in its most recent form, infused with constructivist insights, the study of security communities has close connection with Civilian Power because it assumes that 'a qualitative and quantitative growth of transactions reshapes collective experience and alters social facts', and that this is causally connected to the collective identities that are at the heart of a security community.[28]

Secondly, Civilian Power is not at all restricted to the issue of peace and war. Whereas democratic peace theory is concerned with the hard security of military power, Civilian Power is also concerned with soft security issues revolving around economics, environmental protection, migration and organized crime. Not only in hard security issues but also in soft security issues, 'a qualitative and quantitative growth of transactions reshapes collective experience and alters social facts', leading to the build-up of (soft) security communities. For German policy towards East Central Europe after 1989, these issues were tremendously important, and led to the German promotion of the European Union's eastward enlargement. Democratic peace theory would find it difficult to account for these motivations because it is not concerned with soft security.

This links to the last aspect in which Civilian Power stretches beyond democratic peace theory. Whereas democratic peace theory is exclusively concerned with states, Civilian Power is not. The discussion of the new literature on security communities has already indicated that constructivist liberalism pays attention to new loci of decision making in international politics. That state cooperation creates international institutions which play a role in their own right is of course a traditional claim of liberal international theory. This is reinforced by the Civilian

Power approach. The definition of Civilian Power as consisting of the commitment to democratic rights, to the non-military resolution of conflicts and to multilateralism has already hinted at the primary importance of international institutions. It is therefore fitting that the bulk of this study discusses the application of German Civilian Power in terms of the eastward extension of the Western institutions of which Germany was part. Germany's Civilian Power act could not be a solo performance, but instead was inherited, replicated and critically dependent on the institutional memberships of the Federal Republic.

Civilian Power as the exercise of power

That Civilian Power involves the exercise of power is a fact that Maull treats with great clarity: Civilian Powers, he states, 'want to influence the course of history'.[29] Since a comprehensive treatment of the concept of power would be impossible here, the discussion will be limited to three remarks. The first is that Civilian Power relies only rarely on a Weberian sense of power as coercion. This is particularly true for the use of military force. Yet the *ultima ratio* of a collective security regime is coercion and the Civilian Power approach, by relying on collective security, does not dispense completely with this coercive aspect of power. The second point is that despite the residual importance of coercive power, Civilian Power relies in principle on what Steven Lukes termed 'third-dimensional power', that is the kind of power that prevents conflicts from even making their way onto the agenda.[30] It exercises power in order to affect other states' conceptions of their self-interests. Whereas coercive power attempts to get others to do what they otherwise would not do, Civilian Power is aimed at getting them to want what they otherwise would not want. The exercise of Civilian Power thus relates to Joseph Nye's conception of 'soft power'. In contrast to the realist focus on power as hard resources, Nye defines soft power as the power over outcomes, which is at its most effective if applied non-coercively. Hence Nye argues:

> It is just as important to set the agenda and structure world politics as to get others to change in particular cases. [If a state] can make its power seem legitimate in the eyes of others, it will encounter less resistance to its wishes. If its culture and ideology are attractive, others will more willingly follow. If it can establish international norms consistent with its society, it is less likely to have to change. If it can support institutions that make other states wish to channel

or limit their activities in ways the dominant state prefers, it may be spared the costly exercise of coercive or hard power.[31]

This links with the above discussion about the importance of institutionalized cooperation for the exercise of Civilian Power. Civilian Powers create international arenas for cooperation in order to exercise power. International institutions are thus not just a constraint; on the contrary, they may be enabling and facilitating.

Thirdly, both liberal and constructivist thought have been criticized for paying insufficient attention to the importance of power.[32] Hans-Martin Jäger, for instance, deplored that constructivism does not address sufficiently 'how the power of norms interacts with the norms of the powerful'.[33] It seems that the concept of Civilian Power could address this nexus of norms and power in international relations, not least since it combines the term 'civilian', which relies on norms and values, with the term 'power', which relies on legitimacy and order. In the subsequent chapters, we attempt to meet this challenge in two distinct ways. The first is the conceptualization of foreign policy culture as inherently political, that is as reliant on contest, negotiation and legitimation. The second is a discussion of Germany's endeavours to commit its Western partners to the stabilization and ultimate integration of East Central Europe. In contrast, the power relationships between Germany and East Central Europe (in other words, the power effects of civilianization) will not be considered, primarily because it would overload the argument. The book remains focused on the motivations and mechanisms of Germany's policies towards East Central Europe.

International relations theory and foreign policy culture

Let us recapitulate. We have so far placed the Civilian Power approach in its intellectual heritage and have pointed out a number of theoretical assumptions on which it rests but which it does not make explicit. The Civilian Power approach is deeply embedded in liberal international theory. Sharing with classical liberalism an emphasis on individual rights, the pacific effects of democracy on foreign policy and market economics, it gained from social liberalism its attention on the positive effects of international cooperation. The insights derived from constructivism counter realist scepticism about the limits to cooperation. They can be combined with aspects of liberalism to constitute what we have called constructivist liberalism. This explains the persistence of cooperation among states and prepares the ground for the following two sections, which apply constructivist liberalism to foreign policy analysis.

Constructivism in international relations theory, located in the top right corner of the diagram on page 17, traces the link between state interaction and the constitution of state interests. The present approach relies on this methodology especially in Chapter 2, when it discusses external influences to explain the development of Germany's foreign policy culture after 1945. For the bulk of the book, however, we will reverse the methodology. We will attempt to trace the link between already existing state identities and the formulation of a particular foreign policy when a state is faced with new circumstances. Whereas constructivism in international relations theory is interested in how what states *do* affect what they *are*, this study tries to find out how what states *are* affects what they *do*. In trying to trace how identities affect the definition of state interests, it employs a constructivist liberal approach to foreign policy analysis.

In order to specify what is meant by foreign policy culture, we will first discuss the merits and insufficiencies of a number of rationalist approaches to international relations theory for the question at the heart of this book. In its pure form, neorealism, as developed by Kenneth Waltz, views the state as part of an anarchic international system in which self-help is the surest path to survival.[34] Neorealism considers enduring multilateral frameworks and supranational integration alien to state motivation. State cooperation is seen as unlikely, superfluous at best and pernicious at worst for survival in a hostile and threatening international environment. Hence, as John Mearsheimer predicted in 1990, neorealism would expect Germany to seek independence from all multilateral frameworks after the achievement of unification.[35] Mearsheimer assumed that the removal of the material constraints on West Germany's sovereignty would clear the path for an autonomous, assertive foreign policy. Germany would be unlikely to remain in Nato's integrated military structures, let alone extend them eastwards, where bilateral diplomacy towards smaller and weaker neighbours would enable it to pursue more autonomous and assertive policies.

It is true that Mearsheimer expected the United States to withdraw from Europe and that he made his predictions on German policy on the basis of this expectation.[36] It is also true that Nato did suffer from profound tensions and that the Atlantic seemed to have widened after the Cold War. As Adrian Hyde-Price pointed out, 'it seems to be a geostrategic fact that as Soviet/Russian influence on the region (that is, East Central Europe) declines, that of Germany increases, and vice versa.'[37] By itself, this is true. Germany's influence did increase after 1990. But this fact alone does not allow a conclusion on the nature of this growing influence. For this, one has to scrutinize further the motivations of German policy. Stanley Hoffmann pointed out in reaction to Mearsheimer that one 'ought to ask about the goals of states' rather than their material capabilities alone.[38] Material factors established the preconditions for Germany to act as a Civilian Power, but cannot explain why it actually did so. They explain what was *possible* after 1990, not what actually happened.

In contrast to neorealism, classical realism as developed by Hans Morgenthau does have a place for multilateral frameworks, namely in the form of alliances.[39] In terms of the balance of power Germany's support for enlargement could be interpreted as an attempt to use American power to balance a perceived threat from Russia. Used accurately, however, this reasoning struggles to explain Germany's enlargement policies. Morgenthau believed that 'alliances are typically of temporary duration and most prevalent in wartime'.[40] It seems surprising that Nato, seen purely as a military alliance, should rejuvenate and extend at the precise moment that the Cold War was over. Since Morgenthau assumed that alliances are 'a matter not of principle but of expediency', it seems surprising that Germany should pursue the enlargement of Nato.[41] In line with realist theory, one would instead expect Germany to rely on its own defence capabilities and to acquire nuclear weapons.

The last of the more conventional approaches to international relations theory to be considered here is rationalist liberalism. In the form of regime theory and interdependence theory, it shares with neorealism an emphasis on the significance of the material structures of the international environment and on the primacy of state actors.[42] However, it accepts that states may cooperate, especially for mutual economic gain.[43] In an international environment that is marked by interdependence, states derive benefits from cooperation through a reduction of uncertainty and transaction costs. Rationalist liberalism does make an important contribution to solving the puzzle at the heart of the present discussion. It clarifies in broad terms that Germany had economic interests in the countries to its East, and that those interests could be observed through state cooperation. As we will see, German politicians mentioned frequently that both Nato and EU enlargement were in Germany's elemental interests.

It is questionable, however, whether rationalist liberalism can account for German policies in more specific terms. First, it entails a misconception of the non-economic attributes of the European Union. The EU entails in part significant encroachments on nation state sovereignty.[44] As scholars debate to what extent the EU has actually become a state itself, the view of independent states choosing opportunities according to a strict cost–benefit calculation seems questionable.[45] In addition, it is at least worth noting that German economic interests in East Central Europe could have been observed through looser forms of state cooperation than the EU provided. Secondly, rationalist liberalism struggles to account for Germany's overall European policy after 1990. As we will see, the deepening of integration decided at Maastricht largely dominated Germany's EU enlargement policy. For rationalist liberals this should be astonishing, because the EMS, the previous system of monetary coordination, served Germany rather well, and because the transition to a monetary union, despite its political benefits, also entailed considerable risks and imponderabilities. In this logic Germany would be expected to advocate the stabilization of East Central Europe instead of closer integration within the European Union, a stance that in fact came to be associated with British European policy in 1989–91.

Thus, rationalist approaches to international relations theory share an understanding of the material environment that presented itself to Germany's East after 1990. They point to the room for manoeuvre that was available for German foreign policy. But just as neorealism and realism have problems in accounting for how Germany would use this room for manoeuvre in terms of power politics, rationalist liberalism leaves unspecified through what mechanisms Germany would preserve its economic interests. This suggests that we should pay more attention to foreign policy analysis, that is to the mechanisms of foreign policy making within Germany itself. Here, the bureaucratic politics approach associated with Graham Allison reveals some of the dynamics of inter-ministerial rivalry that affected German policies in both EU and Nato enlargement.[46]

Yet rationalist foreign policy analysis has deficits when it comes to the larger directions of foreign policy. It finds it much harder to explain why deepening the EU should take precedence over widening, why Nato enlargement should be promoted at all and why it should include such leniency towards Russia. Comparing French, British and West German foreign policy in the 1970s, William Wallace concluded that 'in no case can the observer safely ascribe the outcome to bureaucratic politics alone. Foreign policy… emerges out of the continuous interaction between political direction and administrative habit, against the background provided by cultural tradition and constitutional authority.'[47] In the context of the present discussion, this means that rationalist foreign policy analysis cannot explain adequately why Germany should behave as a Civilian Power. It can be assumed that this is so because it has largely neglected the significance of culture and identity for foreign policy.[48]

This points to the puzzle at the heart of the present discussion, which argues that the way German policy makers defined German interests was critically affected by the cultural-institutional setting in which German foreign policy is made.[49] Foreign policy culture can be defined as

> a subset of a larger political culture, as a collective model of nation-state identity, embodied in custom or law, that affects how members of a given foreign policy elite conceive of the aims of foreign policy, and what significance they ascribe to military force, multilateralism, and societal interests for the conduct of foreign policy.[50]

Since foreign policy culture is defined here as being embodied in custom and law, in treaties for instance or in constitutional documents, it is related to the material structures of state organization. As laws are made by those who are in power, it suggests that foreign policy culture is contested, negotiated and legitimated. At the same time, it implies that the process of change and continuity is a political process, which can be traced and documented, for instance, through changes in government. This will be discussed in more detail below, when the introduction of role theory will serve to operationalize the concept of foreign policy culture. Finally, the significance of military force, multilateralism and societal interests are related to the core issues contested in international relations theory in general, and to the concerns of the Civilian Power approach in particular. Military force is the most obvious link to the term Civilian Power, multilateralism is its sine qua non, and societal influences are its domestic foundations.

What is a 'collective model of nation-state identity'? Foreign policy culture is interested in what is collective rather than in what is individual. By viewing the state in terms of the group of individuals that act on behalf of it, it bridges three more classical levels of analysis normally separated from one another in foreign policy analysis: the state, the bureaucratic and the individual. Put differently, foreign policy culture seeks to understand what relates the individual to the structures of which he/she forms part. Individuals are seen as the ultimate agents, but their behaviour is viewed in terms of what connects them to others through time and through institutions.

Identity is a term derived from microsociology and social psychology and refers to the 'academic metaphor for self-in-context', or, to put it differently, to beliefs of personal distinctiveness, usually in relation to some *Other*.[51] Transferring this concept to the state level one can follow Peter Katzenstein's definition of identity as a 'shorthand label for various constructions of nation- or statehood'.[52] Hence, foreign policy is the projection not just of interests but also of identity; it is one way for a nation state to assert what it stands for, what it is distinctive for and how it wants to relate to other states. A change in state identity can change the conception of state interests, and thus of state policy. How this affects any particular policy, and how states change their identity and foreign policy culture, will be explored below in the section on role theory.

For the foreign policy culture of West Germany the question of identity was especially complicated, since national identity and state identity did not coincide. At least in the immediate postwar period, the question of what the West German state stood for had yet to be answered. The values the new state was to embody and its relationship with the past, with the German nation in general and the East German state in particular were fiercely contested. The intimate relationship between the practices of state building and Western integration established a critical importance of foreign policy for state identity. This relationship will be explored in Chapter 2, which outlines West Germany's foreign policy culture.

How does a foreign policy culture change? Material factors, like objective power capabilities, do influence foreign policy and foreign policy culture. The end of the Cold War and German unification as changes in material structures *did* affect German policy after 1990. As pointed out above, they possess indirect explanatory power because they explain what was possible and what was not. Nato and EU enlargement was possible because the Soviet Union had lost its empire in East Central Europe; during the Cold War years, both of these enlargements would have been inconceivable. Yet it is not the objective power capabilities that turn states into Civilian Powers, it is the objectives and methods they choose. This is why it is argued here that foreign policy culture is the crucial intervening variable in explaining how material changes affect policy. It is the prism through which all outside influences, material and normative, must filter before they shape decision makers' view of identities and interests.

The mutability of a foreign policy culture is also affected by its maturity. A nascent foreign policy culture is one in which the set of normative requirements in which individual policy makers are enveloped is still loose and yielding. This means that material structures have a stronger effect on the definition of interests, and thus far greater explanatory power for policy. This explains the strong influence that the constraints of the international environment had on West German foreign policy in the 1950s and 1960s. With time, however, these structural constraints became more flexible, while at the same time, the domestic cultural-institutional setting of foreign policy became more dense and rigid. The increasing maturity of West German foreign policy culture explains that even the turmoil in the international material environment in 1989/90 did not affect German foreign policy as much as it might have done thirty years earlier.

Finally, foreign policy culture is affected by power constellations, since no 'theory of culture – even if it was available – can account for one of politics'.[53] In any pluralistic political system, few beliefs held by decision makers are accepted by all members of the political system. The same is true for the beliefs that make up a foreign policy culture. The core values and beliefs are likely to be contested and compromised before they are accepted as legitimate. This means that foreign policy culture is tied to the formal institutions of government, and therefore to the exercise of political power. In the Federal Republic, the popular endorsement of Western integration largely contributed to the SPD's resounding election defeat in 1957; popular support for Ostpolitik was behind the CDU's defeat at the polls in 1972. The establishment and perpetuation of a foreign policy culture is an intensely political process.

Let us recapitulate. We have found that although traditional theories make significant contributions to the understanding of the material changes that occurred after 1989/90, they find it difficult to conceptualize why German policy makers defined their interests in the way they did. We have examined this process of interest definition with the help of foreign policy culture, which links state identity to state interests, and can therefore supplement existing theories of international relations. Foreign policy culture is linked to material structures. Its changeability depends on its maturity, on political contest and on political legitimation. These are general assertions which, in order to be operational, have to be specified further. Therein lies the use of role theory. Its usefulness is threefold. First, it can specify how the domestic cultural-institutional context manifested itself in particular foreign policy patterns that can be described as roles. Secondly, it can identify the hierarchy between different roles and role conceptions. This in turn will make it easier to explain the political contest over them, and can also elucidate reasons for continuity and change. Thirdly, it will lead to more specific assumptions about how Germany could have, or should have, behaved in its policies towards its Eastern neighbours since 1990.

Foreign policy culture and role theory

The usefulness of role theory for the study of foreign policy lies in the conceptual tools it provides for tracing the link between a state's identity, its foreign policy culture and the particular policies it pursues on a persistent basis. Role theory was developed in social psychology and microsociology, and is much more prolific there than in the study of foreign policy. Here, a role is defined as a persistent pattern in a state's foreign policy behaviour.[54]

State behaviour, what we can describe here as *role performance*, is shaped by influences external and internal to the actor. In foreign policy analysis this is slightly more complicated than in microsociology or social psychology, because the state is an actor, yet made up of a multiplicity of individuals acting on behalf of it. This means that the influences on role performance can be identified as follows. External influences can be separated into material factors and normative factors. As discussed above, material factors seem to have only indirect explanatory power for the question at the heart of this study and are therefore not examined in greater detail. External normative influences, on the other hand, are called *role expectations* by others, who attach norms and expectations to particular positions. Role expectations thus serve as the conceptual bridge between social structure and role behaviour in general, and, focused on foreign policy analysis, between the normative international system on the one hand and its influence on state behaviour on the other.[55] Examples for the importance of these normative influences can be found in the notion of state sovereignty or the respect for human rights.

Yet external role expectations find it easier to explain the similarity between states than to account for the differences that exist between them. If we want to establish why some states are closer than others to the ideal-type Civilian Power, then accounting for differences between states is essential. Let us therefore turn to influences internal to the state. Material internal features of a state, its geographical location and material power capabilities, do affect foreign policy. However, similar to the external material influences discussed above, their direct explanatory value is small. Of course, Germany's geographical exposure to East Central Europe generated its special interest in stability and prosperity there. Yet why this was achieved by multilateralizing its policies towards its eastern neighbours is not clear, and is not written in the laws of 'objective criteria' like the size of its population, its GDP or its military forces. Internal *role expectations* refer to the host of societal influences that affect foreign policy. They are quite distinct, however, from the *role conceptions* that are dominant within the political elite (meaning those who make decisions and affect opinion).

As we look at the state in terms of those acting on behalf of it, we are interested in the government and its most proximate circles. These are influenced by two sets of *role expectations*: external, meaning from the international environment, and internal, meaning from domestic society. The use of role theory for operationalizing foreign policy culture, then, lies in the way different influences on behaviour can be distilled into a much smaller number of role expectations, and in the way the multiplicity of foreign policy activity can be distilled into a much smaller number of roles.

Role conceptions are normed by the values and beliefs foreign policy makers feel committed to and that are expected of them by the outside environment. The multitude of a state's different role conceptions makes up its foreign policy culture. Foreign policy culture is thus the prism through which all other sources of behaviour are seen: internal and external material influences, and internal and external normative influences. At the same time foreign policy culture is not fixed. In order to conceptualize how and when it changes, however, two issues have to be addressed. The first is that of a role conflict, that is a situation in which role conceptions and role expectations have ceased to coincide. The second is that of a hierarchy of role conceptions, that is how a change in one role is related to other roles a state may perform.

It is not uncommon for any actor to occupy more than two roles at any time – indeed this is most likely. Often, these roles do not lead to role conflict. One can be a professor of government, an institute director and a Scot, for instance, just as one can be a professor of government and a connoisseur of classical music. Role conflict arises only when two or more positions that an actor occupies require contradictory performances. If role conceptions and role expectations diverge, the actor is normally pressured to react by adjusting behaviour. This process of adjustment can take a variety of forms, only the most relevant of which will be mentioned here. The first and most superficial is that of *attention deployment*; by ignoring the incompatibility of any two or more roles, actors can pretend that a role conflict does not exist. This will feature prominently in the discussion of German policy on EU and Nato enlargement in subsequent chapters. No matter whether cognitive failure or conscious decision, the sources of role conflict do not usually disappear when they are being ignored. Actors are therefore sooner or later pressured to deal with role conflict through 'instrumental acts': that is to say they are pressured into adjusting their role conceptions and their behaviour.

One way to do this is by *role alternation*. Asked for advice by a graduate student, a supervisor could offer advice as an academic at one point and as a friend at another. This advice would not need to be exactly the same. Indeed the academic could say 'work hard', while the friend could say 'take a break'. Role alternation also featured prominently in the German policies under discussion here. This is perhaps not astonishing, since *role alternation* allows an actor to pursue continuously an already established role while still coming to terms with a new one. Depending on the depth of the role conflict, however, role alternation is unlikely to work in the long term.

Thirdly, role conflict can be addressed by an attempt to fuse roles, that is by enacting them simultaneously. In role theory this strategy is called *role merger*. The professor giving advice to a graduate student would thus attempt to merge his/her roles as a supervisor and a friend, developing a new role to overcome the tensions that had previously riddled his/her relationship with the student. As this merged role is a compromise, it will lead to a new role conception and to new patterns of behaviour. The strategy of role merger also featured prominently in Germany's enlargement policies, especially from 1994/95 onwards.

Finally, if none of these strategies succeeds, or if the old roles simply do not fit an actor's new role conception, role conflict may lead to structural change. In this case, a new role is enacted at the expense of an existing one. By and large, this did not happen in Germany's European policy after 1990. It is a central argument of this book that the collection of role conceptions which had made up West Germany's foreign policy culture were so deeply ingrained that they were not shed for the new roles that arose after 1990. Germany's strategy of addressing role conflict was to avoid structural change. The aim of German policies was to preserve the various roles attached to Western integration and Ostpolitik that existed in the late 1980s, while not ignoring the new ones that arose after 1990.

What are the politics behind addressing role conflicts? Why are some strategies chosen over others? These questions are closely related to the significance that policy makers attribute to different roles. This can be illustrated by a brief preview of the chapters that follow. After 1990 German policy makers had to define how old roles could coincide harmoniously with new ones. In this debate, not only the importance of particular new roles was contested (is Russia more important than Poland? is EU enlargement more important than Nato enlargement?), but also the particular significance of old roles. In other words, in order to meet new challenges, German policy makers also had to establish a hierarchy of their old roles. Only this enabled them to define what priorities to set for the post-Cold War world.

In this debate four main strands could be distinguished. The first consisted of those observers who simply argued that the principles most central to the FRG's foreign policy culture were wrong, and that old roles should be shed in favour of new ones. They contradicted the principle of Western integration in order to root out the core principles of West German foreign policy. Though this was the position of a much discussed collection of essays by foreign policy commentators, it was not the stance taken by the political mainstream.[56] Out of the parties represented in the Bundestag only the PDS were really serious about leaving Nato. No party represented in the Bundestag advocated leaving the EU. Secondly, in contrast to those who argued that the very principles of West German foreign policy had been misguided, others maintained that these principles were correct, but that in following them, German foreign policy had sometimes gone too far. While this had been deplorable before 1989, it had become an untenable position afterwards.[57] This view was voiced by those who favoured a stronger European say in Nato and were sceptical towards EMU.[58] In the political establishment it manifested itself most strongly in the European vision of the Bavarian Minister President, Edmund Stoiber.[59]

The third evaluation of West German foreign policy was by those who argued that the principles of foreign policy were quite correct, but that they were not always carried out correctly. Thus some argued that the principles of multilateralism and Western integration were of primary importance, but those of anti-militarism were only secondary. In this view the reticence to engage in military operations, for instance, could be portrayed as a violation of the core principle of West German foreign policy. In order to stay *bündnisfähig* (alliance-capable), Volker Rühe relentlessly pointed out, unified Germany had to commit troops to international peacekeeping missions. In this view, isolation, a repetition of the German *Sonderweg*, was the truly pernicious option. Finally, the flip side of this argument was made by those observers who ascribed secondary importance to the principles of Western integration and primacy to other principles associated with West Germany's foreign policy culture. Thus many on the Left argued that the main achievement of West German foreign policy had been that of a peaceful foreign policy, and in the notion of peaceful they included the complete absence of military adventures. Though they did not contradict Western integration by advocating a withdrawal from Nato, they argued that it was not being *bündnisfähig* that mattered most, but instead being peaceful to the extreme. Thus the relatively consensual nature of West German foreign policy culture did not preclude disputes over the hierarchy of roles. Germany's enlargement policy was not just about a clash between old and new roles, it was also a profound clash over the hierarchy of old roles which had never quite left the Federal Republic.

Let us conclude. We have introduced role theory as a conceptual bridge between foreign policy culture and state behaviour, and have defined foreign policy culture as the sum of role conceptions collectively held by a foreign policy-making elite. This sum has been conceptualized as a prism through which a host of external and internal influences, material and normative, must filter before affecting foreign policy. We have pointed out that states can suffer from role conflicts, and have identified a number of ways in which they can escape such conflicts, all of which involve a recapitulation of particular roles and an evaluation of their individual significance within the overall foreign policy culture. What, however, was this West German foreign policy culture? Which roles were central to it, which were marginal? Why did West Germany become what Hanns Maull called a Civilian Power, and why did this emerge in the Federal Republic rather than before 1945?

2
Why is Germany a Civilian Power?

Introduction

The purpose of this chapter is to explain why Germany can be categorized as a Civilian Power. This will be no comprehensive history of German foreign policy. All we can offer is a set of brief sketches, emphasizing only the most important elements of continuity and change. We will start with a few observations about German foreign policy after the establishment of the empire in 1871, and link these to the tentative democratization of foreign policy in the Weimar Republic. Identifying 1945 as the key rupture in German history, we will see that before 1945 the exercise of Civilian Power was difficult, if not impossible, because no functioning democracy had come into being. Although German foreign policy before 1945 also contained non-military elements, these lacked the normative basis required of a Civilian Power and were subjected to aggression and military power at the critical junctures of German history. The failure of a civilian foreign policy is thus connected to a much larger failure in German political history, namely that of liberalism and democracy. German society never established the preconditions for the exercise of a Civilian Power foreign policy because it had not established civilianized politics at home. The emergence of Civilian Power in the Federal Republic after 1945 was made possible by the emancipation of civil society from the state, and by the practices of Western integration and Ostpolitik. These practices became part of West Germany's foreign policy culture over time, and established that, for the first time in German history, national considerations were successfully subjected to democratic values. This was the essence of Civilian Power. It established a set of roles that were so deeply ingrained that they survived unification, and critically affected German policies towards East Central Europe after 1990.

Civilian Power before 1945

There is no space here to expand in detail on those aspects of German foreign policy in the last decades of the nineteenth century that existed independently of the more aggressive forms of power projection. The Berlin–Baghdad railway line can serve as an example. Conceived as a purely commercial enterprise, it was encouraged by Deutsche Bank, which was central to the financing and planning stages of the project in the late 1880s and which hoped that the construction of the mammoth project would ensure lucrative orders to Deutsche Bank's industrial customers. There was no interest in turning this into a national issue. 'The German Reich and our German nation', Georg Siemens, the spokesman of the Bank's board of directors said in 1890, 'have nothing to conquer in the Middle East and nothing to desire; we simply have an interest in stabilising the situation there.'[1] This purely commercial view of the Berlin–Baghdad railway was first rivalled by, and later subordinated to, a more assertive approach that sought to instrumentalize it for German foreign policy goals. In the late 1890s, the keen interest of Wilhelm II as well as of officials in the Foreign Office ensured that the railway became what Gregor Schöllgen called 'the most important project of German imperialism'.[2]

The episode encapsulates the increasing politicization of foreign investment in German governmental and commercial circles during the Wilhelmine Empire. Imbued with a missionary sense of nationalism, politicians became increasingly prone to viewing economics in the light of politics. Commercial activities were seen as part and parcel of the nation's struggle for power and survival in a hostile international environment. And vice versa, industrialists sought political support for their aims of expansion. According to Fritz Fischer, German industrialists had a significant influence on Theobald von Bethmann-Hollweg's (the then Chancellor's) September programme of 1914, in which the annexation of Belgium and the creation of a *Mitteleuropa* under German dominance were laid out as German war aims.[3] A similar stance was taken by many liberal politicians before and during the war. Friedrich Naumann was a chief architect of the *Mitteleuropa* to be, and Gustav Stresemann's war aims when lobbying Bethmann-Hollweg in December 1914 amounted to a fundamental redrawing of the map of Europe to allow for German hegemony.[4]

Dominated by *Blut und Boden* (blood and soil) fanatics, the protectionist lobbies of iron and rye and imperialists of all sorts, German foreign policy was rarely non-military and never civilian. Those aspects that were not oriented towards power and domination did not succeed in influencing government and public opinion. And in any case, their normative commitments were not sufficiently developed to make Civilian Power possible. Though this changed with the establishment of the Weimar Republic, it changed only in part. We may recall from Chapter 1 that the civilianization of domestic politics is the precondition for the exercise of Civilian Power. However, a necessary condition is not a sufficient one. Though Civilian Powers have to be democracies, not all democracies are by definition Civilian Powers. This is particularly true for democracies as bruised, battered and ultimately bullied as the Weimar Republic. In addition, the new Republic had a straitjacket in the form of the Versailles treaty – not only because Versailles had imposed the onus of war guilt and had excluded Germany from the League of Nations, nor because it had inflicted the heaviest losses of territory and population in the East, though this was not where the war had been lost, but because the reparations it levied crippled the German economy, destabilized German democracy and thus hampered German foreign policy's chances to develop Civilian Power features.

It was in its attempts to overcome the limitations imposed by the Versailles treaty in Western Europe that the Weimar Republic celebrated its most notable foreign policy achievements, the 1925 treaty of Locarno and the accession to the League of Nations. The spirit of Locarno, culminating in the Nobel peace prize for Stresemann and Briand, the Thoiry agreement and the Briand–Kellogg pact to outlaw war were elevating and contagious. For the period of one or two years in the mid-1920s it seemed as though Europe could escape the vicious circle of great power rivalry, war and armistice, that it could come to an arrangement that would guarantee a veritable peace. Through its Foreign Minister Gustav Stresemann, the Weimar Republic's foreign policy was inseparable from this spirit; it was the closest Germany had come to pursue the policies of a Civilian Power. This illustrates that the exercise of Civilian Power is a continuum, along which states comply more or less to the ideal type. Weimar Germany complied with the ideal type more than Wilhelmine Germany had, but not nearly as much as the Federal Republic would.

Yet Locarno and the League were only one part of the Weimar Republic's foreign policy; revisionism and increasingly rampant nationalism were the other.[5] Not all parts of the political spectrum (the nationalists in the Deutschnationale Volkspartei (DNVP) for instance, and of course the Nationalsozialistische deutsche Arbeiterpartei NSdAP)) had accepted Locarno.[6] There was thus never a consensus on foreign policy in the Weimar Republic, an agreed way of doing things that was to emerge as such a critical variable in the foreign policy culture of the Federal Republic. Alas, after Locarno, revisionism in the West had ceased to be official policy. In the East, it had not. Stresemann was convinced that Poland was a mere *Saisonstaat*, likely to wither away with the next storm. His revisionism, of course, was peaceful. The First World War had demonstrated that war would be an unfeasible option for Germany to take, not only because Germany had lost it, but because the price of war was too high. Revisionism in the East, therefore, had to be achieved through the mechanisms of the League of Nations.

This was the juncture at which Germany's aspirations clashed with what others were willing to concede. It was one thing to argue that peace and stability in Europe were unobtainable without a full German economic and diplomatic recovery. It was quite another thing, however, 'to persuade Britain and the United States, let alone France or Poland, that a stable Europe required territorial revision in Germany's favour'.[7] The treaty of Rapallo between Germany and the Soviet Union can in this light be seen as an agreement of two states with revisionist aspirations vis-à-vis Poland. Gdansk, the 'Polish corridor' and Upper Silesia were integral to the Weimar republic's Eastern policy.

This illustrates that even in Weimar, the tentative roots of Civilian Power were accompanied by a striving for power and mastery. Non-military, multilateral policies, like the Weimar Republic's overt and covert revisionism, do not necessarily qualify as *civilian* in the sense in which it is discussed here. On the contrary, military power, in a collective security system for instance, may well qualify as *civilian*, simply because it may be used to support the normative commitments of managed interdependence. It is thus not the instruments of power alone which a state uses in its foreign policy that determine to what extent it approximates the Civilian Power ideal type, it is also the normative goals for which these instruments are used. In the realm of Civilian Power, it is not what you have that matters, but what you do with it. Hence smaller and arguably less influential countries like Sweden may well approximate the Civilian Power ideal type very closely. The approach is not at all restricted to countries like Germany or Japan.

The reason for the failure of German Civilian Power before 1945 lies in the relations between state and society. They affected the definition of German national identity, which influenced foreign policy; they also failed to establish the constitutional safeguards that could have prevented the worst excesses of German power politics. Not only had, as Michael Stürmer put it, the national question appeared as the *leitmotif* of

German political culture in 1848 (after the failed liberal revolution), it was military victory that became the founding myth of the Bismarck Reich.[8] And the purported need of the *Machtstaat* (power state) to defend itself in a pernicious international environment prevented the build-up of a more mature citizenry.

The pursuit of Civilian Power was thus unlikely. The institutions of civil society, like democratic political parties, trade unions and economic interests, did not influence foreign policy sufficiently to ensure the pursuit of society's interests rather than the aggrandisement of state power. Since society had not emancipated itself from the state, foreign policy remained state-oriented. The establishment of democratic government in Germany remedied this situation only in part. The radicalism at the extremes of the political spectrum, in conjunction with the incomplete revolution of 1918/19, only contributed to the subversion of a possible civilianization of German foreign policy. Weimar, the 'democracy without democrats', suffered from the obstructionism of the remnants of the imperial order, the weakness of its democratic politicians and the disloyalty of the population. The connection between national identity and foreign policy remained a crucial one. The *Dolchstoßlegende* (according to which disloyal and unpatriotic politicians at home had stabbed the brave and unbeaten German army in the back) and the terms of the Versailles treaty facilitated the production of the myth that Germany had been injuriously treated and that the aim of German foreign policy should be to reverse this treatment. This became especially clear in the extensive consensus established in favour of revision in the East. As had been customary since the early nineteenth century, the unity and liberty demanded for the Germans, meaning the inclusion of German minorities in Poland, excluded the unity and liberty of others, namely the Poles.[9] The Germans continued to perceive themselves as a *Kulturnation*, not a *Staatsnation*. German national identity was linked to territory, blood ties and the quest for national grandeur, not to the values that gave the Weimar Republic its domestic constitution. And in contrast to the enlightened policies pursued in the West, territory, blood and the quest for national grandeur informed the policies towards the East. The failure of a civilian foreign policy is thus connected to a much larger failure in German political history, namely that of liberalism and democracy. German society never established the preconditions for the exercise of a Civilian Power foreign policy before 1945, because it had not established civilized politics at home. That was the crux of the matter.

It follows that democracy did not succeed after 1945 simply because integration into the bloc of Western democracies had liberated the Federal Republic from the *Mittellage* (its central position in Europe). Western integration after 1945 gave the illusion of only solving the *Mittellage* problem; its real merit was that it supported a profound and lasting democratization, which in turn had a profound and lasting effect on West German foreign policy. This is the foundation of the argument that unified Germany after 1990 behaved, with qualifications, like a Civilian Power. Despite being in a comparable international position to 1898 or 1926, unified Germany continued to pursue the policies prefigured by the foreign policy culture of the Federal Republic.

State–society relations after 1945

Two factors were decisive for state–society relations in the Federal Re-public in the late 1940s. One was the Basic Law (the Federal Republic's constitution), the other was the development of the Social Market Econ-omy. Both affected not only the course of West German democratiza-tion, but also its foreign policy. They complemented Western integration as the foundations for German Civilian Power. The Basic Law was constructed against the excessive powers of the state and, in the form of the *Grundrechte* (basic rights), gave West German civil society a constitutional basis. This explains that it was not only a guide for deci-sion making, but also functioned as a normative framework of West German democratic politics. This it did in contrast to the Weimar con-stitution. The Basic Law became the cornerstone of West German polit-ical culture. Thirty years after its adoption, it had become such a constitutive part of political identity that commentators began to talk about the 'constitutional patriotism' of their fellow countrymen. To an extent this, of course, reflected the haziness of the concept of the German nation after thirty years of partition. But equally significantly it indicated that the allegiance West Germans felt to the democratic values that informed the Basic Law had become stronger than their allegiance to the nation. In this respect the success of the Basic Law was a precondition for the civilianization of German foreign policy.

A second precondition was the success of the Social Market Economy. With its dual policy of maximum economic competition and decent social protection, the Social Market Economy was as much political order as economic theory. Through the imposition of competition, it broke the extreme accumulation of economic, social and political power that Germany's large industrial conglomerates had enjoyed before the war. West German industry, as Volker Berghahn argued, was 'American-ized' because in 'the American view, a modern industrial society needed an open economic marketplace just as much as it required a free-wheeling political "market". These markets were complementary, and one could not exist without the other.'[10] According to the architect of the Social Market Economy, Ludwig Erhard, the combination of price liberalization, currency reform, and anti-cartel legislation was the Fed-eral Republic's Economic Basic Law which complemented its political Basic Law.[11] The Social Market Economy was no imposition of *laissez-faire* capitalism; in line with the German tradition, it accounted for the need of those too weak to participate in the marketplace. 'The way to acclimatize Germans to a civil society based on a market economy', as Peter Pulzer put it, 'was to reassure them that some of their traditional expectations of the state would remain intact.'[12]

The Social Market Economy was instrumental in redefining the rela-tionship between society and state in Germany, and it was therefore much more than an economic enterprise. It was intrinsically political in its attempt to emancipate society from a state that in the previous eighty years had so often defied its interests. Creating a civil society by unleash-ing the forces of capitalism was a key achievement of postwar West German governance. It was a critical component of the taming of state power that led to the growth of what Peter Katzenstein famously de-scribed as a 'semi-sovereign state'.[13] More importantly for the discussion here, it generated the domestic preconditions for German Civilian Power, and thus affected the Federal Republic's foreign policy. The mutual pene-tration of state and society led to a definition of foreign policy objectives that was concerned with the well-being and prosperity of society.

The specific interaction between capitalism and the state in the Fed-eral Republic generated the unusually strong export performance of West German industry, which has invited the characterization of the Federal Republic as a 'trading state'.[14] This is not the view taken here. To be sure, one should not dispute the strong influence economic consider-ations had for West German foreign policy. But these cannot account for the normative commitments discussed above. They also cannot account for the strong military component of West German foreign policy, which made it the linchpin of Nato. The 'trading state' concept is distortive because it reduces West German foreign policy to an economistic cost–benefit analysis, which neither German security policy nor the normative commitments of West German foreign policy comply with. In contrast, the Civilian Power view employed here holds that the calculation of interests is influenced by state identity, which for

the Federal Republic has involved the recasting of state–society relations, Western integration and Ostpolitik.

West European integration, security and Ostpolitik

The Federal Republic was a child of the Cold War. As the western half of
a divided Germany, the Federal Republic emanated from a European
order that was itself divided, and it depended vitally on the Western
Allies for its security in an overall environment that was itself insecure.[15]
In the first years of its existence, without an army and without sovereignty, it was a mere object in world politics; its predicament was
encapsulated in the Berlin blockade, when the Western Allies stood by
a weak and infant state-to-be that felt under threat and that owed its
statehood to their benevolence. In this context, Konrad Adenauer's
foreign policy aims were threefold: first, security and prosperity for the
fifty million West Germans; secondly, sovereignty for the West German
state and equality in its relations with the Western powers; thirdly,
German unification on exclusively Western terms. Adenauer believed
that all three of these fundamental aims could be attained through
Western integration, and West Germany's cumulative Western integration therefore provided the cornerstone of its foreign policy and domestic order. Although the Western zones of occupation had already been
incorporated into the Western system through the reception of Marshall
Aid and their participation in the OEEC and the European Payments
Union, the most significant arrangements consisted of the Federal
Republic's incorporation into the Western bloc through the ECSC and
the EEC in economic affairs, and through the EDC and Nato in security
matters.

We should remember throughout this discussion that the foreign
policy of the infant West German state did not just limit itself to the
entertainment of sublime ideals. Instead, we can follow Andrei
Markovits and Simon Reich's account. Markovits and Reich argue that
while the collective memory of war, occupation and genocide affected
West German policy, the Bonn Rupublic's policies, strategies, and
actions were guided just like any other state's by efforts to optimize its
interests.[16]

There is no space here to tell in any detail the story of how the foreign
policy of the Federal Republic became civilianized. Instead, we will
reduce the richness of historical material to six principles, pointing
out the connection between Western integration and civilianization.
We will see below that these principles became cornerstones of West

Germany's foreign policy culture and affected German enlargement policy after 1990. The first principle was Franco-German partnership. In many respects, the revolutionary character of Western Europe's postwar settlement lay not just in the integration effort as such, but in the fact that it was piloted by France and West Germany. This was also expressed by the rich symbolism of the relationship between Adenauer and de Gaulle. Since Western integration was also reconciliation, especially with France, it established the indispensable moral foundations on which all German foreign policy after 1945 had to be built. The discussion of Germany's EU enlargement policy in the 1990s will illustrate that the German stance did not only depend on France – that might not be surprising – but cannot actually be understood without constant reference to French policies.

The second principle, and this is related, was the turn away from balance-of-power politics. Both the ECSC and the EEC were arrangements that provided advantages for all participants. Even though interests were not necessarily identical, ways were found of pursuing these interests in an amicable rather than an adversarial way. This meant that, thirdly, state interests were no longer viewed exclusively in terms of relative gains. State cooperation would generate overall positive gains that would make these states more secure. Fourthly, nation states would shed important decision-making powers to the Community level. Though not all these functions were carried out by supranational institutions, the practice of pooled sovereignty limited the autonomy of individual nation state policy. However, in conjunction with the third principle, this was acceptable because it was seen to generate overall benefits.

Fifthly, integration was a process. It was a voyage into the unknown, its end point was indistinct. For some, this end point was a federal West European state. For others it was a loose alliance of nation states. For others still, it was an Odyssean adventure in which the journey mattered, not the destination. Although the haziness of the aim of integration contributed to the success of the project, it did at times provoke fierce debate. This was especially so when the process seemed to have come to a crossroads, as it did for instance in the 1950s, concerning the geographical scope of integration. The debate over British membership and the Efta countries was one of its aspects; the debate over the effects Western integration would have on German unification was another. Yet common to both was the approach that the integration process should develop both functionally and geographically. Sixthly, and related to this, the fact that integration was a *process* was concomitant with the belief that it was *progress*. This belief was essential for West

German policy, not least because of its concern over unification. For only if Western integration was conceptualized as progress could one claim that it laid the foundation for German unification on Western terms. One by one, these principles became part of West Germany's foreign policy culture. They were essential for its civilianization, not only because they stabilized West Germany's infant democracy but because multilateralism is a cornerstone of Civilian Power. As the discussion in the remainder of this book will show, they affected Germany's enlargement policy after 1990.

The Federal Republic's Western integration would have been incomplete without the security dimension and the link to the United States. At the height of the Cold War in the early 1950s, no issue was as emotionally charged as rearmament, and for the future course of Western integration none had as far-reaching consequences. Proponents of West German rearmament advocated three reasons. The first was a reaction to the Cold War and the perceived Soviet threat; the second was that rearmament would cement West Germany's ties with Western Europe and the United States, helping to anchor democratic values; the third – emphasized in West Germany in particular – was that rearmament would turn West Germany into a proper state. It would accelerate West Germany's attainment of sovereignty, and would thus prevent the Potsdam nightmare of the victorious powers negotiating about Germany's future over and above the Germans' head.

Opponents of rearmament argued that the Weimar experience with the armed forces had hardly been a happy one, and that the Army's disloyalty (for instance during the Kapp Putsch in 1920) had been one of the reasons for the failure of the Republic. In any case, rearmament within a decade after the end of the war seemed simply unbearable. After Germany had brought war over Europe twice within thirty years, peace should now emanate from German soil. This argument was popular in West Germany, but it also reflected the deep-seated reservations of some West European countries, notably France. Secondly, opponents pointed out that the absorption of the two German states into their respective military alliance would seal the partition of Germany. To have the two German states oppose one another with nuclear weapons and a huge potential of conventional weapons would make their dissolution and eventual unification highly improbable. This was an argument put forward most fervently by the SPD, which after having been accused of betrayal by the centre-right parties in the Weimar Republic, was determined not to open itself up to such criticism again. In the event, the proponents of rearmament won.

Striving for unification would have entailed neutralization (which was in fact what Stalin offered in 1952) and, in the eyes of the Adenauer government, would thus have destabilized the nascent democratic system. The West German leadership at the time feared that a neutral and unprotected Germany would not be able to withstand the lure and pressure from the Soviet Union for long. Democracy and freedom for the fifty million Germans of the Federal Republic were thus more important than the unification of the two German states. This argument succeeded because its proponents were in government, because they offered a credible protection from Communism and because they enjoyed the support of the Western Allies. There was nothing inevitable in their victory. The fact that they won, however, established the single most important principle of West Germany's foreign policy culture: that the adherence to the values on which the Federal Republic was founded, and on the grounds of which it was tied to the West, were more important than German unification.[17] Democratic values took precedence over national ones. This was the essence of civilianization.

The success of West German foreign policy until 1990 was therefore intimately linked to Nato. Due to the patterns of civil–military relations, and due to its Western integration, the *Bundeswehr* contributed significantly to West Germany's civilianization. One reason for this was the fact that state formation preceded rearmament. Whereas the army had represented a key element of continuity between the Imperial Order and the Weimar democracy, the Federal Republic had been founded as a state without an army, to be defended at first exclusively by the Allies and later with their indispensable support. Its eventual rearmament was thus a manifestation of its adherence to the Western bloc, which in turn it cemented. Not least because the *Bundeswehr* had no independent command structure, West Germany's military power was neither conceivable nor functional without the Western military alliance. And if it was true, as Adenauer claimed, that West Germany only became a state when it had the ability to defend itself, then it also only became a state as a part of the Western alliance. One of the essentials of Civilian Power, the multilateral conduct of foreign policy, was thus present at the Federal Republic's creation and a midwife at its birth.

The notion that the Federal Republic violated Civilian Power principles because it featured such significant armed forces is therefore potentially misleading. We have already seen that Civilian Powers are committed to the defence of the values for which they stand. Although they do so primarily with non-military instruments, we have no reason to assume that they must not defend themselves. This reveals a tension in the Civilian Power ideal type between the defence of democratic, civilian values on the one hand, and the peaceful pursuit of foreign policy on the other. West German policy reflected this tension repeatedly. Part of the West German political establishment and the population favoured the defence of the democratic principles on which the West German state was founded. Others elevated peace to the most important principle of foreign policy. The potential tension between these two principles manifested itself clearly in the early 1980s, when the adherents of the peace movement opposed the modernization of Nato's nuclear weapons with the argument that it endangered peace, while first the Schmidt and then the Kohl government maintained that the democratic order in West Germany was threatened, and that in order to defend it the Nato weapons had to be modernized. We may hold, however, that it is precisely this tension that ensures that Civilian Power principles are guarded. The commitment to peace corresponds to the non-military instruments of policy; the commitment to democratic values establishes the normative principles which foreign policy has to adhere to. Although one might argue that not all steps of Nato policy, say, in the early 1980s were prudent, Nato remained at heart a defensive alliance, which tied its members freely to one another, and which, despite exceptions, was built on democratic values. Although Nato membership is no precondition of Civilian Power, in the German case it laid some of the foundations that turned West German foreign policy into its distinctive self.

Again, the history of rearmament and of West Germany's relations with the United States is far too complex to be related here in any detail. In order to identify what really mattered, we will therefore again extract from the stream of historical events a set of principles that guided West German security policy. The first is the principle of indivisible security. Article 5 of the Nato treaty establishing that member states treat an attack on one member as an attack on the whole organization was, given the situation at the height of the Cold War, of tremendous benefit for the Federal Republic. It is significant for the Civilian Power argument because the collective exercise of military power is at the heart of conceptions of collective defence and security. In essence this amounted to an American nuclear security guarantee to West Germany. The security partnership that was the foundation of West German–American relations can therefore serve as our second principle.

Thirdly, this in turn meant that the Federal Republic would have to master a diplomatic juggle between France and the United States, since both countries fulfilled indispensable functions for its foreign policy. The tensions this frequently generated, and the lofty rhetoric it gave rise to, were as integral to the foreign policy culture of the Federal Republic as any of the principles listed above. This came to the fore especially in the early 1960s when an underlying insecurity grew in the Federal Republic about the reliability of the American nuclear guarantee. Our final principle is the fact that West Germany's accession to Nato and the concomitant American military presence in Western Europe had a profound and paradoxical effect on the process of European integration. On the one hand, the American security shield offered reassurance to France against the possibility of West German rearmament, and thus allowed the process of European economic integration to flourish. On the other hand, the fact that after the failure of the EDC European integration was devoid of military aspects also saved European nation states from biting the bullet and integrating further in these highly sensitive areas of their power. Unwittingly, American policy on Western Europe delimited the minimum and maximum of European integration. As we will see in Chapters 3 and 4 these principles became integral to West Germany's foreign policy culture and affected Germany's enlargement policies after 1990.

Whereas the progress of European integration and the 'economic miracle' testified to the success of *Westbindung* and the transformation of state–society relations, by the mid-1960s it seemed as though Adenauer's Eastern policies, based on the non-recognition of the status quo in Eastern Europe, were a resounding failure. The 'magnet theory', whereby West Germany's prosperity and domestic liberty would pull the GDR out of the Soviet orbit, had not materialized. Moreover, the Federal Republic's claim of sole representation (that is, of not recognizing the GDR) and its Hallstein doctrine (according to which it severed diplomatic relations with states that recognized the GDR) became increasingly untenable as relations between the superpowers relaxed, and as Charles de Gaulle pursued a French version of détente vis-à-vis the Soviet bloc. Policies that had been devised to isolate East Germany threatened now to isolate the Federal Republic. As Wolfram Hanrieder put it:

> Bonn's aspirations and policies became an uneasy mix of conflicting attitudes about international politics and the meaning of the 'national' interest, embracing a territorial mode of thinking in one context and rejecting it in another, looking forward and backward in history at the same time, being both in and out of tune with fundamental political, economic, and psychological developments in the postwar European order.[18]

In its Eastern policies, the real adjustment of West German foreign policy came with Willy Brandt's Ostpolitik in 1969.

Ostpolitik established five new principles in West Germany's foreign policy culture. The first, as mentioned, was the turn away from the territorial politics of the past, adjusting the Federal Republic's Eastern policies to the progressive policies of the West. The second was that it established more independence. Ostpolitik was new and daring not only because it suggested that the Federal Republic should recognize the GDR, but because it clarified that not all its foreign policy priorities were necessarily congruent with those of the Western powers. It is true that Nato's Harmel report in 1967 had already prescribed the diplomatic injunctions which, in a sense, Ostpolitik followed. But it is also true that the Western allies, in particular the United States, entertained considerable disquiet over the aims and intentions of Brandt's Eastern policies. The fact that Ostpolitik equipped the Federal Republic with room to manoeuvre, which in fact only manifested itself in actual policy in the early 1980s, is significant for tracing the origins of Civilian Power because it established the slice of autonomy within which the Civilian Power priorities could be developed. That Ostpolitik was routinely enacted and established as an integral part of foreign policy was the best hint that West Germany did not just behave according to the constraints of the international environment, or to put it differently, that it had developed its own foreign policy culture. This leads to the third principle, continued Western integration. Ostpolitik was as significant for what it did not do as for what it did. Bonn did not pursue a more active Eastern policy at the expense of Western integration but as its natural supplement. Indeed, only continued Western integration provided the strength and diplomatic vigour in the tough negotiations with the Soviet Union. That this was the case cemented and completed the foreign policy culture of the Federal Republic.

Fourthly, Ostpolitik re-established the supreme importance of the Soviet Union for West German foreign policy. Not least since the Soviet Union had started to entertain diplomatic relations with the Federal Republic, and was thus in effect exempted from the Hallstein doctrine, it had had a special place in West German diplomacy. But this was now supplemented by the increasing evidence that the key to German unification lay in Moscow, and that all *Deutschlandpolitik* would therefore have to be triangular in nature: from Bonn via Moscow to Berlin.[19] Good relations with Moscow were from now on important for Bonn, despite the uncertainty this provoked in the West, and despite the new Cold War in the early 1980s. This preoccupation with Moscow continued

after German unification and played a crucial role in Germany's enlargement policy afterwards. It was not merely a preoccupation of power
politics, however, in the way that it had been so often in the past.
Instead it was closely linked to the desire for peace, reconciliation and
interdependence.

This links to the fifth and final aspect of Ostpolitik, namely its moral
significance. Due to the outbreak of the Cold War and the non-existence
of diplomatic relations, one of the key functions of Ostpolitik was
dealing with the history of war and occupation inherited from the
1940s. Here, the Federal Republic had a lot of ground to cover. On top
of the Third Reich's enormous brutality in the East, the Federal Republic
had until then been portrayed as a revanchist state by the regimes in
Eastern Europe. Thus, Ostpolitik was also an initiative to improve the
image of the German in Eastern Europe. In this it corresponded to
deeply held desires on behalf of many West Germans, especially those
of the younger generation, to dissociate themselves from the evil that
was the German past, and to act and be perceived as 'good'. This was a
tremendously powerful input into the civilianization of German foreign
policy. It informed not only the social consensus that was established
around Ostpolitik and led to the SPD/FDP election victory in 1972. It
also motivated the peace movement that swept through the Federal
Republic at the time of the missile deployment in the early 1980s and
has had a strong influence on the foreign policies of the SPD and the
Greens ever since.

What can we expect?

We have seen that by the 1980s an all-party consensus carried the
essentials of foreign policy. This was a key feature of the Federal
Republic's foreign policy culture. Twice the respective opposition party
had to accept a policy against which it had originally fought in order to
make itself electable. The SPD's acceptance of Western integration is
usually associated with Herbert Wehner's speech in 1960; the CDU/
CSU's acceptance of Ostpolitik was a protracted process lasting the
better part of the 1970s. This meant that the key principles outlined
above were adhered to once the change of government took place.
Whereas the SPD did not challenge Western integration in the 1970s,
the CDU/CSU did not challenge Ostpolitik in the 1980s. This was the
substance of consensual politics. However, there is no denying that
major disagreements riddled the debate about how to proceed with
foreign policy. In the 1980s, for instance, there was a strong dispute

about how much further to take Ostpolitik, especially since few of the original aims concerning the unification of Germany established in the 1970s appeared within reach.[20] The respect for the integrity of established arrangements did not include a consensus on how to proceed with them, especially when different principles clashed with one another.

How do these principles of West Germany's foreign policy culture help in understanding the policy unified Germany pursued towards its Eastern neighbours after 1990? In what respects, precisely, was the past likely to influence the future? Having established that due to its domestic transformation and international embeddedness the Federal Republic would behave like a Civilian Power, we can try to specify this in terms of policies. How does a Civilian Power behave towards a set of nascent market democracies right on its border? First, it would be likely to eliminate all bilateral problems, like territorial questions and the status of minorities. Secondly, it would attempt to stretch Civilian Power to these countries, that is it would attempt to incorporate them into the network of interdependence in order to stabilize their democracies and to support their prosperity. Such a stabilization would be unattainable through bilateral arrangements, since managing interdependence requires institutions and organizations that are predominantly multilateral.

Hence, civilianization occurs through stabilization, which in turn occurs in multilateral frameworks. These multilateral frameworks could, in theory, be founded from scratch. It would be possible for a completely new organization to replace the EU and to manage economic affairs for the whole of Europe, and that an organization like the OSCE would be founded for the management of military security. In the case study under observation, however, the strategy of institutional inception was always unlikely because the unification of Germany in 1990 had occurred through the strategy of institutional extension, meaning the extension of the Federal Republic's domestic political arrangements and international commitments to the Eastern Länder. A Civilian Power seeking the civilianization, stabilization, and multilateralization of East Central Europe would therefore have to embark upon the course of institutional extension. For Germany as a Civilian Power, enlargement was the name of the game.

However, the Eastern enlargement of Nato and the EU was an entirely novel process. It did not sit naturally with the foreign policy culture of a state that had learned to conduct its foreign policy in the stalemate of the Cold War, under the working assumption that, for the time being, an extension of its multilateral commitments into Eastern Europe would be perfectly impossible. In order to formulate working hypotheses about how Germany's enlargement policies may have sat with the principles of West German foreign policy outlined above, we will first of all identify six of the roles typical for the Federal Republic's foreign policy.

Of the roles related to European integration, the first is that of *integration deepener*. As mentioned, the exercise of state building had, for the Federal Republic, gone hand in hand with West European integration, and its gains in sovereignty had been resubmitted at the European level in order to deepen integration. The second role is that of *integration widener*. It was crucial for eventually attaining German unification, and also for the enlargement of the European Community in the 1970s and 1980s. Out of Nato related roles, the *security consumer* identifies the dependence on the nuclear guarantee of the United States, which affected all conceptions of Western integration. Related to this directly was the role of *Atlanticist*, which gave primacy to the United States precisely because of the security dimension. The fifth role is that of *Gaullist*, emphasizing the importance of France not only in European integration but also in security matters. This shows that the role of *security consumer* – even under the changed circumstances of post-Cold War Europe – could either be closely associated with that of the *Atlanticist*, as in effect it was for the duration of the Federal Republic, or with that of the *Gaullist*, which it was not. The sixth and final role was that of the *Muscovite*. Entailing a strong focus on Moscow, this went hand in hand with conceptions of a genuine, pan-European security framework, in which aspirations to unification could be maintained just as easily as the desire to be good and truly 'European'.

These roles were not necessarily congruent with one another at all times. Indeed, they were at times highly contradictory. One role conflict occurred between the *integration deepeners* and the *integration wideners*, a second between *Atlanticists* and *Gaullists* (especially prominent in the CDU/CSU in the 1960s), a third between *Atlanticists* and *Muscovites*. The last erupted especially over the most likely path leading to the attainment of unification, but was really decided in favour of Atlanticism, first by the Adenauer government in the early 1950s and later by the Brandt and Schmidt governments in the 1970s. This leads to the concluding observation that in the three role conflicts of West Germany's foreign policy culture, two roles dominated the other four. These two roles were those of the *integration deepener* and *Atlanticist*. Their continued presence, one can safely assume, would critically affect Germany's enlargement policy after 1990. This leads to the following three expectations.

First, the commitment to deepening integration would predominate over the desire to widen integration, especially immediately after unification. *Secondly, the role of the Atlanticist would continue to predominate over that of the Gaullist.* This affects the security arrangements made for East Central Europe, since Atlanticism entails the continued military presence of the United States in Europe, so that the security arrangements for East Central Europe are likely to be made through Nato. Yet Atlanticism would be undermined by the weakened significance of the role of *security consumer*, which would decline because of the diminution of the Soviet/Russian threat with the end of the Cold War. A role change for unified Germany would only be a departure from Nato, which in turn of course would entail no enlargement of Nato, and instead an arrangement for the military security of East Central Europe based on beefed up versions of the OSCE, the EU or the WEU.

Thirdly, a heightened role conflict would erupt between Atlanticists and the Muscovites over NATO enlargement. Though Atlanticism would persist, the preoccupation with Russia would function as a strong incentive to refrain from any policies that could endanger good relations with Moscow. How this role conflict is solved cannot be assumed from the roles defined here and from the hierarchy in which they have been placed. Nevertheless, a really new self-conception of German policy would have occurred if Germany either decided to oppose Nato enlargement completely, because that would contradict the principles of multilateralized stabilization typical for a Civilian Power, or if it went ahead with Nato enlargement completely irrespective of Moscow's stance. To sum up, then, the foreign policy culture of the Federal Republic leads to the expectation that Germany will react towards its Eastern neighbours in terms of multilateralized stabilization that is in essence civilianization, and that this civilianization will be critically affected by its role as *integration deepener*, *Atlanticist* and *Muscovite*.

3
Bilateral Relations

Bilateral diplomacy and Civilian Power

After 1989, bilateral diplomacy between Germany and the smaller Eastern neighbours was charged with two tasks: to overcome the burdens of the war, and to subdue the flawed notions of a political *Mitteleuropa*. Despite Ostpolitik, relations between the Federal Republic and its Eastern European neighbours had been marred by memories of the Second World War until the late 1980s. Communist power in Eastern European satellite states had relied on depicting West Germany as revanchist and dangerous. The Soviet Union had portrayed itself as the protector against West German aggression; Communist parties in Eastern Europe had legitimized the proximity to the Soviet Union as a prerequisite for state survival. This was the case especially in Poland and Czechoslovakia, where the scars left by the German occupation in the war were deepest, and where territorial revision and expulsions after the war heightened fears of German revanchism.[1] In addition, reconciliation between Germans and Eastern Europeans was bound to remain partial and incomplete as long as a free exchange between people was impossible, and as long as West German foreign policy was geared towards regimes in Eastern Europe that were not representative of popular preferences.

After 1989, West German foreign policy therefore still had a lot of ground to cover. It had to persuade its Eastern neighbours that German unification would not be dangerous. It had to solve a whole host of outstanding bilateral problems pertaining to the legacy of the war, especially the final recognition of the Polish–German border, the treatment of the Sudeten Germans forced to leave Czechoslovakia after 1945, the treatment of German minorities in all three countries and their reassurance on dispensing with reparations.

Finally, Germany had to initiate a process of real reconciliation with its Eastern neighbours, this time at the level of society, which had been precluded as long as the Communist regimes were in power. Bilateral policies were therefore intimately linked to Civilian Power policies. For Germany, it would be impossible to portray itself as a Civilian Power as long as it was perceived through the lens of the Second World War. It would also be extremely difficult to contribute to the stabilization of the Eastern neighbours if bilateral problems were not solved.

The solution of bilateral problems was essential for Germany after 1990 for a second reason. This had to do with the term *Mitteleuropa*, and the connotations it has for the conduct of German foreign policy.[2] Peter Stirk has observed that in the past, German economic and military power was at the heart of the 'inherent disequilibrium of Mitteleuropa'.[3] Friedrich Naumann had proposed a *Mitteleuropa* dominated by Germany in 1915 as part of the war aims discussion in the early years of the First World War.[4] Assuming that this was beneficial for the smaller Central and Eastern European states, which by themselves were too weak to survive, he argued that Germany could use its hegemony over its Eastern neighbours in order to propel itself to world power status in terms of territory and population, where it lagged behind Russia, Britain and the United States. After the defeat in the First World War the revisionism directed at the Central European countries became even more aggressive than Naumann's concept had been. After 1933 economic links were fostered through bilateral treaties between Germany and its Eastern neighbours. The treaties establishing the exchange of raw materials and agricultural products for Germany's manufacturing goods were geared towards German autarchy and rearmament, and are widely seen as having been detrimental to the economic modernization of East Central Europe.[5]

In the first half of the century, the term *Mitteleuropa* therefore suggested German hegemonic ambitions in Europe, if not the world; it was the antithesis of Civilian Power. This changed when the concept was revived in the mid-1980s. *Mitteleuropa* now sought to contradict the notion of East and West in Europe in order to overcome the continent's division. This time the concept was revived by intellectuals from countries belonging to the Eastern bloc, by people like Gyorgy Konrad, Milan Kundera, Vaclav Havel, but was readily picked up by West German thinkers like Peter Glotz and Peter Bender, who saw it as an opportunity to overcome the strict division of Germany and Europe.[6] For Glotz and Bender *Mitteleuropa* was less a cultural consideration than a political one, seeking to overcome the American dominance of West Central

Europe as much as the Soviet dominance of East Central Europe. This was not an attempt to dominate the countries to Germany's East, but to foster cultural links, human contacts and, especially, disarmament.[7]

There was, however, a parallel to the earlier concept of *Mitteleuropa*, namely an uneasy relation to tight Western integration and the security partnership with the United States. The discussion on a political *Mitteleuropa* in the 1980s questioned the key principle of West German foreign policy: that a defence alliance based on indivisible security and common democratic values was superior to the concepts of nationhood and national unity. In this sense the common strand that ran through discussions of *Mitteleuropa* was its offer of an alternative to the West: as an alternative to Locarno and the League in the 1920s, to the recalcitrance of the West to be dominated economically and politically in the 1930s, and to the principles that cemented the Western Alliance in the 1980s. It was precisely for this reason that commentators from East Central Europe were uneasy about the political use of the concept *Mitteleuropa* after 1990. Janusz Reiter, Poland's ambassador in Bonn, observed:

> The idea of *Mitteleuropa* should be left to artists and historians... A *mitteleuropäisch* Germany would not shorten the path to European integration that Poland and other Central European countries seek. It would only prolong it and make it more complicated.[8]

By extending the principles of Western integration eastwards after 1990, Germany fundamentally negated the notion of a revived political *Mitteleuropa*. Similar to Ostpolitik, then, *Mitteleuropa* in a political sense is obviated in the post-Cold War Europe by the dynamics of European integration. For this, as we will see, German policy was instrumental.

Hungary

In the 1980s West German relations with Hungary were more relaxed than with other countries of the Soviet bloc in East Central Europe. The fact that Hungary had belonged to the 'axis' powers during the war may have contributed to this, as may the absence of an 'expellees' question', geographical distance and the Hungarian affinity to Austria and, by extension, to the German cultural heritage. The Kadar regime had initiated the process of political and economic liberalization very early so that by 1989, social and commercial links were already well developed. Liberalization also came to dominate Hungarian foreign policy. As early as 1987, the Federal Republic made a DM 1 billion loan available to

Hungary, which brought in return the opening of a Goethe Institute in Budapest and an even better treatment of the German minority in Hungary. Liberalization continued when a group of reform communists around Prime Minister Miklos Nemeth oriented Hungary away from the Soviet bloc, culminating in the cutting of the barbed wire on the Austro-Hungarian border at the end of June 1989.

These developments became extremely propitious two months later, when tens of thousands of East Germans sought to use the hole in the Iron Curtain to flee, still illegally, to Austria and then to the Federal Republic. This situation had been unforeseen by the Hungarian leadership, who had only allowed for its own citizens to travel freely. The fact that a huge number of East Germans now picked up on the issue confronted the Hungarian leadership with a difficult choice. Letting the thousands of East Germans that had gathered on Hungarian soil leave was a violation of a 1968 agreement with East Germany, while sending them back to East Germany meant propping up a sick dictatorship with whom the Hungarian leaders already felt they had little in common. Hungary stopped sending East Germans without exit visas back to the GDR on 9 August, thus encouraging a further influx and rendering the situation more tense. On 21 August an East German refugee was shot by Hungarian border guards not knowing how to deal with the situation. At a subsequent secret meeting near Bonn on 25 August between Nemeth, his foreign minister Gyula Horn, Kohl and Genscher, the Hungarians clarified that Hungary would refuse to close the border despite East German pressure. This meant that there would indeed be a mass exodus from East Germany, with a further 40 000 people leaving before the end of September. Hungary thus contributed significantly to the destabilization of the East German regime and set the path for German unification only a year later.[9] It is hard to overestimate the extent of German gratitude to Hungary for this assistance. Kohl recounts that he was in tears when Nemeth told him at Gymnich that he planned to let the East Germans on Hungarian territory leave within three weeks.[10] Hungary did not accept direct remuneration, but a DM 500 million loan was passed and visa regulations were abolished. Perhaps most importantly for this discussion, Kohl assured the Hungarians of his support for their accession to the EC. 'I thought it went without saying...that we helped those who helped us.'[11] It is remarkable how cordial German–Hungarian relations became over the following years.

The bilateral treaty signed in February 1992 cited Hungary's contribution to 'surmounting the division of Europe' in its preamble; in their speeches on German unification or European policy, German politicians unfailingly mentioned the Hungarian contribution.[12] In per capita terms, Hungary received more technical aid from Germany than any other state in Central Europe. This led to the joke that Hungary had once again turned into a *K. und K.* country, though this time *K. und K.* did not stand for *Kaiserlich und Königlich* but for Kohl and Kittel, Walter Kittel being the senior civil servant in charge of Germany's *Transform* programme that coordinates technical assistance. In 1995, at a time when German public finances had already plunged into turmoil, Hungary was granted another DM 500 million loan.

Poland

The relationship between Germany and Poland took quite a different path. In addition to the fact that Germany's legacy of war and occupation in Poland was horrific, the Communist governments in Poland had also instrumentalized this legacy in order to drum up popular support. For in their logic, only the Soviet Union could protect Poland against a revanchist Germany, and only the Communist Party, through its close links with the powerful in the Soviet Union, could defend Poland's territorial integrity. Tensions decreased after the signing of the Warsaw treaty in 1970, in which the Federal Republic recognized the Oder–Neisse line as the border between Poland and the GDR, and that those German territories which had been placed under 'Polish administration' at Yalta had in fact become part of Poland. Though contacts between Poland and West Germany proliferated after 1970, they were bound to remain limited as long as they were not properly devolved to the level of society. When the government of Tadeusz Mazowiecki, Poland's first non-communist prime minister since 1947, assumed power in September 1989, both sides, West German and Polish, increased their efforts at improving bilateral relations. This occurred on different levels. One was 'general reconciliation', or the art of apologizing and forgiving. This was by no means insignificant, but had to be tested when it came to the crunch. The crunch, the second level of bilateral relations, were particular cases of bilateral problems such as the status of minorities, the bilingual naming of Silesian towns and streets, reparations and, most importantly, the recognition of the Oder–Neisse line as the final border between unified Germany and Poland. The third level was the numerous congruent interests, for instance in commercial matters, border operability and international affairs.

It seemed at first as though the considerable energy the Kohl and Mazowiecki governments had devoted to these issues would pay off. Between 9 and 14 November, only some ten weeks after Mazowiecki had come into office, Kohl and Genscher paid a state visit to Poland, concluding a number of agreements on the protection of the German minority in Silesia, the bilingual renaming of the German cultural heritage in Silesia and a comprehensive economic aid package for Poland. At the end of the visit, Kohl and Mazowiecki celebrated a mass together at Kreisau. The photo of their embrace went around the world as a symbol of Polish–German reconciliation. Few people thought at that time that a deep and bitter deterioration in bilateral relations was only weeks ahead.

Alienation set in after 28 November 1989. On that day, Kohl presented his ten-point plan on German unification in the Bundestag, omitting a mention of the Oder–Neisse line as the final Eastern border of a unified German state.[13] In Warsaw, this omission caused consternation. 'Mazowiecki was shocked at first, then alarmed,' the then Polish Foreign Minister Krzysztof Skubiszewski recalled in an interview with the author, 'and he was determined to do something about it.'[14] It is sometimes argued that the omission of the Oder–Neisse line was an oversight, that Kohl and his advisers had merely forgotten to mention that unified Germany would exist within the borders of the two German states plus Berlin, because this was seen as a matter of fact. Indeed, the Federal Republic had signed the Warsaw treaty in 1970 recognizing the inviolability of Poland's frontiers, and Kohl had said in the Bundestag only a day before he left on his state visit to Poland that his government would abide by that commitment.[15]

This argument is not persuasive. The ten-point plan was, to all intents and purposes, the most important speech in Helmut Kohl's political life. It was intensively discussed in the Federal Chancellery. Kohl knew full well that it would place him at the helm of the domestic and international debate on the future of the two German states, and that every single one of his sentences would be closely watched. The speech was meticulously drafted by Kohl's closest advisers in the Chancellery and finalized by Kohl himself on the weekend before it was given. It is quite inconceivable that a point as essential as the borders of the future state should not have been deemed important enough to be included. Other, arguably less important, points were elaborated in some detail.[16] Moreover, the omission of the Oder–Neisse line in the ten-point plan was perfectly consistent with Kohl's stance in the months to come. If this had been an oversight, Kohl could have made up for it within days. But he chose not to.

The reason was a mixture of genuine legal concerns and domestic political calculations. The legal concerns should not be underestimated. There was a general consensus that West Germany was not the appropriate legal entity to negotiate a treaty on behalf of the unified state. Since West Germany had signed the Warsaw treaty, Kohl argued, the problem was solved. Yet legal concerns were only one part of the calculation; domestic politics and the consideration of the expellees' organizations in the Federal Republic were another, especially in an election year. The territorial losses that had been imposed on Germany after the Second World War had gone hand in hand with the expulsion of Germans and their resettlement in the Federal Republic. By some accounts, this was a group of ten million people. Their expropriation and expulsion turned them into a potentially radical electorate, supporting policies towards the possessors of their former territories, especially towards Poland and Czechoslovakia, that contained at least some chance that they would eventually be allowed to return to their homes, or at least receive financial compensation. Ever since Adenauer had opened Christian Democracy for the expellees' parties in the 1950s, the CDU/CSU had relied very heavily on the expellees' votes. While this repeatedly swung CDU/CSU policies in favour of the expellees, it also meant that these did not have their own, more radical political parties. This explains Kohl's manoeuvring. Although Kohl seems to have been unequivocal on the inviolability of the Oder–Neisse line in private, he was conspicuously quiet about it in public.[17] For months, all the Chancellor said on the topic was a constant reiteration of the legal positions that served as a welcome argument against doubters at home and abroad.

Mazowiecki's scepticism towards German promises and legal positions was exaggerated but not entirely unfounded. A state has to be prepared to defend its territory if it is to survive. The border topic was therefore by definition a highly sensitive one, not least because the Soviet Union, which for decades had portrayed itself as a guarantor of Yalta Poland, was about to withdraw its troops. If German legal positions doubted the finality of the border, would they not also doubt the finality of the entire postwar settlement on which Poland's territorial integrity was based? Ever since the signing of the Warsaw treaty, successive West German governments had maintained that, though West Germany respected Poland's territorial integrity, the final settlement of borders in Europe could only be achieved as part of an overall peace treaty. The implication of this was of course that a peace treaty would also have to address the German question. Keeping open the border question, at least legally, was therefore also a way of keeping open the German question, at least legally.

At the time, such a legalistic position appeared to be petty-minded, but for successive West German governments it was the only fall-back position to keep the German question open in face of an overwhelmingly adverse reality. In addition, German policy makers were bound by the 1973 ruling of the Constitutional Court. West German politicians therefore tended to make an explicit link between all borders in Europe. One day before the wall fell, Kohl repeated this old position on the Warsaw treaty in the Bundestag:

> Each of us knows what this means, knows that we do not yet have a peace treaty... The national right to self-determination is recognised in the charter of the United Nations. He who defames our claim to the realisation of that right for all Germans as 'revanchism' is really opposed to this basic law of the community of nations.[18]

As the destabilization of the East German regime accelerated and the flood of refugees to the Federal Republic increased, however, it suddenly seemed possible to use the momentum of the situation in order to attain unification much more quickly. The critical impetus for the decision to press ahead and take the initiative was probably the desire to stabilize the situation in East Germany. But there was also an international aspect. The pressure of the people could be utilized to avoid a peace treaty which, because of the likelihood of reparation claims and the large number of victor countries involved, would have delayed the process of unification and increased its costs to Germany. From the German position, developments in East Germany were a golden opportunity to drop demands for a peace treaty quietly and rapidly. From the Polish position, this seemed threatening. Therefore the Polish position hardened in the first two weeks of February 1990, that is after the announcement of economic and monetary union between East and West Germany, and the decision at the Ottawa CSCE conference that the external aspects of German unification would be dealt with in the 2+4 negotiations, which excluded Poland. What had been a German position for 19 years had changed literally overnight. Without any ill-feeling or wish to do harm, the constellation of priorities between the West German and Polish governments was extremely unfavourable: whereas Kohl was preoccupied with unification, Mazowiecki was preoccupied with the border. Both had only a limited understanding of the other's point of view.

Despite a constant increase of domestic and international pressure on Kohl, no significant breakthrough in the West German position had occurred until the end of February. At this time Kohl was under intense pressure from the SPD, the FDP and from parts of his own party. The matter assumed such significance that the coalition between the CDU/CSU and the FDP threatened to break up. An agreement was hammered out in a coalition round on 5 and 6 March 1990, proposing a joint declaration of the two German parliaments to be issued after the East German elections on 18 March. These declarations were to be endorsed by the two German governments. A final treaty, however, would only be negotiated and signed by an all-German government. When Kohl introduced the proposal in the Bundestag on 8 March, he said:

> It lies in our best self-interest not to burden the path towards unity with border questions. Only thus can we receive support for our national concern – the unity of the Germans – from our friends and neighbours in West and East.[19]

Kohl's emphasis that unified Germany would refrain from territorial claims vis-à-vis Poland only as part and parcel of a deal on German unification had a twofold audience. One comprised those in the international community sceptical about unification, especially in the Soviet Union. To them, the quotation read that the final recognition of the border would exact a price, namely unification. The second audience were the expellees' organizations in the Federal Republic. To them, the Chancellor inverted the argument: unification would be possible, but came at a price – the finalization of the Oder–Neisse line. In the weeks that followed, Kohl had a gargantuan task in bringing the expellees' organizations, especially their representatives among the CDU/CSU Bundestag deputies, to accept the declaration. Presenting the expellees with the stark choice between unification and the final recognition of the Oder–Neisse line, thus turning a national argument against a national grouping, was the most powerful weapon in Kohl's political repertoire. When the Bundestag voted on the declaration on 21 June 1990, Kohl said:

> There are many in our country who are deeply affected and pained by the declaration we give today... We have respect for them and their feelings and we can understand them well. But we also have to say clearly: He who wants to use the chance of completing Germany's unity in freedom has to give a clear answer to the question of the

Polish Western border. No one should deceive himself. We stand today before an entirely clear choice. Either we confirm the border as it exists, or we gamble away the chance of German unity for now.[20]

By hesitating for so long and by increasing the stakes, Kohl virtually forced the expellees' organizations to consent to his policy. In this respect, his line was a political masterstroke that weakened irredentism vis-à-vis Poland on the German political scene. This is not to say that Kohl's policy had no downside, especially with regard to Polish–German relations. As we shall see, however, the downside was in the short term only. Freeing German policy from the shackles of irredentism, on the other hand, was a long-term gain.

The Kohl/Genscher proposal of 8 March 1990, though calming the situation within the coalition, did not have a similarly placatory effect on the Mazowiecki government. In these circumstances, the close links between Kohl and the Bush administration proved propitious. On a visit to Camp David on 24 and 25 February, Kohl had assured the American President that he did not intend to question the finality of the border. Bush understood Kohl's legal reservations, and trusted that the border issue would be resolved finally after unification.[21] Whereas Bush was benevolently disposed towards German unification, however, those that were not translated their disquiet about the impending unification of the two German states into vociferous demands about the Oder–Neisse line.

This was true especially for Margaret Thatcher and François Mitterrand, both of whom remained hesitant about German unification and who channelled their opposition to Kohl's diplomacy into support for Mazowiecki.[22] On 8 and 9 March 1990, Mitterrand received Jaruzelski, Mazowiecki and Skubiszewski in Paris, with the clear intention of lending support over the border issue. Diplomatically, this was a peculiar visit, not only because Jaruzelski was tainted with the declaration of martial law in Poland in 1981, but also because he was the last Communist ruler in office in the whole of Eastern Europe. In a press conference on 9 March, Mitterrand not only supported Polish demands on participation in the 2+4 negotiations on the external aspects of German unification, he also endorsed Mazowiecki's claim that a binding declaration of the border should be negotiated and passed before unification.

For Kohl this was a severe breach of trust, especially because it had the potential to derail the international aspects of the unification process. The Franco-Polish rapprochement created a *cauchemar des coalitions*, in which Kohl suspected Mazowiecki of attempting to drive a wedge into the Franco-German partnership.[23] Kohl arranged for President Bush to broker a deal between Mazowiecki and himself, according to which the key parts of the text of the final settlement would be negotiated before unification, and would be incorporated into the two parliamentary declarations. The final treaty would be signed after unification. As Mazowiecki reluctantly accepted the deal, the zenith of the crisis had been overcome, though its tremors continued to shock Polish–German relations for the better part of the year.

Kohl's hesitation to commit himself on the border violated the objectives of Civilian Power policy. As mentioned above, good bilateral policies are essential for multilateral civilianization. In the case of Germany and Poland, this general principle had an additional tangle, because the latent fear of Germany contributed to a deceleration of transformation in Poland. In February 1990, Mazowiecki suddenly announced that it was no longer in Poland's interest to enforce the withdrawal of the Red Army, obviously implying that the Soviet Union could balance a resurgent Germany. Interestingly, the British Prime Minister supported his view, presumably for the same reason. It is hard to measure causally just what effect the Polish–German border dispute had on the pace of Polish transformation. But it was clearly not in Germany's interest to have Soviet troops stationed in Poland.

Recognizing precisely why Kohl chose to contradict the principles of West German foreign policy culture (the principles of Civilian Power) is therefore significant. Territorial revision was never an objective. Electoral tactics mattered, as did legal concerns, but the former should not be overestimated and the latter should not be underestimated. After all the border treaty was signed very rapidly after unification, on 14 November, which, it must be emphasized, was only two weeks before the elections. A point which is often missed in the discussion of the legal constraints affecting Kohl's policy is that the border dispute was most intense when it seemed as though the constitutional instrument of unification would either be the build-up of confederative structures (as mentioned in Kohl's ten-point plan) or the Basic Law's Art. 146, according to which the Basic Law would lose its validity if the German people freely decided on a constitution replacing it. In these cases it would not have been obvious that the new legal entity would assume the legacy of the Federal Republic's international commitments, which is why Mazowiecki insisted on a legally binding guarantee before unification. Had it been clear from the start that the constitutional mechanism of unification would be Art. 23 of the Basic Law, implying the accession of the GDR to the FRG, it would also have been clear that the unified German state was legally no different from the Federal Republic. And since the Federal

Republic had recognized the Polish Western border in the Warsaw treaty, it could in early 1990 easily have concluded a treaty on behalf of unified Germany reaffirming its own former commitment.[24] None of this changes the fact that neither the legal nor the electoral considerations of the Kohl government were directly linked to foreign policy calculations. Their purpose was not a particular aim within the context of bilateral or multilateral relations like the increase of power or the revision of the border. A set of domestic concerns external to foreign policy culture negated German Civilian Power, not a new principle of foreign policy culture. This does not change the effects of policy. In the episode under consideration, the Federal Republic failed to behave like a Civilian Power. But the reason for this failure was not a change in foreign policy culture, but a set of circumstances external to it.

It would be biased to blame only the German side for the acrimony of German–Polish relations in 1990. Criticisms of the Mazowiecki government's stance abide both in Poland and in Germany, pointing out that the Mazowiecki government left the consensus on policy towards Germany that the democratic opposition had worked out in the 1980s (according to which a free and unified Germany was compatible with the aspirations of a free and independent Poland), that the Soviet Union was instrumentalized in policies towards Germany (weakening Poland's diplomatic credibility as well as the pace of its transformation), and that the Mazowiecki government achieved nothing that would not otherwise have been achieved, but risked relations with Poland's most important European partner instead.[25] We cannot discuss these various claims here for lack of space. What is significant in this context is just how precarious Germany's position in Central and Eastern Europe was, despite the efforts of Ostpolitik in the previous twenty years. The alienation between Kohl and Mazowiecki was not one of incongruent interests, as the rapidly improving relations after 1990 proved. To a great extent it was one of personal estrangement.[26] Genscher and Skubiszewski, for instance, were much closer all through the crisis, and developed a veritable friendship afterwards. In this sense, the crisis between West Germany and Poland, between Kohl and Mazowiecki, was a matter of trust. George Bush trusted Kohl's private assurances over the border, although these were not fully in line with Kohl's public stance. But Bush had reason to trust Kohl, not least because of the missile deployment in the early 1980s which will be explored in Chapter 4. For the United States, Kohl had been a reliable partner in Nato ever since he had assumed office. Mazowiecki did not share this trust, not because of personal misgivings, but because Kohl was the head of a

German government. This mistrust towards Germany, despite the troubles of Ostpolitik, showed how deeply fear and resentment towards Germany continued to touch the Polish collective psyche in 1989 and 1990. As the Polish writer Andrzej Szczypiorski remarked in June 1990:

> The overwhelming majority of Poles ... experiences a reunified Germany as a threat to Poland. Whereas in personal contact every Pole will treat a German in a friendly manner, thinking and acting at a political level will be determined by fear, insecurity and scepticism towards all questions related to Germany.[27]

The significance of the border issue was, in a sense, greater than it should have been. We have seen that there was no fundamental incongruence of interests but a change of German objectives, highly disconcerting for Poland, because the rapid destabilization of East Germany obviated the West German desire for a peace treaty. This was a short-term discord, resolved on 14 November 1990 when Genscher and Skubiszewski signed the border treaty in Warsaw. As the border issue assumed such disproportionate significance, it clouded the underlying congruence of interests between Poland and Germany. Above all, this congruence consisted of a shared interest in removing the Soviet dominance over East Central Europe, which for Poland promised the realization of a free society and for Germany the achievement of unification.

Starting from the assertion that neither of these aims would be attainable under the Yalta order, even under the conditions of détente, the transformation in Poland and the unification of Germany were in fact causally linked.[28] The Solidarity movement in Poland destabilized the East German regime and thus promoted German unification. In turn, Poland could only hope to escape the iron cage of Soviet power if Germany unified on Western terms. Poland therefore advocated full Nato membership for a unified Germany earlier than any other state in the Warsaw pact. The proximity of a Western state on its western border would facilitate Poland's Western orientation in foreign policy matters, and anchor its domestic transformation externally. It was due to such calculations that Skubiszewski spoke of a 'community of interests' between Poland and Germany. This community transcended the joint interest in removing Soviet influence from East Central Europe, and stretched into the post-Cold War European order. Both Poland and Germany had an interest in Germany's continued Western integration, first to tame German power, and secondly to facilitate Poland's Western integration. This Western integration was also a congruent interest and emerges as one of the defining features of German enlargement policy as discussed below. It was much easier to see this congruence once the veil of the border dispute had been removed.

Reconciliation developed at a surprising pace after 14 November 1990. A treaty on good neighbourliness and friendly cooperation was concluded in Bonn on 17 June 1991. Among other things, the treaty established regular consultations between heads of government, security cooperation, a positive treatment of the minorities and a Polish–German Youth Organization modelled on its Franco-German counterpart; most significant for the Polish side was Germany's pledge to support Poland's accession to the EC, the first such clear and unequivocal commitment beyond association.[29] In addition, Poland benefited enormously from Germany's financial assistance. The Kohl government had already made considerable financial pledges two days after the first semi-free elections in Poland on 4 June 1989, clarifying that financial aid would depend on democratic reform. Of course, this was also intended as a signal to other countries in the region, not least East Germany. Although in December 1990 Germany did not agree to the Polish request for an 80 per cent debt relief in the group of public creditors that constituted the Paris Club, it did, in July 1991, agree to a 50 per cent relief in order to counter the impression that Poland's significance for Germany had declined after unification.[30] Germany thus contributed considerably to Poland's debt relief within the Paris Club. The first stage of debt relief agreed in 1991 remitted 30 per cent of Poland's $33.5 billion debt to the creditors of the club. In April 1994, Poland was released from a further 20 per cent. By the end of 1994 Poland's debts amounted to less than 40 per cent of GDP, a significant amelioration of its public finances, and a situation with which many EU member states struggling to fulfil the Maastricht criteria would have been delighted. This change in Poland's debt structure influenced positively the reputation of the zloty, and the confidence in the Polish economy by foreign investors. Germany contributed significantly to this debt relief. It credited Poland with DM 4.5 billion in the context of the change in Poland's debt structure, and remitted DM 6 billion.[31] This sum of more than DM 10.5 billion corresponded to more than a third of Poland's overall debt relief. In addition to these bilateral programmes Germany of course paid its share of 28 per cent of Phare, the EU's technical assistance programmes in Eastern Europe.

At the political level, relations between Poland and Germany developed well, leading to increasingly regular and relaxed consultations between ministers and high civil servants. An important psychological hurdle was overcome by a speech the new German President, Roman Herzog, delivered in Warsaw on the fiftieth anniversary of the Warsaw uprising. Germany, Herzog said, would sincerely support Poland's accession to Nato and the EU since 'We can do nothing better for our children and grand-children.' But the thrust of Herzog's speech was an apology for German actions during the war.

> August 1st reminds us what immense suffering was caused to Poles by Germans...It fills us Germans with shame that the name of our country will for ever be tied to the pain and suffering that was inflicted on Poles in millions of cases...But today I bow before the fighters of the Warsaw uprising, and before all Polish victims of the war: I ask for forgiveness for everything that was done to you by Germans.[32]

The symbolic value of Herzog's words was immense. It shattered, as Andrzej Szczypiorski commented, the stereotype of the German in Poland.[33] To be sure, even the most emotive words, the most moving gestures, could not change the relationship between Poles and Germans within a few years. But by 1993/94 Polish–German relations at governmental level had become a platform for the future rather than a continuation of the past.

This surely had to do with the fact that in 1993 and 1994, German support for Poland's Western integration manifested itself with particular clarity, while the issues surrounding EU enlargement were not yet specified enough to expose the latent sectoral conflict of interests between the two countries. It might also have had to do with the fact that both sides were so relieved with the relaxed relationship that they consciously refrained from addressing difficult issues. By 1997 Aleksander Kwasniewski, the new Polish President, openly joked that relations between Poland and Germany were so good that in fact the political elites of the two countries had very little to talk about.

This was a misguided assumption. The acceleration of the EU enlargement process in the first months of 1998 focused attention on a number of issues that had hitherto been neglected. In part, these were multilateral. Many of the really tricky issues of the enlargement process had to be resolved between Poland and Germany. The fear of migration from new to old EU member states, especially to Germany, was one of these issues. The selling of real estate in Western Poland to a flood of foreign investors, especially Germans, was a parallel fear in Poland, since prices there were substantially lower than in Germany. In both cases, national politicians addressed the issue by placating the fears of their electorates, that is by unilaterally declaring the need for transition periods. These claims were not without problems, for in a multilateral negotiation process like EU enlargement, a quick resorting to exceptions and derogations risks watering down the final result. If the Single Market established the free movement of goods, services, people and capital, the particular wishes of Poland and Germany stood in marked contrast to the general legal principles that were at the heart of the European Union. On the other hand, however, the popular fears connected to the issue of labour migration in Germany and real estate purchase in Poland were so grave that they threatened to undermine the enlargement process as such. In Poland, accession to the EU would occur only after the population had voted 'yes' in a referendum. If fears about the selling of land were too strong, the part of the population in favour of EU accession would shrink and thus possibly endanger the positive outcome of the referendum. Though in Germany there was no need to win a referendum, popular opinion, voiced and put forward especially by the trade unions, called for a slowing down of the enlargement process with a view to the tense situation on the German labour market. In other words, although the demanding of transition periods was risky in principle, it was in this case politically prudent. As each side had an interest in its own transition period, it was more lenient towards the needs of the other.

The truly contested topics were therefore not the conditions of EU enlargement but older bilateral issues, which the impending enlargement brought to the fore but did not cause. Above all, there was the treatment of the German expellees. The conclusive definition of the Oder–Neisse line as the border between Germany and Poland had weakened the German expellees' organizations. For answering the border question – in so far as it ever was a question – meant at the same time asking the pertinent question about the expellees' organizations' *raison d'être*. There was little they could now offer to their members apart from a sense of belonging. And in the same way that their issue was gone, the generation that had dominated their politics throughout the postwar period was also in retreat.

If one thought, however, that the ultimate closure of the border issue, in conjunction with the weakening of the membership base and the generational shift in the leadership would silence the expellees' organizations completely, one was mistaken. In part, this was a consequence of the fact that their closest political links were to the CDU (leaving the special links between the Sudeten Germans and the CSU aside for the moment), and that the CDU was in government. Tying the expellee vote in was a structural imperative of CDU postwar politics. As we have seen from the discussion of Kohl's treatment of the border issue, this imperative always affected the CDU's policy towards Poland, whether in government or in opposition.[34] The CDU mainstream's fear that the expellees would drift to the extreme right did not subside after 1990. That the election victory in 1994 had been such a narrow one therefore only reinforced a structural imperative that already existed. If the CDU/CSU wanted to stand any chance at the election in 1998 it had to mobilize its classical milieus to go to the voting booths, and it had to ensure that those who turned up did not vote for parties on the right of the CDU. The new generation of expellees' leaders could therefore expect a sympathetic ear from the CDU mainstream, though not necessarily one that was encouraging.

The proximity to the CDU was not the only reason for the expellees' organizations' increasing vociferousness in 1997 and 1998. A further reason was, paradoxically, their internal generational change. In particular, Erika Steinbach, the new leader of the Federation of Expellees and a CDU Member of Parliament, sought to drum up internal support by returning attention to so-called 'unresolved issues' between Germany and Poland. Throughout the summer of 1998, Steinbach characterized the legacy of the expulsions in terms of 'wounds' and 'pain', which were after all a 'thorn in the flesh' of Polish–German relations. Her language was decidedly more inflammatory than that of her predecessor, Fritz Wittmann. The expulsion became a *Vertreibungsuntat* (expulsion atrocity) and the essence of the Polish and Czech states was expulsion: they were *Vertreiberstaaten* (expelling states). Despite proclamations to the contrary, this was the language not of reconciliation but of accusation.

The rallying cry of the German expellees' organizations was that every injustice had to be seen in its own right, had to be treated as isolated from other acts, just or unjust, committed before or after. In a sense Steinbach's words mirrored those that Poland's Foreign Minister Wladyslaw Bartoszewski had said in the German Bundestag in 1995. Citing the Polish writer Jan Jozef Lipski, Bartoszewski said that 'the evil committed against us, even the greatest, is not and cannot be a justification for the evil that we ourselves have done to others.'[35] In contrast to Bartoszewski, Steinbach never spoke about the historical context of the expulsions. Though she agreed that 'the most dramatic injustices were committed by Germany', she did not admit a causal connection between them and the injustices that were later committed against Germany.[36] In a sense, this was understandable. The overwhelming majority of the expelled had committed no crimes; they were the ultimate victims of an aggressive regime. But this was only one side of the coin.

For although Germans were not collectively guilty, the aggression of the Second World War had been committed in Germany's name. All Germans therefore had to ask themselves how they had behaved in the face of these injustices. This was a question that had above all to be answered individually, but assumed, in the case of the expellees, also a collective significance, because the expellees acted as a collective voice in the dialogue with Poland and the Czech Republic. *Vergangenheitsbewältigung*, coming to terms with the past, was therefore as important for the expellees' organizations as it was for the rest of German society, with one important difference. The expellees saw themselves primarily as victims.[37] Guilty were others, the Hitler regime, the Czechoslovak and Polish states, perhaps the Soviet Union. Erika Steinbach's moral superiority in dealing with Poland and the Czech Republic exhibited the psychology of the victim. In contrast to the rest of German society, she spoke with the absoluteness of someone with a clear conscience.

It was precisely this partial view, the obliviousness to the historical context of the expulsions, which was so difficult to take in Poland and the Czech Republic. Not only were Poland and the Czech Republic thrown into a war in the unleashing of which they had no part, they also had to bear the brunt of it in the form of forty years of communism. At least in the case of Poland, the expulsion of the German population had been decided by Britain, the United States and the Soviet Union while the war was still being waged and was later sanctioned at Potsdam. Poland had been shifted westwards as a result of the war, it had lost territories itself, and millions of those who now lived in former Eastern Germany used to live in the former Eastern Poland. If the German expellees really argued on moral grounds alone, their addressee should have been the four powers that participated in the Potsdam conference. Russia should have been an addressee alongside Poland and the Czech Republic, because the Kaliningrad *oblast* also used to be German territory. The fact that Erika Steinbach referred to Poland and the Czech Republic alone led many to conclude that not morality but more cynical calculations of strength and weakness, of power and interests, were the decisive factors in her calculations.

This observation was supported by the fact that next to the change in rhetoric, Steinbach also toyed with a change in demands. Arguing that 'violations of human rights had to be healed', she demanded a

compensation for the expropriation of the Germans in the former Eastern territories. One 'would have to talk' about state compensation,
either in terms of financial compensation or in terms of state property.
The fact that the German Foreign Ministry under Klaus Kinkel did not
press these claims with Poland and the Czech Republic, was, according
to Steinbach, a clear indication that Kinkel was incapable of defending
'German interests'.[38] The real crux of Steinbach's comments however
was neither the sharpness of her rhetoric nor the claims for compensation per se, but the demand that German foreign policy should link
the demands for compensation with the accession negotiations to the
European Union. It was time, Steinbach argued, to resolve the 'open
questions' between Germany on the one hand and Poland and the
Czech Republic on the other in the run-up to EU enlargement. Germany
did not need enlargement 'at any price', and if Poland and the Czech
Republic were reluctant to offer compensation, one would have to build
alliances with those member states of the EU that were also critical
about enlargement.[39] This, in effect, was blackmail.

If one wants to appreciate the way in which these comments were
received in Poland, one has to link them to two phenomena occurring
literally at the same time. The first of these were the activities of an
obscure extreme-right splinter organization, the *Bund für Gesamtdeutschland* (Federation for Pan-Germany), which issued pre-printed letters and
compensation claims to hundreds of thousands of expellees with the
encouragement to sign them and send them on to the local Polish
authorities. These letters asking for compensation attracted considerable
attention in the Polish media and generated great concern among the
Polish population living in the former German territories. The second
was a Bundestag resolution on 27 May 1998 declaring expellees, outsettlers and German minorities a 'bridge between Germany and its
Eastern neighbours'.[40] Passed with the votes of CDU/CSU and FDP
(the SPD abstained, the Greens and the PDS opposed), the resolution
opined that EU accession for the Eastern neighbours also meant the
acceptance of 'basic European freedoms for all citizens in old and new
member states, meaning also for the German expellees. The German
Bundestag nurtures the hope that in the process of acceding to the
European Union, the adoption of the *acquis communautaire* by Poland
and the Czech Republic will facilitate the solution of those bilateral
questions that are still open.'

In the weeks before and after the passing of the German resolution,
the machinery of Polish–German political contacts failed completely.
The Bundestag text was not cleared with the German embassies in

Warsaw or Prague and tested for its possible reception in the countries that would be most affected by it. It was not even translated and made available to the political elites of the Eastern neighbours. The Polish–German parliamentary group failed to act as a mediating body. It turned out, as Janusz Reiter observed, that the bilateral relations between Poland and Germany were more superficial than it had seemed in the honeymoon years after 1994.[41] On 4 July 1998 the Sejm passed a short resolution in which it described the Bundestag text as 'unhelpful for the development of Polish–German cooperation' and containing 'dangerous tendencies'. The Polish parliament would not accept a questioning of 'the territorial order in East Central Europe'. The accession to the European Union 'must not endanger the Polish border or Polish property'. One has to be surprised that this resolution was possible at all, that the Sejm could seriously question the status of the border after everything that had happened between Germany and Poland in the previous nine years. After the border dispute in 1990, the 'war of the resolutions' was the nadir of Polish–German relations.

Few in Germany understood the reason for the Sejm's sensitivity and the use of such powerful language: in the end, the Bundestag resolution had, in asking for an inclusion of the expellees into the process of reconciliation, only reaffirmed a practice that already existed, and had, in emphasizing the right to settle freely, only ascertained a fundamental principle of the Single Market. Realizing that the damage was done, Klaus Kinkel sought to reassure Poland that 'there was no border question between Germany and Poland'. Kinkel distanced himself clearly from Steinbach and the idea that bilateral questions should be connected to the EU enlargement process.[42] At the end of July, Rita Süssmuth, the Bundestag President, went to Warsaw to assuage Polish fears. Her message was the same as Kinkel's: there was no border question, there were no 'dangerous tendencies' in the Bundestag; if anything, there had been misunderstandings that had to be cleared up. Süssmuth's trip to Warsaw did as much good as, given the circumstances, it could have done. But the circumstances were poor. For the first time since 1990, the overall intentions of German policy were received sceptically in Poland.

Now in order to do justice to the German side, one does have to mention that the German government had at no point undertaken a change of tactics or of rhetoric. Neither the Chancellor nor the Foreign Minister had said anything that gave rise to fear or antagonism in Poland. The Bundestag resolution contained nothing new or noteworthy if one saw it in its own right. But this was precisely the problem. The resolution was a text, and texts have both authors and audiences.

The failure of German politicians lay in the inability to see that the interpretation of the audience could be very different from the intention of the authors. And the interpretation of the Polish audience was affected by the circumstances of the text's publication. As we have seen, the reception of the Bundestag resolution in Poland coincided with the activities of the obscure *Bund für Gesamtdeutschland* and Erika Steinbach's campaign for linking compensation payments for German expellees to Poland's EU entry. In this atmosphere, the Bundestag phrase that 'the adoption of the *acquis communautaire* by Poland and the Czech Republic will facilitate the solution of those bilateral questions that are still open' was bound to be misinterpreted. Though Steinbach did not speak for the government or for the Bundestag as a whole, she was a CDU deputy. She was also backed politically by voices in the CSU who demanded a postponement of EU enlargement. And not once throughout the Polish–German summer crisis did Helmut Kohl distance himself from the stance of the Bund der Vertriebenen (BdV) and its leader.

If the Bundestag authors had not reckoned on the interpretation of their text by their Polish audience, the Polish audience did little to understand the intention of the authors. Anyone who in 1998 assumed that there was any doubt about the Polish–German border lived in a different world. If they voted for the Sejm resolution nevertheless, they either sought to instrumentalize the 'German factor' in order to slow down Poland's Western integration, or they were under intense domestic pressure not to be seen as weak in the face of the stronger German neighbour. One is therefore tempted to conclude that the Sejm resolution was no *pièce de résistance* of parliamentary dignity, any more than its Bundestag predecessor had been.

As the Polish–German summer crisis sits uneasily with the Civilian Power argument we may ask why Kohl did so little to ameliorate the situation in the weeks after the Sejm resolution. Since the association was between Steinbach as a BdV leader and Steinbach as a CDU deputy, only the party leader and Chancellor Helmut Kohl could have put her remarks into perspective. That he chose not to was reminiscent of the border dispute of 1990. In both cases Bundestag elections provided the political background to foreign policy decisions. As Karl-Rudolf Korte noted in his analysis of Kohl's policy towards Poland in the 1980s: 'Kohl projected the premises for action unambiguously onto his role as party leader, and only subsequently onto that of the Chancellor.'[43] When it came to the choice of risking a clash with the expellees and risking a dispute with Poland, Kohl chose the dispute with Poland. As per usual, the public effect of his stance in Germany, as well in Poland, was highly damaging.

Yet the summer crisis of 1998 should not distract from the fact that bilateral relations between Germany and Poland were exceptionally good. In large part this was a consequence of the bilateral understandings of the early 1990s, of border recognition, of the lifting of visa restrictions and of the treaty on good neighbourliness and friendly cooperation. In large part, it was also a consequence of the German support for Poland's Western integration. Many of those who remembered the state of Polish–German relations in 1989–90 were amazed by the solid relationship at the end of the decade. What remained to be observed was that German diplomacy always benefited when it was linked to the future-oriented aspects of European integration, and always lost out when it was linked to the inevitably divisive memories of the Second World War.

Czechoslovakia, the Czech Republic, Slovakia

The relationship between Bonn and Prague had been icy despite the 1973 treaty in which the Federal Republic and Czechoslovakia had established diplomatic relations with one another. Since the Husak regime feared contacts with the West, political and societal contacts with West Germany had scarcely existed, and even rudimentary reconciliation had been impossible before 1989. It was therefore quite notable that Vaclav Havel, only three days after assuming office, was to travel to Munich to apologize for the transfer of the Sudeten Germans after 1945. Havel met both von Weizsäcker and Kohl in Munich – a location chosen on purpose, because it suggested that the transfer of the Sudeten Germans after 1945 could not be separated from the Munich agreement in 1938. Both sides moved quickly to negotiate a treaty on good neighbourliness and friendly cooperation, which was signed on 27 February 1992. The treaty excluded those issues of the past that could have complicated the process of negotiation. In a nutshell, these were *Munich* and *Vertreibung*, summing up the events in that awful decade in bilateral relations between 1938 and 1948.

Munich represented a Czechoslovak claim, namely the recognition by Germany that the Munich agreement had been invalid from the start, and that the Czechoslovak state had existed continuously between 1938 and 1948. The Munich agreement had been negotiated and guaranteed by Britain, France, Italy and Germany; it had credited Germany with possession of the so-called Sudeten German territories in the

north-west of Czechoslovakia bordering on Germany. Though negotiated and concluded without Czechoslovak participation, it was recognized as legally valid by the four powers, which at the height of
appeasement convinced themselves that they had remedied one of the
failures of the Versailles treaty. Of course it became evident within
months that the Munich agreement had been not only a profound
injustice vis-à-vis the Czechoslovak state but also a diplomatic failure.
When Hitler's Germany invaded Czechoslovakia it was clear that
Czechoslovakia had died hand in hand with the policy of appeasement.
Its doubtful moral justification notwithstanding, the Munich agreement
had in the German view been valid from the day of its signing (29 May
1938), though invalidated when broken by Nazi Germany on 15 March
1939. In this interpretation, the treaty itself was legal, not least since it
had been signed by Italy, France, Britain and Germany. If the treaty had
been declared illegal from the day of its signing, the Sudeten Germans
would never have been German citizens, and could, for instance, be
charged with treason by the Czechoslovak state because of their service
in a foreign army.[44]

The term *Vertreibung* represented a German claim. It described the
expropriation and expulsion of all Germans from the territory of
Czechoslovakia, which became government policy in Czechoslovakia
when announced by President Benes on 19 May 1945 and lasted until
1947. In contrast to Poland, Benes could not point towards the decisions
of Teheran and Yalta in order to link the expulsions to the decisions of
the four powers. That he acted without their consent, however, is improbable, not least because Art. VIII of the Potsdam agreement legitimized the 'transfer' of Germans 'in an orderly and humane manner'. It
long ago entered mainstream history that of course the 'transfer' was
often far from 'orderly' and 'humane', and that the revenge of the
victims of German aggression was often brutal, in the Soviet Union, in
Poland and in Czechoslovakia. As Ferdinand Seibt put it, the horrors of
the war had affected ordinary people in a very similar way:

> In those diabolical seven years, threatening voices in front of the
> house, shots on the street, fear in the dark, the cries of the persecuted,
> sadistic irony and the pitiful, trembling failure of one's own powers
> roared again and again like an infernal symphony through the heads
> of people in the Bohemian lands. Only, not at the same time; only,
> that at different times the front lines ran differently, and were en-
> grained so deeply that even today, after fifty years, one does not easily
> want to recognise how much one has in common.[45]

In line with the language of the Potsdam agreement, the Czechoslovak side denied that an expulsion had ever taken place and spoke instead of an ordinary 'transfer' of the Sudeten population. The Sudeten German associations in Germany, as well as consecutive West German governments, spoke of *Vertreibung* (expulsion). The Sudeten Germans did not welcome the signing of the Czechoslovak–German treaty, because they felt that it did not account for them and their interests. What precisely these interests were, however, was never entirely clear. In the early 1990s at least, it appeared as though the Sudeten Germans did not claim financial compensation for their property, demanding moral restitution and the right to return to their homeland (including the purchase of real estate) instead.[46] Probably this was the view of the grass roots within the Sudeten German organization. At the same time, however, questioning the moral justification and legal validity of the Benes decrees was also a prelude to more, namely restitution or at least financial compensation. As the situation was confused, the negotiating parties had decided to exclude all concerns related to the population transfer, reparations and the Munich agreement in the Czechoslovak–German treaty.

This was meant well, but exacerbated tensions in the medium term. The Sudeten Germans were disappointed that their interests had not been accounted for in the treaty, and feared that their claims would never be addressed if they did not step up the pressure. After the treaty had been ratified, Kohl therefore decided to make the Sudeten claims a *Chefsache* (a matter for the boss), removing the more lenient Foreign Ministry from strategic decision making.[47] As the pressures from the Sudeten expellees' organizations became stronger, Kohl sought to ensure that whatever was decided in negotiations with Czechoslovakia would be compatible with his domestic interests.

After Czechoslovakia split on 1 January 1993, the Czech Republic inherited the problem. Whereas Slovak–German relations slid into insignificance, assisted by the limited respect the Meciar government paid to Western integration, Czech–German relations now seemed dominated by the Sudeten issue.[48] As German intransigence came to be matched by an increasing disappointment on the Czech side, the issues unsolved by the treaty in 1991 were a heavy burden on bilateral relations. This development is perhaps best illustrated by Vaclav Havel, who, through his timely visit to Munich in January 1990, had invested so much into reconciliation and had provoked considerable domestic criticism. In a speech at the Charles University in Prague in February 1995, Havel exhibited an uncharacteristic impatience with the Sudeten Germans' clout within the CSU:

> We can have different views on the postwar transfer of the German population – my own critical opinion is widely known – but we can never take that step out of its historical context . . . I therefore deem it my duty to say here in the clearest of terms that the Czech Republic is one of the legal heirs of the Czechoslovak statehood born out of two dreadful wars in the unleashing of which it had no part. Our republic will therefore never negotiate about a revision of their outcome, about any infringement of the continuity of its legal system, about any corrections of history to the detriment of our contemporaries.[49]

The clarity of Havel's speech notwithstanding, the beginning of 1995 did mark a new initiative on behalf of the Czech government to put a lid on the bottle of the past. Havel's speech specifically addressed the need for a lasting reconciliation, and Josef Zielienec, the Czech Foreign Minister, launched a new diplomatic initiative. Negotiations now concentrated on drafting a bilateral declaration, without legal force, which could address all outstanding issues. Vladimir Handl has perceptively pointed out that although both sides shared an interest in drafting a declaration, they did so for very different reasons.[50] While Czech motivations revolved around the desire to protect the state and its citizens from compensation claims, to find a just solution for Nazi victims, and to ameliorate Czech–German relations with a view to Czech EU accession, Germany shared an interest in the latter two motivations, but not in the first. In addition, there was no clear position in Germany on how to deal with the Sudeten German issue. Hence, although the Foreign Ministry seems to have been eager to press ahead in search of agreement, German domestic politics hampered foreign policy once again. In December 1995 the German negotiating side reversed a number of positions which had already been agreed upon, possibly because of Sudeten German pressure.[51]

To make matters worse, Klaus Kinkel mentioned in a newspaper interview in January 1996 that Germany had never accepted the legal validity of the Potsdam agreement – thus questioning the Czech reference to the agreement's Art. VIII about the population 'transfer'. This unfortunate comment, though legally justifiable, prompted the victorious powers of the Second World War to issue declarations asserting the Potsdam agreement's validity. Kinkel's comment had not only produced a situation where Germany was legally isolated from its most important partners and allies, it also generated considerable disquiet in the Czech Republic. The opposition in Prague spoke of a 'fundamental turnaround' in German policy which, so the argument ran, once again questioned the results of the war.[52] In Prague, constitutional and legal certainties derived from the assumption that the Benes decrees had been embedded in a multilateral framework (the victorious powers at the end of the war), which produced a legally binding justification (the Potsdam agreement) for Czechoslovak domestic law (the Benes decrees). Questioning the multilateral framework therefore shook the legal and constitutional order of the Czech Republic to its foundations.

The most important difference of opinion revolved around financial compensation for the expelled Sudeten Germans. While the Czech governmental stance was that this was not necessary because the expulsions had been a legally valid governmental act, the stance of the German government was that the expulsions had contradicted international law. What was more important, however, was that the German government, though upholding the financial claims of the expellees in theory, did nothing to press them in practice. There existed an extensive political consensus in Bonn's foreign policy establishment that pressing the expellees' demands would have had unforeseeable consequences for Germany's international reputation – quite regardless of the demands that others could then also press against Germany. Officially denouncing the legal right to compensation was held impossible, however, because the Bonn government's lawyers feared that the expellees would then press their claims against the German state – and possibly win. The outcome was an essentially hypocritical situation: Bonn never pressed for compensation, but could not withdraw from its legal position. German politicians therefore continued to assert that 'certain issues' were 'open', but did nothing whatsoever in order to close them. As so often in German foreign policy, political and legal considerations were incompatible. In principle, this would of course have been a politically acceptable modus vivendi for both sides if overall relations between Germany and the Czech Republic had been so full of trust that the Czechs felt they had nothing to fear. While the Sudeten Germans had such strong influence on the CSU, and thus indirectly on the CDU, this feeling never settled very deeply in the Czech Republic.

Despite ups and downs, the Czech–German declaration that was signed in January 1997 was an expression of political will, not a treaty with legally binding force. The declaration featured a number of very delicately drafted phrases on mutual dealings with the past, and established a Czech–German Fund for the Future as well as a Czech–German

Discussion Forum on the model of the Königswinter Conference and the Polish–German Forum. It is perhaps not surprising that interpretations of the declaration varied a great deal. The Czech side perceived it to be a *Schlußstrich*, a final settlement, at least at the highest diplomatic levels, which in a sense could initiate the process of societal reconciliation in the form of youth exchanges, historical commissions and so forth. The declaration was not perceived as a *Schlußstrich* in Germany. Indeed the CSU interpreted it as a possible opening for the recognition of the Sudeten Germans' right to settle in the Czech Republic.

The two phrases that provoked the most strikingly different reactions in Germany and the Czech Republic were the vow that the two countries would not burden their relationship with 'political and legal questions resulting from the past' (Art. V) and the German pledge to support the Czech Republic's accession to the EU and Nato. While in the Czech Republic these were welcome promises, the German expellees were dissatisfied. As Fritz Wittmann, the leader of the BdV, noted accurately (and angrily):

> While for a long time the Foreign Ministry emphasised its readiness to 'address the issues at an appropriate time and in an appropriate manner', while always stressing 'that in conducting foreign relations the Federal Government has to consider both norms of international law and foreign policy interests' – it has now emerged that the Federal Government is not prepared to link what it calls 'strictly bilateral property questions' to the question of EU enlargement.

Wittmann was not the only one to complain. 'It is quite inconceivable', Christian Schmidt, the CSU's foreign policy spokesman in the Bundestag, said in an interview with the author, 'that we have an EU member state that has elevated a clear breach of international law to its *raison d'état*.'[53] This position was a prelude to the more hard-line position taken by Wittmann's successor, Erika Steinbach, in the summer of 1998. Perhaps most significant in this context is the observation that the Czech Republic's negotiation and accession process with the EU was profoundly affected by bilateral relations with Germany. In this sense, the Czech Republic and Poland were very similar cases. Although the overall quality of relations with Germany helped the pro-integrationist course, as we will see below, there also existed a great sensitivity to any deterioration in these relations. In the Czech Republic, this affected the discussion on the European Union *and* on Nato. At the height of the diplomatic crisis with Germany in February 1996, some opinion makers in Prague wondered whether Nato enlargement was anything but a German plot designed to push the Czech Republic into a similarly exposed geopolitical position as it had occupied during the Cold War.

Nevertheless, a comparison with the Polish border dispute is only edifying in part. First, the border dispute and the expulsions from Poland were closely related to the international diplomacy of German unification and were solved as part and parcel of it. This was not the case with the issue of Sudeten grievances, which were a bilateral problem. Secondly, the relative size of the Czech Republic and Poland contributed to their different status for German policy. Whereas Germany developed a clearly articulated policy vis-à-vis Poland, the Czech Republic was catered for primarily within multilateral frameworks. Arguing cynically, one could maintain that Germany forewent its legal principles in favour of its overall political interests vis-à-vis Poland, whereas it stuck to its principles regardless of overall political interests in the case of the Czech Republic. Another way of putting this is that Polish–German relations benefited from their timely concern with multilateral issues. The ingenuity of Skubiszewski's 'community of interests' lay in its focus on the nexus between bilateral and multilateral interests. This never happened in Czech–German relations. Whereas multilateral cooperation functioned adequately, bilateral relations suffered. The nexus between the two, however, was neglected.

Thirdly, Kohl's handling of the Silesian expellees' associations was facilitated not only by mounting international pressure, but also by the fact that they were represented in the CDU. Kohl's proficiency at handling internal party affairs had always been a cornerstone of his political success, and the handling of the border issue was no exception.[54] This was infinitely more difficult in the case of the Sudeten Germans, because they had predominantly settled in Bavaria after having been forced to leave, and were concentrated in the CSU. Whereas Kohl was highly capable of managing affairs in his own party, he found it impossible to manage those inside the CSU.

How did the Civilian Power perform?

In its bilateral relations with its eastern neighbours Germany failed, in part significantly, to approximate Civilian Power ideals. This was particularly so with regard to Poland and Czechoslovakia, later the Czech Republic, where German policies did not match the foreign policy culture outlined above. It was not at all the case for Hungary, where bilateral relations achieved an unusual degree of cordiality. Yet Hungary almost seems the odd one out. Its contribution to German unification was unique, something other states could never aspire to. If Germany were a Civilian Power, surely it would establish good bilateral relations with all countries, regardless of their contribution to the German national cause?

It is questionable, however, whether what we have found illustrates a change in Germany's foreign policy culture induced by the removal of the structural constraints that had characterized Cold War and partition. German legalism in foreign policy was hardly a new phenomenon. Moreover, if a change in German foreign policy culture really had occurred in the months following November 1989, it would be difficult to explain the rapid improvement in Polish–German relations that set in after the border treaty was signed.

In contrast to the argument that a change had occurred in Germany's foreign policy culture, the explanation one arrives at is that German foreign policy can at times be hampered by a legalism that is also typical of its domestic political culture. True, some time has passed since Ralf Dahrendorf asserted in the mid-1960s that Germans preferred legal solutions to political problems, since these were seen as more authoritative.[55] But excessive legalism has remained an integral part of German political culture. Whereas in domestic politics, this no longer seems surprising, it continues to confuse when applied to foreign policy matters. Witness, for instance, the argument, propagated most forcefully by Hans-Dietrich Genscher in the Gulf War, that the Basic Law prohibited the participation of Bundeswehr forces in out-of-area missions. The decision whether or not this was so, perhaps the single most important change in the foreign policy of unified Germany, was made by the Federal Constitutional Court, not by the political establishment elected to decide upon it. At the same time, this produced the absurd situation whereby the Foreign Minister (as the FDP leader) supported the FDP's case at the Court, thereby ending up suing himself as a member of the government – a truly remarkable state of affairs even by German standards.

This legalistic political culture, reinforced by a particular set of domestic interests, explains Germany's deviation from Civilian Power policy in bilateral relations with Poland and the Czech Republic. One can therefore follow Torsten Krauel's argument that 'in particular questions, Germany's foreign policy is still not entirely free from a historical culture of legal reservations, volatility, and foreign policy interests seemingly motivated by short-termism and party politics'.[56] Although this is not particular to Germany, it is especially evident in the German case because it sits uneasily with the ethos of Civilian Power. He who sits on the moral high horse runs the risk of falling a long way when confronted with the hurdles of practical politics.

Although Germany's legalism has significant effects for German foreign policy, it is not integral to foreign policy culture, and sets the limits of Civilian Power rather than undermining it. This will be illustrated by the following two chapters, which demonstrate how Germany promoted the multilateral stabilization of East Central Europe, regardless of the state of bilateral relations. One might also argue, however, that legalism is in itself a profoundly civilian principle, both in domestic politics and in international relations. The civilianization of domestic politics depended decisively on the imposition of the rule of law. Equally, liberal international theory has – as discussed in Chapter 1 – since its very beginning argued for the legalization of international relations. In this view only adjudication could free the world from the dangers of balance-of-power manoeuvres and cabinet politics. What we observe in Germany's bilateral diplomacy with its East Central European neighbours, then, is a manifestation of a contradiction within Civilian Power itself. The legalization of social relations that is at the heart of civilianization can at the same time act as an obstacle to it. German policy makers were tripped up by the institutional constraints that had been put in place in the early days of the Federal Republic to ensure that civilianization would succeed. In this case, the obstacle was the Federal Constitutional Court or, to be more precise, a political establishment which was supremely aware of the limits the Court's rulings established, and whose political will was weakened because it had become accustomed to judicial superiority.

4
Germany and EU Enlargement

Germany and stabilization

In its European policy, Germany pursued a number of highly divergent aims in the 1990s. Germany found it difficult to reconcile these aims, and to both widen and deepen the process of European integration. Initially, the tension was merely latent. Germany's priority was deeper integration in the West; its aim vis-à-vis East Central Europe consisted of stabilization. The more German aims towards its eastern neighbours came to be formulated within the context of integration, however, the more hard-pressed German leaders became to define their priorities. It emerges from the following discussion that one of the obstacles of attaining Civilian Power objectives lay in the domestic institutions, which hampered German policy makers in a way unforeseen by those who created the institutions in the early years of the Federal Republic.

The stabilization of the emerging market democracies in East Central Europe was a task too large to be achieved by Germany alone, even, or especially after, unification. This is why establishing links between the East Central European countries and the EC was the cornerstone of any policy of stabilization. Such links had a symbolic aspect, because they represented the return to Europe for those countries, which, as Milan Kundera put it, had under the Yalta order been culturally in the West and politically in the East. It also had a financial aspect, because the EC was likely to provide aid and technical assistance, not in humanitarian terms, though for certain countries this became important, but for administrative reform and investment in infrastructure. Moreover, links with the EC were likely to have benefits through access to the EC's huge market. This would generate pressures of adjustment for the process of economic transformation in East Central Europe, which, so the economic argument ran, would result in long-term benefits despite the undoubted harm done by short-term costs. Finally, links with the EC could enhance the security of East Central European countries. As Nato enlargement was out of the question at this early stage, ties with the Western community would enhance both the military security of these states – since it was unclear how long Gorbachev would last – and their economic and social security, by stabilizing transformation.

The European Council had first discussed a concerted EC response to the changes in East Central Europe at the December 1988 summit in Rome. It was decided at the G7 summit in Paris in July 1989 that the European Commission should coordinate the technical assistance towards Poland and Hungary, the most advanced countries, for all G24 countries in a fund called Phare.[1] This illustrates that the Commission under Jacques Delors pursued an active policy vis-à-vis East Central Europe at this early stage, moving ahead of member states and, in a sense, dragging them along. At the December 1989 European Council in Strasbourg, Mitterrand proposed the foundation of the European Bank for Reconstruction and Development (EBRD) in order to make loans available for East Central Europe. Like Phare, the EBRD would also administrate funds from the G24. It is significant for the further discussion in this chapter that Mitterrand's support for East Central Europe consisted exclusively of technical assistance and diplomatic support.[2] It did not encompass proposals for enlargement.

Ironically, the Kohl government at this time did not share the enthusiasm shown by the Commission and the French President. First and foremost, of course, it was preoccupied with events in the GDR. The ever accelerating race to unification subsumed all other matters between the summer of 1989 and the elections in December 1990. The Kohl government agreed to the Commission proposal in April 1990 of negotiating so-called association agreements with the East Central European states, but this had not been a West German initiative. West German politicians emphasized their readiness to support the transformation processes in East Central Europe financially; they also mentioned the notion of *Heranführung* (the leading into) of East Central Europe to the EC, but this was not a prominent feature of their speeches.[3] In October 1990 Helmut Kohl said no more on the topic than 'Our offer is aimed at the reform states of Central, Eastern, and South-eastern Europe, to guide them to the European Community as early and closely as possible through an association geared at their needs.'[4] Instead of the term enlargement, German politicians at this time pointed out that the East Central European states needed a 'European perspective'.[5]

There was also a second reason why enlargement towards East Central Europe was not a German priority at the time. This was the absolute priority awarded to a further deepening of integration in the EC, most notably political union. This had been a top priority of the Kohl government ever since 1982, but came to particular prominence in the late 1980s because the overall conditions for integration had improved strikingly. 'Our aim remains Europe's Political Union,' Kohl said in his first governmental declaration in October 1982.[6] Against the widespread resignation about the integration process at the time, Kohl asserted, citing Adenauer: 'Europe is like a tree that grows, but that cannot be constructed.'[7] Seven years later the tree had shot up and was about to blossom: the Single Market programme was well under way, the budgetary situation had been solved (mainly due to Kohl's generosity), the Commission was the driving force behind the process and member states debated anew proposals for a monetary union. But Germany's view of European integration remained wedded to the Western half of the continent. As Kohl said in his governmental declaration in January 1991:

> Germany is our fatherland, Europe is our future. For us the European Community, which we want to build up into the European Union, forms the core and foundation for the unification of Europe. On the path to a united Europe, France and Germany have to remain the driving forces.[8]

The Chancellor's thinking on European integration reveals a clear distinction between support for the transformation processes in East Central Europe on the one hand, and the desire to foster political integration inside the European Community on the other. In the same speech in the Bundestag, Kohl laid out his objectives in European policy in terms of eight points prioritized as: the completion of the Single Market, the removal of border controls, subsidiarity and cultural diversity, empowering the European Parliament, a common foreign and security policy, economic and monetary union (*sic!*), the social chapter, and the close connection between the two intergovernmental conferences on monetary and political union. Only then, so to speak after his elaboration on Europapolitik, Kohl mentioned that the Community had to remain open for other European countries and that the East Central European countries needed a 'European perspective'.[9]

Two months later, the distinction between policies to the East and policies to the West was already less rigid, but support for the East Central European states' accession to the EC remained non-committal:

The political unification of Europe remains our aim. But the European Community is not the whole of Europe. *In principle* the Community has to be open for other European countries. This does not mean that we can accept all European countries tomorrow or the day after tomorrow. But it does mean that we do not exclude anyone if the conditions for membership are fulfilled . . . [my italics].[10]

The italics highlight the use of the subjunctive mood: enlargement to East Central Europe, at least at this juncture, was treated as a hypothetical scenario only. Of course, one may assert, Kohl was right. The East Central European states, the 'reform countries' in the official German language of the time, were not yet ready for membership. They had none of the administrative tools in place that would make the implementation of Single Market directives possible; their products were uncompetitive; their markets would have been swamped by EC products; free movement of people would have flooded the European Community with cheap labour. These were insurmountable difficulties in the face of immediate enlargement.

Nonetheless, rapid enlargement did have proponents, most notably the British Prime Minister. In August 1990 Margaret Thatcher came out unequivocally in favour of widening the Community: 'If we set off down the path of giving more power to highly centralised institutions, which are not democratically accountable,' Thatcher stated, 'we should make it harder for the East Europeans to join.'[11] And *The Times* commented for those who had not realized: 'Eastern Europe is Mrs Thatcher's Trojan horse. Wheeled into the cosy corridors of Brussels, it will disgorge a thousand threats to the oligopolies of the EC.'[12] In a sense, Thatcher was entirely correct: deepening would make enlargement more difficult. But she missed the point. The overwhelming majority of EC member states, Germany included, feared not a delay in enlargement but a dilution of integration in the wake of German unification. The dilution of (West) European integration was precisely what Germany did not want, either before or after unification, and especially not under a Chancellor whose aims, after the attainment of unification, were much more focused on European integration than on a particular version of domestic social or economic order.[13]

Instead of rapid enlargement, Germany supported the Commission initiative of negotiating bilateral 'Association Agreements' with Poland, Hungary and Czechoslovakia. In order to emphasize their special nature for the East Central European countries, these were called 'Europe Agreements'. In principle, they were economic accords that consisted of the removal of trade barriers. The idea was that this would be undertaken asymmetrically, with the EC removing its trade barriers more quickly and more comprehensively than the East Central European countries. This would increase the competitiveness of East Central European products, help production, generate employment and would therefore assist the transformation processes in the associated countries. In theory, this was a good idea. In practice, it failed.

Although trade was liberalized quickly in an overwhelming majority of products, EC negotiators proved highly intransigent when it came to a set of specific 'sensitive' sectors: agriculture, coal, steel and textiles. This was not due to the intransigence of the Commission's negotiators, but to the very limited negotiating mandate the Commission had received from EC member states. In those sectors where the East Central European countries were most competitive, where they had chances to export to EC markets, domestic interests in individual EC member states pushed successfully for an erection of trade barriers.[14] This had detrimental effects on the transformation processes in East Central Europe. It decreased exports, had a negative effect on the balance of payments and the balance of trade, and led to the renewed erection of protectionist barriers by the East Central European countries.[15] Both exacerbated the shortage of capital. But capital in East Central Europe was a scarce commodity, badly needed to finance public and private restructuring. The protectionism of the 'Europe Agreements' in the sensitive sectors, therefore, had adverse consequences for the pace of transformation in the associated countries.

Surely, this was detrimental to the EC's enlightened self-interest, which had vowed to stabilize its East Central European neighbours. How could this have occurred? And what was the German responsibility for this outcome? The negotiations of the Europe Agreements were simply not prominent on the agenda of European politics in 1991. Matters related to the EC were aggregated in the two intergovernmental conferences on political and monetary union to be concluded under the Dutch Presidency in December. Apart from the intergovernmental conferences, policy makers were also distracted by the after-pains of the Gulf War and the outbreak of the Yugoslav war, in particular towards the end of the year when member states battled for a common stance about whether or not to recognize Slovenia and Croatia. Finally, to the extent that Western attention was focused on the former Warsaw Pact at all, it concentrated on the Soviet Union: its economic decline, nationality problems, the August coup and its final implosion. It is perhaps not surprising that under these circumstances, Western politicians did not devote sufficient time or energy to ensuring that the to-be-associated countries received a fair deal.[16]

There is also a second reason why the Europe Agreements did not come to a more positive conclusion for East Central Europe. This was that in the sensitive sectors, domestic interests were sufficiently assertive to influence the Commission's negotiating mandate, circumventing the more benevolent disposition of foreign policy establishments. Agricultural producers' lobbies influenced the negotiating stance through the Agricultural Ministries and the General Directorate for Agriculture in the Commission; other organized interests focused on their respective ministries and General Directorates.[17] This led to an extremely intransigent negotiating stance on the part of the Commission, because its room to manoeuvre was limited. Every change of position had to be sanctioned by the relevant Council of Ministers. This prolonged the conclusion of the agreements, originally planned for June 1991, considerably. Disappointed by the Community's intractability, Poland walked out of the talks on 7 July; the Community responded by a suspension of talks on 29 July.[18] France, whose agricultural interests were at stake, refused to resume the talks for weeks, and only agreed to their continuation after a triangular deal was struck that arranged for Polish meat products to be exported to the Soviet Union. That the French representatives returned to the negotiating table at all was due to Delors's negotiating skill.[19] The August coup in the Soviet Union may also have contributed, at least in so far as it reinforced the need to press ahead with external support for the stabilization of East Central Europe.[20] Its failure, however, led to the relaxation of pressures on the negotiators of the European Community.

The German stance during the negotiation procedure was badly co-ordinated at best, contradictory at worst. If one accepts that Germany had a strong political interest in the stabilization of its Eastern neighbours, one would expect its support for a favourable deal for them in the Europe Agreements. This was so only in part. The German government's main interest seemed to lie in the political inclusion of its Eastern neighbours into the Community's framework, and it was therefore in part extremely reluctant to lower trade barriers in those sectors where domestic German interests were threatened.[21] This was the case especially in agriculture and steel. Whereas France actually blocked the agreement on agriculture in September, the German negotiators could conveniently hide behind the French position. This weakened Germany's resolve to persuade France to return to the negotiating table. The same was true for the coal and steel sector, where Germany was reluctant to agree to liberalization. The Franco-German negotiating stance also encouraged other countries to assert their national positions very strongly, as Portugal did with regard to textiles, to the detriment of an overall fair deal for the East Central Europeans.

The denial of role conflict

The outcome of the Europe Agreements in the sensitive sectors was so undesirable that a further probing into the German negotiating position seems necessary. Did Germany pursue policies in Brussels that were detrimental to its policies vis-à-vis Prague, Warsaw and Budapest? The key to answering this question lies in the nature of the European policy-making process in Germany. It has been observed that this process is often little more than the domestic policy process responding to external events.[22] When the EEC was founded in 1957, responsibility for the negotiations leading up to it were divided between the Foreign Ministry and the Economics Ministry. The German Permanent Representation in Brussels is headed by a representative from the Foreign Ministry, whereas overall responsibility for European economic policy lies with the Economics Ministry. Negotiations in the Europe Agreements were led by a representative of the Economics Ministry, since as with the Lomé agreements they were mainly concerned with trade issues. It is perhaps not surprising that the Economics Ministry, pressured by specific domestic concerns, should take a different view of Germany's overall interest in the stabilization of East Central Europe from the Foreign Ministry. 'All departments were delighted that the Economics Ministry bore responsibility for negotiations,' a top civil servant said in an interview with the author, 'because the Foreign Ministry has a tendency to privilege the interests of others to our own.'[23]

This institutional dynamic in German European policy is reinforced by a constitutional one. According to Article 65 of the Basic Law, the Chancellor has the prerogative of setting down the guidelines of policy (*Richtlinienprinzip*), whereas ministers are responsible for their individual departments (*Ressortprinzip*). This division of responsibility holds for European policy just as it holds for domestic policy, and indeed it may be especially strong in European policy because many issues cut across foreign and domestic interests, which only the Chancellery can aggregate adequately. The Chancellor therefore has a strong device in the institutional resources of the Chancellery. In addition, Kohl had from the start taken a great interest in European policy and devoted much time and energy to it. His dominance over the European policy-making process was reinforced in the process of German unification leading up to the Maastricht treaty, and by Genscher's resignation in May 1992. For all intents and purposes, European policy was Helmut Kohl's special domain. No German policy vis-à-vis Brussels would be fundamentally changed in the absence of a guideline from the highest level.

In the negotiations of the Europe Agreements this set of institutional, constitutional and political factors led to a negotiating stance that did not benefit the stabilization of East Central Europe. German agricultural interests were at stake, and these have had a special electoral importance for the CDU/CSU since the Federal Republic's inception. The German farmers' union (Deutscher Bauernverband – DBV) counts as Germany's best organized interest group with the most powerful links to government and administration. The German agriculture minister, who is normally a member of the DBV, is both vulnerable and sympathetic to its pressure. In previous attempts at reforming the Common Agricultural Policy (CAP), Kohl managed to reconcile his government's European vocation with domestic political interests only by seeking exceptions for German farmers, at considerable expense to the Federal Republic's public purse.[24]

In this light it does not seem surprising that German negotiators at the Europe Agreements, faced with the opportunity, chose to hide behind the much more forcefully asserted French position. There is no evidence to suggest that this unambiguous decision was actually stated explicitly in the brief for Germany's negotiating position. In the inter-ministerial meeting to determine Germany's negotiating stance, the Agriculture Ministry had reaffirmed its classical position clinging to price support, over-production, and external protection.[25] Thus old positions remained unchanged in the absence of a guideline from the Chancellor that they should be revised. This strategy was mirrored in other 'sensitive' sectors, where the German negotiating position also featured protectionist elements. Here, however, it was not the Agriculture Ministry that asserted them but the Economics Ministry, which is in fact known for its free trade vocation. Germany's negotiating position was therefore far less rigid, aiming to attain longer transition periods rather than a fundamentalist blocking of trade.

Against the evidence presented here it seems quite reasonable to contend that Germany's stance in the Europe Agreements contradicted its official policy of stabilizing the East Central European neighbours. Noting this contradiction, one observer concluded:

Although Germany as a whole has the strongest interest among EU members in stability in CEE [Central and Eastern Europe], concessions to some sectors of domestic industry led to a highly restrictive stance on market access in the EA [Europe Agreements] negotiations. Not only does this contradict a strictly economic logic, if one takes into account the considerable future export opportunities for German industry, but in the broader political context it undermined an otherwise consistent political strategy which combined substantial financial aid with support for eventual membership.[26]

If the civilianization of East Central Europe was supposed to be multilateral stabilization, Germany's Civilian Power policy was impeded by both domestic interests and its continuous Western orientation. Although the congruence of political interests between Germany and its eastern neighbours was a historical novelty, sectoral interests remained incompatible. One could therefore argue that in this early stage Germany did not behave like a Civilian Power at all.

The question is whether this was really so. Germany would have had to exert enormous pressure to make a complete opening of markets possible; in agriculture, an opening of markets would have exceeded all costs if unaccompanied by CAP reform. But was it really in Germany's interest to throw its weight around? Would this not have violated the 'culture of reticence' that had become such an integral part of German foreign policy? Did unified Germany not have to demonstrate its readiness to cooperate, its modesty even, to gain the trust of its Western partners, most of whom had had severe reservations about unification in the first place? If the Kohl government had pressed for rapid enlargement at this early stage, it would have risked a profound diplomatic rupture with its Western partners, especially with France. Although Germany would have been hugely popular in East Central Europe, it would have paid a price in the form of the destabilization of Western Europe. With all this, we have to remember that Germany is an entirely different country than Britain. Because of its size and its past, it is much more distrusted. Germany would not have been well advised to push for rapid enlargement, in the way Margaret Thatcher did, if it wanted to keep its European credentials. Margaret Thatcher had never really had European credentials, and to the extent that she did, had thrown them away with her Bruges speech in 1988. For a German government to throw away its European credentials would have been singular folly. A push for a more rapid stabilization of East Central Europe, either by advocating rapid enlargement or by promoting an early opening of EC markets, would have endangered the very stabilization that a Civilian Power would have wanted to promote.

It is thus difficult to establish precisely to what extent Germany approximated Civilian Power in this early phase of its policies towards East Central Europe. This leads to an important observation about the Civilian Power concept as a whole, because it drives home the point that it is not sufficiently narrowly constructed. When testing Germany's foreign policy culture against the background of decision-making processes, it becomes evident that the nature of the German policy-making machinery allows a considerable degree of flexibility in the interpretation and application of the Civilian Power ethos. Furthermore, the Civilian Power concept also contains methodological difficulties. These lie in the hazy distinction between German and EC policy. The Europe Agreements were an EC policy, they were supported, not initiated, by the German government. Does this mean that it was Germany that behaved like a Civilian Power, or was it really the European Community? To what extent can unified Germany take credit for the association policy that the EC pursued?

These questions are extremely difficult to answer. They provoke a discussion of the relationship between the EC and the nation state, and this varies by policy area. In external trade, which the Europe Agreements fall under, the Commission's clout is far stronger than in institutional reform, which assumed increasing significance in the run-up to the Amsterdam summit. These questions are too broad and too intricate to be discussed here in any detail. As the author's view on them, however, is likely to inform any further discussion, two observations can be offered. First, the Commission appears to have provided leadership in the absence of initiatives led by individual countries or by the European Council. Perhaps it was more acceptable to the whole Community to follow initiatives proposed by the Commission rather than by individual countries understood to have a vested interest in enlargement. There is no evidence to suggest that the Commission pressured member states into an association policy they did not support. But although member states determined the Commission's negotiating mandate for the Europe Agreements, the Commission succeeded in establishing common positions. One may recall, for instance, that in September 1991 France seemed quite prepared to let the entire agreements fail because of its discontent over the proposed import of Polish beef or, to be precise, over whether or not blood sausages counted as beef. Secondly, in a multilateral framework, national policies are difficult to disentangle, not least because high-level discussions often occur over the phone, in informal settings and in the Council of Ministers where consultations are secret. It is therefore difficult to establish just to what extent the conclusion of the Europe Agreements was down to German policy. All we can do is to establish where German priorities lay.

These priorities testify to Germany's basic dilemma after unification. On the one hand it had long-standing, actual commitments in the West. On the other it had desirable, new commitments in the East. Its primary foreign policy orientation remained the West. Yet the primary risks to its security and well-being lay in the East. These conflicting foreign policy aims explain why much of what German foreign policy makers did in their Europapolitik was contradictory, and why much of what they said was an attempt to conceal the contradiction. The years 1990 and 1991 marked the emergence of a role conflict between Germany's old role as *integration deepener* and its new role as an *integration widener*.

This conflict explains why German European policy in these years was confused in comparison to those architectural designs proposed by the French President and the British Prime Minister. Whereas Mitterrand gave a clear priority to the deepening of integration inside the EC, Thatcher, as discussed above, preferred a rapid enlargement to East Central Europe. Kohl's vision of the EC's role for Europe as a whole was stuck in the middle. He shared Mitterrand's view that deepening should take priority over widening, but agreed with Thatcher that enlargement was a necessary and desirable project. Official German rhetoric at the time was marked by a clear denial that the objectives of policies to the East and of policies to the West conflicted. The concept by which this was achieved was a revived Adenauerian magnet theory: the European Union would attract and stabilize the East Central Europe countries. It is enlightening to hear Helmut Kohl's version of this:

> The radical change in Central, Eastern, and South-eastern Europe entails recognisable risks and imponderables. The whole of Europe needs a secure anchor now more than ever before. This role and task can only be assumed by a strong European Community. This brings me to one, if not the, essential aim of the Maastricht treaty. This treaty is not just a European answer to the collapse of the dictatorships in Central, Eastern, and South-eastern Europe. With it we take up our responsibility for the whole of the European continent.[27]

One may assert of course that at this juncture Germany's role conflict was only latent because its established role of *integration deepener* took clear precedence over the new role as *integration widener*. Germany's immense commitment in the Maastricht treaty, not least in sacrificing the Deutsche Mark, contrasted sharply with the tentative support for enlargement. In this sense Kohl and Mitterrand shared a clear view not only of the EC (soon to become the EU), and of the role Germany should play in it (namely that of an *integration deepener*). But considering that Germany had given a commitment to enlargement, which France had not, one wonders how this commitment would sit with the commitment to deepening given in Maastricht. German politicians neither recognized publicly the contradiction of their aims nor propounded a plan of how to solve them.

This was by no means impossible. As early as July 1989, two of Kohl's main advisers had published an early draft of a European architecture of concentric circles, in which France, Germany and other EC countries would establish one circle, Britain and other more reluctant member states a second, and the more reformist East Central European countries a third.[28] This design recognized the tension in the deepening–widening scenario, and realized that West Germany's European policy could not be all things to all people. The same clarity of thought was not demonstrated when the need to reconcile conflicting objectives sprang up two to three years later. This denial of role conflict had, for the time being, two main effects. It allowed Germany to pursue its conflicting priorities concomitantly, pretending that nothing had changed and that nothing would have to change. Secondly, it did not attack the root cause of the dilemma, did not alter the subject matter itself. The denial of role conflict, as discussed in Chapter 1, was always likely to dramatize the conflict itself.

The first enlargement phase

December 1991 marked the signing of the Maastricht treaty (on the 11th and 12th) and of the Europe Agreements (the 16th). It can conveniently be chosen as the beginning of the first enlargement phase, because the former set the course of European integration in the West, whereas the latter recognized the wish of the associated East Central European countries to become members of the EC. The East Central Europeans had to fight for this recognition, because some EC negotiators felt that the commitment that this entailed was more than they could support. Moreover, the recognition was phrased very cautiously.[29]

However, enlargement towards East Central Europe was now firmly on the agenda.[30] This forced German policy makers to think much harder about how the various aims of European policy were to be reconciled than they had previously done. At the September 1992 CDU party conference, the new Defence Minister Volker Rühe asserted:

> It seems to me that the discussion about the deepening and widening of the European Community has been conducted too superficially so far. I also have to say quite honestly that I cannot permanently deal with the formula 'both-the-one-and-the-other'. Priorities have to be set, decisions have to be made. I have to say to you: I do not believe that we can continue to perfect the club of the twelve at a high level – which we have already reached – by essentially persisting with the high financial transfers from North to South, without doing more to reduce the drop in prosperity in the whole of Europe.[31]

Volker Rühe, of course, is an outspoken politician. Although it is instructive to cite him because he makes things that little bit clearer than others, he is not a representative of the CDU mainstream. The quotation illustrates, however, that there was an awareness towards the end of 1992 that the deepening–widening dilemma needed to be addressed, though naturally opinions differed as to how this should be done. The fact that there was a role conflict could now no longer be denied, not least because the denial of role conflict hitherto had only exacerbated the problem. Yet due to uncertainty about how to combine old and new roles, Germany chose a strategy of role alternation, opting for the role of *integration deepener* at one moment and *integration widener* at the next. While Germany's ratification and support of the Maastricht treaty were never in doubt, the first phase of enlargement was marked by the growing strength of Germany's role of *integration widener*, which came increasingly to sit side by side with the old commitment to deepening. Only the second phase of enlargement, from August 1994 onwards, yielded proposals for a merger of the two roles.

Already in the course of 1991 the EC's recalcitrance in the negotiations of the Europe Agreements had been criticized in the public sphere, by journalists and scholars alike. Criticisms concentrated on two main points: that the West had been selfish and unfair in denying the East Central Europeans wider access to its markets, and that its selfishness was foolish because it imperilled stabilization. After France had refused to continue its negotiation over the Europe Agreements in September 1991, William Pfaff wrote that the episode provided another reason for the East Europeans to think that in matters involving sacrifice or risk the West's attitudes towards them have not really changed very much since 1938, or 1945. Eastern Europe was then considered expendable and seems now to be . . . One may hope, of course, that this will not be so. But Czechoslovakia, Poland and the other Eastern Europeans countries could once again find that they are on their own.[32]

Equally, it was pointed out that the EC's intransigence was harmful for Western Europe itself, since the increasing interdependence that marked the continent after the Cold War would bring East Central European problems right into the West, whether or not the West wanted them. Doing more for East Central Europe was therefore in the West's enlightened self-interest. In this vein, Timothy Garton Ash, Dominique Moïsi and Michael Mertes argued:

> In 1989 the dominoes fell in the direction of democracy. But could they not fall again the other way? Although the coup has failed in Moscow, the situation in the former Soviet Union remains highly volatile and potentially threatening . . . East Central Europe has urgent need of both protection from external threat and moderation of internal conflict. Enhancing their security will also enhance ours.[33]

Interestingly, the criticism of German or EU policy towards East Central Europe coincided with an increasingly lively debate on the nature of German foreign policy in general, and the conception of German 'national interests' in particular.[34] Almost all contributors to the debate noted that, whereas it was not in Germany's interests to forsake Western integration, the stabilization of East Central Europe was a vital German interest which had to be recognized clearly and portrayed unambiguously. This was summed up neatly by Günther Nonnenmacher, a co-editor in chief of the *Frankfurter Allgemeine Zeitung* and highly influential contributor to the debate:

> Germany owes its prosperity to the integration with the other West European democracies. For the maintenance of security and prosperity this alliance has to be deepened, stretched incrementally towards the new democracies in Central and Eastern Europe, and kept open for free global trade. These are aims that do not always concur. But it is in the German interest to mediate and, as much as possible, to work towards a balancing out.[35]

These changed role expectations coincided with a change in Germany's geopolitical situation. First and foremost, the dissolution of the Warsaw Pact and the implosion of the Soviet Union at the end of 1991 created a fundamentally different security environment. This was reinforced, secondly, by the outbreak of the war in Bosnia in the spring of 1992, which proved to be even more of a quagmire than the war between Serbia and Croatia had been in 1991. Both of these developments increased the fear in Germany that large-scale instability in Eastern Europe was quite possible and that, if it was to come about, Germany would bear the brunt of it. This view was supported by an exponential rise in asylum seekers in Germany, most of them from the former Soviet bloc; in 1988 approximately 100 000 people applied, and in 1992 the number had risen to almost 440 000.[36] Although the obvious response to the asylum problem would have been to develop a new migration policy, the connection to a more active foreign policy in East Central Europe was made. This contributed to the pressure for a reconsideration of foreign policy priorities. It is again instructive to quote Volker Rühe:

> Without stability in the East of our continent there will be no stability for the continent as a whole, and especially no stability for Germany. Germany at the moment is in a situation of being a bolt, a cordon towards the problems of Eastern Europe and Central Europe. We cut many other countries in the European Community and in Western Europe off from these problems, whether they are asylum problems or other. It cannot be in the German interest to remain permanently in this position and therefore we have to commit ourselves as a matter of priority to eliminating the rift of prosperity between Western Europe and Eastern Europe.[37]

Finally, growing role expectations from published opinion and changes in the geopolitical situation were complemented by increasingly vociferous demands from the East Central European countries themselves. These role expectations focused on a rapid accession to the EU, that is to say on accession by the end of the decade as a realistic aim. In September 1992 all three countries, Poland, Hungary and Czechoslovakia, issued a declaration in the context of their Visegrad summit expressing profound dissatisfaction with the progress on closer association, and calling

> upon the Communities and the member states to respond to our efforts by clearly stating that the integration of our economies and societies leading to membership in the Communities is the aim of the

Communities themselves. This simple, but historic statement would provide the anchor we need.[38]

Interestingly, the Visegrad cooperation ceased to function shortly afterwards, primarily because Vaclav Klaus, the Czech Prime Minister, assumed that it would delay the Czech Republic's accession.[39] All three countries planned to apply officially for membership in the course of 1992, but then chose not to do so in order not to endanger the ratification of the Europe Agreements in EU parliaments. Since the ratification process took much longer than had been anticipated, official applications were only submitted in the summer of 1994. The message, however, was clear: the East Central European countries wanted to accede to the EU, and they expected German support. In the bilateral treaties with Poland (signed in June 1991), and Hungary and Czechoslovakia (both signed in February 1992), Germany had, of course, committed itself legally to support the East Central European efforts.

Part of the East Central European focus on Germany also had to do with the inactivity of other countries. France spoke of enlargement in terms of decades rather than years; Britain lacked diplomatic influence in general and on enlargement in particular, because everyone suspected a Trojan horse; Italy had to cope with the breakdown of its domestic political system; and the Mediterranean countries made their budgetary concerns about a rapid enlargement quite explicit. In these circumstances it was hardly surprising that the role expectations from East Central Europe focused on the immediate western neighbour. Germany became an *integration widener* partly by design, partly by default. To a considerable extent, civilianization was a demand-led strategy.

Germany as integration widener

The new role of *integration widener* manifested itself above all in a rhetorical shift. The term *Heranführung* (leading up to) was shed in favour of *Erweiterung* (enlargement). In terms of actual policy, it manifested itself in three different ways: the Weimar triangle, the Copenhagen declaration of June 1993, and the initiation of the Structured Dialogue at the Essen summit in 1994. The creation of the Weimar triangle was a remarkable piece of diplomacy, not only because of its novelty value, but because of the unique mixture of the personal and the institutional that made it possible. The idea to have regular annual meetings between the Foreign Ministers of France, Poland and Germany was Genscher's idea, first realized in August 1991. Though there was a complex combination of motivations behind the three countries' decision to go ahead with this, the good personal relations between the three ministers helped. Genscher and Dumas were notoriously close, and had remained so despite the row between Kohl and Mitterrand in the first months of 1990. The same came to be true for the relationship with Skubiszewski, with whom Genscher developed, in his own words, a 'profound human relationship' that remained untouched by the problems Kohl and Mazowiecki had with one another.[40]

The Weimar triangle proved Monnet's dictum that nothing starts without people, but nothing lasts without institutions. The informal meeting of the three foreign ministers, who had become friends, had not been planned as a regular event. Though the three decided to meet again in Bergerac in May 1992, it would have been far-fetched at this juncture to predict that the idea would survive their departure from office, be copied by the ministers of defence from 1994, and by the chief executives from 1996 onwards. According to his memoirs, Genscher's motivation was simply the realization of the significance the three countries had for the future of the continent.

> If Germans, Frenchmen, and Poles act together as Europeans and do not give another chance to nationalism, this will have a trust- and peace-building effect for the whole of Europe.[41]

The geopolitical importance of the Warsaw–Berlin–Paris axis surely did have something to do with the inception of the Weimar triangle. We can, however, also discern a more narrowly defined set of national goals. Poland's objectives, perhaps most easily identifiable, were threefold: first, to be upgraded in diplomatic status by participating in the Franco-German tandem; second, to awaken a French interest in East Central Europe, thereby spreading Poland's diplomatic influence and diluting the German position in the region. 'One of the reasons that we hope to tie France into East Central Europe', Bronislaw Geremek said in an interview with the author, 'is that to us, France ensures that we will deal with a European Germany. And because France has this function and is the only country that can fulfil it, we would never aspire to breaking up the Franco-German alliance.'[42] Third, and perhaps most importantly, Poland saw the Weimar triangle in terms of its use for Western integration. If France and Germany had been the tandem for integration, perhaps Poland, France and Germany could be the vehicle for enlargement.

In a nutshell, the German motivation was to ensure that the desired multilateral stabilization of East Central Europe really was going to be perceived as a multilateral task. Part of this had to do with the belief, inherent in the Civilian Power view, that multilateralism is per se a desirable framework of policy. Part of it also had to do with the fact that East Central Europe came to be seen as a bottomless pit. By the end of 1994 Germany had paid a total of $57 billion dollars to East Central Europe and the former Soviet Union, a full two-thirds of the total these countries received from the West.[43] Since the stabilization of East Central Europe was a Herculean task as it stood, utterly unmanageable by Germany alone, it was indispensable to tie the Western partners in if it was to succeed. France was particularly important for this endeavour.

The French interest in the Weimar triangle was to be aware of, and perhaps to exert influence upon, German policies towards East Central Europe. If this was so, it backfired. Since the purpose of the Weimar triangle was so clearly focused on Poland's Western integration, a purpose that Germany and Poland shared, the amount of pressure France could exert in order to slow this process down was always going to be disproportionate to the amount of pressure it would have to endure from the other two partners. In this sense, the true ingenuity of Genscher's plan was selling Germany's new role of *integration widener* to France. By familiarizing France with German and Polish concerns for EU enlargement, Germany not only affected the role expectations from a country to which it related as an *integration deepener*. It also affected the external role expectations towards France by confronting it with demands to behave like an *integration widener* itself.

The Weimar triangle was not solely responsible for the French change of position towards EU enlargement. The change in government in 1993 also contributed to this, as did the passage of time and seeming inevitability of the process. But it is important to recognize how much the resolutions of the Weimar triangle committed the three countries to work towards Poland's Western integration. In 1991 this was largely non-committal – 'France and Germany support all efforts to guide Poland and the young democracies towards the European Community' – and was undermined dismally by the French negotiating stance on Polish meat imports only days later.[44] But by November 1993, now at a meeting between Klaus Kinkel, Alain Juppé and Andrzej Olechowski, the language of the communiqué was already far more specific: 'Germany and France will firmly support Poland in the process' of accession to the European Union.[45]

In addition, following this meeting Kinkel and Juppé urged their fellow WEU members to grant associated status to Poland and other East Central European countries, a status that had been unobtainable for the previous two years.[46] According to Andrzej Olechowski the meeting played an instrumental role. 'It did not take long to figure out that if an initiative had the backing of France and Germany in a European context, it had extremely good chances of success.'[47] A similar cooperation was achieved in preparation for the Structured Dialogue initiated at the Essen summit in 1994.[48] Hence, the picture that emerges is one of a unique conjunction of bilateral, trilateral and multilateral politics. Not least because it was extended to meetings of defence ministers and chief executives, the diplomacy of the Weimar triangle proved a remarkably effective vehicle for Poland's Western integration. It offered Germany a perfect mechanism to exercise its new role of *integration widener.*

As discussed above, the Europe Agreements had only offered the associated countries a very tentative perspective for eventual accession to the EU. The increasing criticism this attracted from East Central Europe, in conjunction with the awareness in some member states of the enormousness of the task, pushed for a more explicit acknowledgement that the East Central European countries would eventually be welcome to join the EU. This featured prominently in the consecutive British and Danish EU Presidencies, which had worked hard for progress on enlargement.[49] The Edinburgh summit in December 1992 had already announced that the Copenhagen summit in June 1993 would come to agreements 'in order to prepare the accession of the associated countries'.[50] This received strong support from the German government, where the Chancellery had asserted itself in support of the Foreign Ministry over the Economics and Agriculture Ministries.

This gathering of forces in member states was also supported by a change in the Commission's position following the conclusion of the Maastricht treaty. Not only was the Commission now freed from the extreme work overload from which it had suffered during the negotiations of the Europe Agreements, but also the change of personnel and organizational structure in January 1993 provided impetus for reform. The split in responsibility for East Central Europe between DG I for external commercial affairs and the new DG IA for external political affairs provided the Commission with the administrative freedom and ability to provide leadership.[51] The result was that trade restrictions were more rapidly reduced than originally offered, and that a perspective for membership was included in the Copenhagen communiqué for all those countries that fulfilled the necessary criteria. These, rather vaguely, were determined to be a stable democracy and respect for human and minority rights, a functioning market economy, and the capacity to absorb the *acquis communautaire* and to promote fully the objectives of the Maastricht treaty. Especially the last two criteria meant that the hurdle for EU accession was high for the associated countries. The full adoption of the *acquis* necessitated a considerable acceleration of administrative reform in order to implement Single Market directives. The full endorsement of the Maastricht treaty entailed readiness for Economic and Monetary Union in terms of inflation, public debt and budget deficit criteria. Copenhagen established neither a catalogue of criteria nor a starting point for negotiations. It determined a set of high hurdles – they made plain that the associated countries would be granted no special treatment – but their advantage lay in the encouragement they provided for the East Central European countries to attempt to jump. Copenhagen was widely hailed as the breakthrough for enlargement.

Again, it is difficult to evaluate the precise German input. Again, the Commission and other member states seem to have been as instrumental to the final outcome as Germany. Again, we can therefore only look at the priorities of the German government. Genscher had asserted for almost a year that Poland, Hungary and Czechoslovakia should be EU members by the end of the century.[52] Kohl had assured Skubiszewski at a private dinner in 1992 that he would be Chancellor of Germany until the Visegrad three acceded to the EU – surely a remarkable demonstration of confidence in one's political longevity by anyone's standards.[53] Publicly, German politicians began to assert that the Oder–Neisse line could not be allowed to remain the Eastern border of the European Union.

This increasing outspokenness in favour of enlargement was matched by the assertion of the ministries with an interest in the long-term stabilization of East Central Europe (the Chancellery, the Foreign Ministry and the Economics Ministry) over the ministries with a primary interest in the protection of domestic economic interests (chiefly the Ministry for Agriculture, the Ministry for Labour and Social Affairs, and the Ministry for Transport). This facilitated the breakthrough made on market access at Copenhagen. It also vindicates the previous assertion about the Chancellery's centrality in German European policy. Just as it had been the Chancellery that had tipped the balance in favour of domestic protection in the Europe Agreements, it was now the decisive factor in favour of liberalization. The role of *integration widener* had become an official German position. Yet this position remained riddled with tensions. On the one hand, the East Central European countries were assured that they would soon accede to the EU; on the other, the West European partners were assured that deepening remained a priority and that EMU would go ahead on time. How East Central Europe would ever be able to catch up with a group of states that had advanced so far down the road of integration, however, remained unclear. Especially since the hurdles determined at Copenhagen were high, the tension between deepening and widening could hardly be disguised. Germany alternated between the roles of widener and deepener.

Role alternation was also demonstrated with the strategy of increased political cooperation between the associated countries and the EU that culminated in the Structured Dialogue agreed at the Essen Summit in December 1994. As early as spring 1993, Kohl had called for an invitation to the heads of government of the Visegrad states to the next European Council.[54] There was a realization that not enough had been done for East Central Europe, and that a political overture might give a sign of encouragement. A symbolic sign would not be costly – an important point at a time when the state of public finances of EU member states in general and Germany in particular was becoming increasingly dire. Finally, German politicians had the desire, already touched upon above, to ensure that the stabilization of East Central Europe was seen as an obligation for the whole of Western Europe, not just for Germany.

Horst Teltschik, Kohl's main foreign policy adviser until December 1990, recalls that Kohl had made attempts as early as 1988 to create a common Franco-German Ostpolitik. At the time this was unsuccessful and led to competition rather than cooperation in the policies vis-à-vis the Eastern bloc.[55] Similarly a resolution agreed at a meeting between Kohl and Mitterrand in September 1990 proposing a joint Ostpolitik came to very little, if one excludes the Weimar triangle. In preparation for the consecutively held EU Presidency by Germany and France in 1994/95, Germany made another attempt to tie France into its foreign policy towards East Central Europe. Kohl reiterated in the spring of 1994 that relations with the associated countries would be one of the priorities of the German presidency. Kinkel called for a joint Franco-German effort when in Paris in March.[56] The German initiative received special momentum because the proper association agreements were now in place clearing the road for an application from the associated states for EU membership. Hungary and Poland applied in the spring of 1994, increasing the pressure on the EU to respond. The German announcement encouraged the Commission to come up with new proposals, like a new use for Phare money and first proposals for the adoption of Single Market legislation.[57]

The proposals for a regular inter-ministerial dialogue were endorsed in a joint article in *Le Monde* by Kohl and Eduard Balladur, the French Prime Minister, in May 1994, whence it was fairly predictable that the German initiative would be adopted at the Essen summit in December.[58] The Structured Dialogue passed there envisaged the regular participation of ministers of the associated states in the EU's Council of Ministers, and participation of heads of states in the European Council once a year. Whereas the Europe Agreements had been bilateral, that is between the EU and a particular associated country, the Structured Dialogue was a multilateral forum. Its aim was to give a further and more substantial perspective of membership to the East Central European countries, and to familiarize their policy makers with the often complex EU mode of decision making. Though practically it was deeply flawed, its ingenuity lay in its symbolic dimension, signalling to both East and West that enlargement was, in principle, a decided matter, while not straining public finances or sectoral interests and thereby provoking the type of resistance that had proved so detrimental in 1991. The Structured Dialogue was a considerable German achievement, especially in the form of its initiation at Essen, where the heads of state from the associated countries attended the European Summit at Kohl's invitation. Whereas the Southern member states and France seem to have remained wary about raising expectations that could not be fulfilled – *il ne faut pas brûler les étapes* – the German position was that a clear perspective both for enlargement and for a mechanism working towards it were badly needed.

At the same time, German politicians became increasingly outspoken about their role as an advocate of the East Central European states in the West. This had originally been refined to German policies vis-à-vis its immediate Eastern neighbours. By 1994 it had become customary with reference towards almost the entire former Soviet bloc.[59] The expectations that Germany behave as *integration widener* had obviously affected the role conceptions German policy makers entertained about their European policy. The basic dilemma of German European policy after unification, however, remained unsolved. The deepening and widening of European integration were not naturally reconcilable. This only became clearer after the Scandinavian enlargement in January 1995, in conjunction with the 'enlargement of the enlargement' process, that is the extension of association to Cyprus, Malta, Romania, Bulgaria and the Baltic states. What had started off in 1990 as an EU of 12 members enlarging to 15 or 18 had turned into an EU of 15 members enlarging to 30.

The second enlargement phase

As the strategies of denial and role alternation had hitherto failed to solve Germany's role conflict, the new strategy employed was the attempt to merge the role of *integration deepener* with that of *integration widener*. This was to be achieved through 'flexible integration' – a term used to indicate that not all member states would have to share a particular level of integration at a particular point in time.[60] In other words, some EU member states would go ahead with integration in a specific policy area, while those unable or unwilling to participate would not, at least for the time being. This would facilitate the integration of East Central Europe into the EU.

The discussion of flexible integration achieved a prominent status in Germany for the first time with the publication of the so-called Schäuble-Lamers paper in September 1994.[61] Officially published by the CDU/CSU Bundestag caucus under the deceptively modest name 'reflections on European policy', the paper came to be regarded as a fundamental text in German European policy. Schäuble and Lamers explicitly acknowledged for the first time that a tension between deepening and widening existed. In order to solve this tension they proposed that a close group of states – France, Germany and the Benelux countries – become a vanguard of integration. These countries would form an inner core that shared not only monetary union but also a common foreign policy. While the 'hard core' of Western countries would take the opportunity to integrate tightly, the EU would open its doors for the first wave of associated East Central European countries by the year 2000. These countries – Poland, Hungary, the Czech Republic, Slovakia and perhaps Slovenia – would not participate in all common policies right from the start, for instance in EMU, but would gradually join those common policies for which they fulfilled the necessary conditions.

There is no room to discuss the different aspects of the Schäuble-Lamers paper in detail. It received an unusual amount of attention, much of which was due both to Schäuble's involvement and to its omission of Italy from the core of countries likely to join EMU in the first wave. The significance of the paper for the present discussion is twofold. First, Schäuble and Lamers emphasized that deepening Western integration remained a vital German aim. Secondly, they asserted clearly that EU enlargement was also an important German aim. The ingenuity of the paper, the attempted *role merger*, lay in the fact that the 'formation of a core group of countries is not an end in itself but a means to reconcile the two ostensibly conflicting goals of widening and deepening the European Union.'[62]

If other EU member states chose not to support the stabilization of East Central Europe, Schäuble and Lamers warned, 'Germany might be called upon, or tempted by its own security concerns, to try to effect the stabilization of Eastern Europe *on its own and in the traditional way*' (my italics).[63] This sentence in itself did a lot of damage to the paper, most probably because it was interpreted as a scarcely veiled threat. This interpretation is understandable, but unjustified. One can follow Gunther Hellmann's analysis on this point, according to which Schäuble and Lamers framed their fears in realist categories, like regressive nationalism and balance-of-power politics, and prescribed liberal principles, like integration and interdependence.[64]

Although Schäuble and Lamers were exceptionally clear in their analysis, their proposals were hardly new. Only seven days before the publication of their paper, Kinkel had stated in a speech:

> The question for the 1996 Intergovernmental Conference is: should the convoy focus on the slowest ship? Or should those who want to proceed more quickly be allowed to do so?[65]

Of course, this is much more diplomatically phrased than the assertions of the CDU/CSU paper, yet the idea of a core Europe is already there. A further difference between Kinkel and the Schäuble-Lamers paper was Kinkel's reference to Britain (the slowest ship in the convoy) whereas Schäuble and Lamers deduced the necessity for flexibility not just from British recalcitrance but from the tension between deepening and widening. Especially with reference to Britain, German proposals for flexibility went back to the late 1980s. On the twenty-fifth anniversary of the Elysée treaty in January 1988, Kohl had included a discreet reference to flexible integration as a warning for Thatcher:

> Together the Germans and the French must form the core of a European union . . . We sincerely invite our European partners to cooperate in this project – but we will not cease to develop this Union further and to achieve it with those who want to participate in it.[66]

Against the argument that closer Western integration would endanger the chances of German unification, two of Kohl's closest foreign policy advisers had proposed in July 1989 that a flexible solution for integration should be found. This could accommodate the reforming countries of East Central Europe – at the time Poland and Hungary, but of course also the GDR – in an outer circle.[67] In short, the concept of flexibility was not at all new. The reason why it kicked up a fuss in September 1994 was because of Schäuble's involvement, its explicitness of language, its clarity of analysis, and the naming of countries for the first wave of EMU and the first wave of Eastern enlargement. These provocative elements, however, were not what the paper was really about. They were only included in order to assist the true purpose of the authors: to provoke a debate on German European policy. The first meeting of the reflection group preparing the 1996 intergovernmental conference was little more than six months away, while no debate on Germany's aims and interests for the intergovernmental conference had as yet been initiated.[68] Although Kohl had seen the paper and had discussed its contents with the authors, the paper was in this respect implicitly critical of the Chancellor, too. Kohl's approach to European policy relied on elite bargains on the model of those that had produced the Single European Act and the Maastricht treaty. Schäuble and Lamers on the other hand, aware of the popular backlash that had haunted the ratification of the Maastricht treaty, perceived an urgent need to trigger a comprehensive public debate.

The failure of role merger

They only achieved this in part. In Western Europe the paper generated enormous publicity, sometimes outrage, depending on whether or not a specific country was deemed qualified for first-round membership of EMU. In East Central Europe the paper experienced a mixed reception. On the one hand, a close core of tightly integrated countries was seen as a guarantee of a 'European Germany', which was perceived to be a good thing. On the other hand, it triggered latent fears that the process of catching up would be rendered even more difficult.[69] In its most extreme form, this was translated into fears of a 'second-class membership', which would terminate the (financial) solidarity that had accompanied integration for the previous forty years.[70] On the German domestic political scene, the Schäuble-Lamers proposal received lukewarm support from some, but was rejected by most. SPD representatives accused the CDU/CSU of 'creating an upper and a lower class Europe' that 'would destroy the European Union', had undermined the 'credibility and reliability' of German European policy, and should therefore be retracted.[71] Though the intensity of these attacks can at least partly be explained by the ongoing election campaign, the Social Democrats did have a point in recognizing that the paper had embarrassed the Foreign Minister. Asking who actually made European policy in the Kohl government, the opposition jibed: 'The government's spokesman manoeuvres, the Foreign Minister dissociates himself, the Finance Minister agrees, and Helmut Kohl is tacit on all of this and holds an altogether different position at EU meetings.'[72]

Kinkel dissociated himself from the paper early on. He was wary about embarrassing the pro-integration side so shortly before the impending Swedish referendum on accession, which could have swayed into a negative vote had the controversial proposals appeared as an official German position. In addition, the paper's pithiness was a scarcely concealed attack on the conceptual haziness of Kinkel's European policy. Although he had elaborated on the idea of a core Europe only days before the Schäuble-Lamers paper was presented, the poignancy of the paper made it unacceptable for support by either the FDP or the Foreign Ministry. In his position as FDP leader, Kinkel then used the negotiations on the coalition agreement that ensued after the October 1994 election in order to water down the Schäuble-Lamers proposals.

Alas, even Kohl saw fit to distance himself from the paper, disquieted in particular by the possible effects it could have on the Swedish referendum. Kohl emphasized that the paper was not government policy. That, in a formal sense, was true. But it clouded the fact that under Kohl, the lines of distinction between party, parliamentary caucus and government had become blurred, as virtually all important decisions had come to be made in a meeting of party leaders, the *Koalitionsrunde*, rather than in Cabinet or Cabinet committees. Due to his position as head of the CDU/CSU parliamentary caucus and his proximity to Kohl, Wolfgang Schäuble was Germany's second most powerful politician. If he took an interest in European policy, people were only too right to be observing what would come of it.

The conception of flexibility eventually found its way into formal governmental policy. In the coalition agreement after the 1994 federal election, the parties stated no more on the issue than that although all member states should be able to partake in integration, 'the refusal of individual member states must not prevent progress in integration'.[73] This phrasing reverted the concept of flexible integration back to a warning for Britain, rather than picking up the Schäuble-Lamers proposal of accepting it as the answer to Germany's deepening–widening dilemma. However, proposals for flexibility did find their way into Germany's official policy after all. Interestingly, these were presented as Franco-German initiatives. In a joint letter preceding the Madrid European Council, Jacques Chirac and Helmut Kohl explained:

> ... we regard it as desirable and possible to include a general clause in the treaty that opens up the opportunity for those countries that so wish and that are capable of it to develop an enforced co-operation while maintaining the Union's single institutional framework.[74]

Of course the language of 'enforced co-operation' was much more evocative of an open avant-garde than the exclusive metaphor of a 'hard core' had been. Yet the 'hard core' had been an ill-chosen metaphor in the first place, and did not actually reflect adequately how open Schäuble and Lamers had envisaged the core group to be. Indeed in 1997, the Amsterdam summit decided that 'flexibility' would enter the Treaty on European Union as 'enforced co-operation'. This could occur only as a result of a unanimous decision, that is to say with a veto for those member states that decided not to participate, which actually defied the original Franco-German plan. Although the mentioning of flexibility was an achievement, the Schäuble-Lamers initiative could therefore not claim success in replacing the old model of integration with a new one. If anything, the Amsterdam summit made it extremely improbable that a hard core of countries would go ahead with closer integration, thereby facilitating the East Central European countries' accession to the outer circle. The question is why this was so.

First, some member states, especially Britain and Greece, were vehemently opposed to a flexible model of integration, because they feared that they would be marginalized from the core of integration. But this was only a superficial reason. Flexibility never became the main issue of negotiations at the intergovernmental conference, and never exposed deep rifts between member states in the way other issues did. Consider, for instance, the different approaches by France and Britain on an incorporation of the WEU into the EU. Franco-German momentum for flexibility had been tentative in the first instance, regardless of the joint letters by Kohl and Chirac, Kinkel and de Charette. That this was so had other causes than British or Greek defiance.

One was an element of doubt in France, not least since Gaullism – back in office since 1993 – has a more natural affinity to a looser confederation of states than to a tightly integrated core. The 'hard core' countries would, according to the German plan, have cooperated especially in foreign policy matters, and whether this was to the French taste was extremely doubtful. If France could persuade Germany to start up a genuinely European foreign and security policy, that is one with minimal American influence, a tight core might have been acceptable. As long as Bonn was staunchly Atlanticist, however, and as long as Britain opposed the approximation of the EU and the WEU, these plans were doomed to failure. A second element was the growing number of countries that were set to qualify for EMU from the outset. Schäuble and Lamers' starting point had been the small number of countries that seemed ready for EMU. In one sense, their paper had merely affirmed the absolute German commitment to proceed with EMU even if only a small group of countries was set to qualify. Their proposal to broaden the EMU base to include foreign policy matters in this tight core was a desperate attempt to achieve the aims of a political union that had been disappointed at Maastricht. As soon as more countries seemed qualified to participate, most notably Austria, Finland and Ireland (but also Spain and Italy), the argument in favour of a small, tightly integrated core group had lost its basis. A third element was the hesitation from the FDP, which, not least because it was in charge of the Foreign Ministry, hampered the CDU/CSU policy proposals.

Quite regardless of the FDP's and the Foreign Ministry's objections we therefore have to return to the observation that at least strategically European policy was determined in the Chancellery, and that Kohl could have made flexibility his project had he wished to do so. But he chose not to, and this constitutes the fourth reason for the failure of the Schäuble-Lamers proposal. Kohl had been hesitant about flexibility from the start. Although he is often seen as an idealist, even a visionary, in his European policy, his track record in office is also one of pragmatism. As do many great statesmen, Kohl combined a clear vision of where he wanted to go with an acute sense of the possible. Pragmatism in 1995/96 suggested that EMU was a sufficiently intricate process on its own, that the mobilization of all political forces was demanded to achieve it in the face of adversity, and that much of the proposed political union would follow from EMU anyhow. Hence, flexibility never entered the mainstream of German European policy. This meant that for the time being, the old model of integration would endure. Germany's role conflict between deepening and widening, which had been solved conceptually by the Schäuble-Lamers proposals, would persist in practice. How does this sit with the attempted stabilization of East Central Europe? Was the proposal for deepening compatible with the Civilian Power ethos?

The persuasiveness of the Schäuble-Lamers argument was derived in large part from its realization that for Germany, policies to the East and policies to the West had become two parts of the same coin, a coin called Europapolitik. Whereas German policy had hitherto distinguished clearly between stabilization and Western deepening, this distinction had now become obsolete. Schäuble and Lamers exaggerated when advocating flexibility as an answer to a perceived large-scale instability emanating from East Central Europe. By 1994, the first phase of trans-formation had already been accomplished. If instability was not impending in Germany's Eastern neighbours by this stage, it was un-likely to be so in the future. However, it is noteworthy that the authors related their 'hard core' to the stabilization of East Central Europe through a modern, updated version of Adenauer's magnet theory. The core idea of enforced cooperation, Lamers said, was 'a belief borne out by the entire course of European unification – that if a smaller group of countries press ahead with particularly intensive and far-reaching eco-nomic and political integration, this group or core has a centripetal or magnetic effect on the other countries'.[75] The East Central European countries needed a magnet by which to be pulled into the EU. Once inside, they would become part of the magnet and pull others in. Integration remained a process that widened and deepened by defin-ition. By allowing some countries to proceed with integration more quickly, the tension between Germany's different roles could be solved. For a Civilian Power, extending the core of interdependence is impos-sible without maintaining internal stability. In this respect, Germany would have corresponded closely to its Civilian Power ethos by following the road of flexible integration as proposed by Schäuble and Lamers.

Managing role conflict, 1995–97

The failure of the Schäuble-Lamers initiative advertised the continued tension between deepening and widening. This manifested itself in the German position for the 1996/97 intergovernmental conference, the so-called Maastricht II conference, charged with perfecting and extending the agreements reached in the Treaty on European Union. At this junc-ture, we ought to discuss one of the terms most frequently used in this chapter, namely 'deepening'. On the one hand, one can view deepening as the introduction of policy areas into the realm of EU decision making. Monetary policy can serve as an example for such deepening, as can foreign policy and immigration policy. On the other hand, one can also view deepening as an institutional reform reducing any one member state's influence over the EU's institutions. The reduction of the Commission to ten members would be an example of this – though in theory Commissioners are of course independent of the governments that appointed them – as would be a reduction in the blocking majority in the Council of Ministers or an extension of rights for the European Parliament.

When discussing the tensions between deepening and widening, one must clarify which one of these meanings of deepening one refers to. This has a particular relevance for enlargement, since some forms of deepening are much more easily compatible with it than others. Deepening in the sense of institutional streamlining, for instance, can be seen as the natural correlative to enlargement. If the EU's institutions, originally created for six member states, are to function for 15 or 20 they have to be adjusted. Such adjustments may be painful – smaller member states may have to dispense with the right to a Commissioner, for instance – but are indispensable nevertheless because dysfunctional institutions would undermine the legitimacy of the entire EU order.[76]

The compatibility of 'policy communitization' and enlargement is more questionable. In the early 1990s, the building of the Single Market as part of the Community's 1992 programme raised severe doubts about the ability of non-community countries to catch up. The same was true for the decision to 'communitize' monetary policy in EMU. Since the difference between the EU and East Central Europe was especially stark in economic terms, the obvious question about the provisions of the Maastricht treaty was whether they would effect a magnetism towards East Central Europe, as Kohl had claimed, or whether they would propel Western European countries into a sphere of integration that would remain unattainable for the rest of the continent. This argument, however, also has a flip side, because the incorporation of East Central European countries into the second and third pillars of the Maastricht temple, foreign policy and justice and home affairs respectively, was comparatively easy. To put it bluntly, it proved much more difficult to improve the hygienic standards of Czech dairies than to vote for a common resolution on Yugoslavia in the UN Security Council. Of course the EC/EU was predominantly about economic affairs: its heart was the Single Market, in future it would be a common currency. Other policy areas, in contrast, had only experienced rudimentary integration. This means that even in communitization, one has to clarify the relationship between deepening and widening. In Single Market matters and in EMU, pressing ahead with integration made it more difficult for the associated countries to catch up. In foreign policy and domestic security affairs, deepening was more easily compatible with widening.

Against this background, German proposals for reform in the 1996/97 intergovernmental conference appear modest. Germany was content not to form ambitious positions that would then prove untenable in the course of negotiations. Rather, the German position, as traditionally it has done, sought the middle ground in order to investigate which positions could gain majorities.[77] In early 1995 Kinkel defined German aims as proximity to the people, competitiveness, domestic security, qualified majority voting in foreign policy matters and institutional reform, warning that national 'thinking about prestige has to retreat for the necessity to increase the efficiency of institutions'.[78]

Leaving aside the first two of Kinkel's aims, it is noticeable that the emphasis on 'communitization' in foreign policy and domestic security matters mirrored the German ambition in the run-up to Maastricht. Back then, the aim had been to complement EMU with a political union, that is with closely integrated policies involving pooled sovereignty and Commission authority. The fact that a review conference was scheduled for 1996 was not least due to the German disappointment that a political union had been unattainable at Maastricht. As illustrated by Kinkel's proposals, however, the German position for the 1996 intergovernmental conference was actually quite reticent. It focused on pragmatic deepening in the form of communitizing further in foreign policy and domestic security matters. This included qualified majority voting, progress on Europol and the incorporation of the Schengen Agreement into the EU's policy-making framework.[79] None of these aims was incompatible with the rapid incorporation of the associated East Central European states. German proposals for institutional reform were also vague, geared primarily towards a reform of the voting system in the Council of Ministers. The noble aim of a political union was neither mentioned nor backed by ambitious policy proposals.[80]

The modesty of German designs for the intergovernmental conference was accompanied by an increasingly vociferous demand for the timely incorporation of the associated East Central European countries. In October 1995, Karl Lamers proposed enlargement even before the EU had accomplished some of the reforms planned for the end of the century. Since the East Central European countries needed a realistic perspective, and since the EU would need time to reform some of its policies, he maintained, one had to devise a form of enlargement that would not disappoint East Central European hopes and would not overburden existing EU policies.[81] Thus for Lamers enlargement provided a welcome opportunity to tackle the EU's institutional immobilism. Rather than being detrimental to deepened Western integration, Lamers asserted, widening would actually accelerate political-institutional deepening, since this was long overdue anyway.[82]

How does this relate to the role conflict in Germany's enlargement policy? First, Germany's reform proposals for the intergovernmental conference advocated a deepening that did not obstruct concomitant widening, because it was geared at the communitization of those policy areas where East Central European countries could participate. Secondly, Germany was more cautious on institutional reform, that is in those areas that would maintain the Union's workability in the case of enlargement. This is not to say that Germany did not favour institutional deepening. But the Kohl government was cautious not to establish a conjunction between institutional reform and enlargement. For if this were the case, a failure to reach agreement on institutional reform would automatically delay enlargement. This would give those countries with little interest in enlargement considerable leverage over the process, a leverage that at least from the German point of view must have appeared undesirable. It is therefore not surprising that instead of a conjunction, German policy makers established an inverse causality: enlargement was unstoppable, they argued, and the pressures of the process made institutional reform inevitable.[83] Thirdly, German policy makers were firmly intent on distinguishing clearly between enlargement and the reform of EU policies. They were eager to keep policy reform off the intergovernmental conference's agenda, because they feared that the complex web of national and sectoral opposition this could mobilize would hamper the promotion of enlargement.

These last two points seem to suggest that Germany's role of *integration widener* had by now become more important than that of *integration deepener*. In order to push through enlargement, Germany appeared to be willing to sacrifice institutional reform and shut out all questions of finance and policy issues. This proposition is tenable only in part. German policy makers were adamant that EMU would go ahead on time. EMU was defended vis-à-vis a sceptical domestic audience not simply as a massive catalyst for economic restructuring and modernization, but as the first step to political union. Instead of the idealistic designs for political union flouted in the course of 1991, the German stance in 1996 was pragmatic. The aim of EMU, which had for much of the 1980s and in the early 1990s taken second place behind the designs for a political union, was now seen as an instrument to attain this political union despite the obstacles involved. The intergovernmental conference was not the main focus of Germany's, or anyone else's, thinking on European policy. Since EMU attracted all German hopes for closer economic and political integration, it reconciled German aspirations not only for deepening but, because it would effect a pragmatic flexibilization, also for widening.

This development was highly significant. The centre stage EMU assumed in European policy cannot be ignored in any account of Germany's enlargement policies. It affected the discourse on European policy not only in Germany itself, but also in France, and had a number of significant consequences for Germany's enlargement policy. Some consideration of EMU is therefore indispensable. The recession of the early 1990s had made it painfully clear by about 1994 that most EU member states would struggle to make the public debt and budget deficit criteria laid down in the Maastricht treaty. Austerity was especially difficult for France. Ever since 1983, when Mitterrand and Delors had decided to launch the *franc fort* policy, French monetary policy had been tied to the Deutsche Mark via the fixed exchange rate in the European Monetary System (EMS) and via the inflation target.[84] This became a problem in the early 1990s, when the inflationary pressures of German unification induced the Bundesbank to raise interest rates to levels far higher than the stage in the economic cycle warranted.[85] This caused enormous deflationary pressures not only in Germany, but in all Western European countries that were tied to the Deutsche Mark through the EMS. These pressures contributed to the severity of the British recession in the early 1990s, to Britain and Italy's ejection from the EMS in September 1992 and the force of speculation against the franc in August 1993.

The restrictive monetary policy, in conjunction with austerity packages related to EMU and a host of structural and demographic factors, exacerbated unemployment and other social problems that riddled French society. The French budget deficit surged from 1.6 per cent in 1991 to 6 per cent in 1994.[86] Jacques Chirac won the presidential election campaign in 1995, not least because he ran on an inclusive, quasi social-democratic ticket promising 'La France pour tous'. The adjustments imposed by the EMU straitjacket, however, forced Chirac's turnaround in the autumn of 1995. This culminated in a set of reforms proposed by the Juppé government that provoked, in December 1995, the most bitter and extensive social protests that France had experienced since May 1968.

At the same time, scepticism in Germany about the monetary reliability of some of its partners increased. Although scepticism was mostly directed at countries like Italy and Spain, which did not seem to follow the German monetary gospel, the real cause for concern was France. The doubts over EMU in the media and, more camouflaged, in the political establishment clearly affected the Kohl government.[87] It prompted Finance Minister Theo Waigel to devise the 'stability pact', adopted at the Dublin summit in December 1996, according to which EMU member states could be penalized if they transgressed the Maastricht deficit criteria once EMU was in place. When President Chirac called a snap parliamentary election for May/June 1997, the hurried Parti Socialiste ran on a platform remarkably similar to Chirac's two years before, and won. Since fiscal prudence and monetary restrictiveness had become associated causally with high unemployment and social malaise, the Socialists called for an *autre politique*, which, because it promised to alleviate the burden of unemployment, was also implicitly directed at the conditions of EMU. Thus, as Ulrike Guérot noted, Franco-German tensions can in principle be explained by the fact that a part of France's political elite, under public pressure, proposed an escape from the contractual conditions that had been agreed at Maastricht, returning to the original French designs for EMU.[88] In the event, the dog barked but did not bite. The Jospin government made its agreement to the stability pact conditional on the creation of a *gouvernement économique*, consisting of national finance ministers, which would complement the purely monetary bias that the provisions for EMU and the European Central Bank had hitherto entailed. Though this was irritating for some of France's partners, notably Germany, it was a considerably more amicable condition than the rhetoric of the election campaign had suggested.

The significance of these developments for the present discussion lies in their effect on the French negotiating stance at the Amsterdam summit. Pressured by promises made during the election campaign, the Jospin government's main aim was the agreement on a *gouvernement économique* and a chapter on employment in the treaty. This left aside the areas that the intergovernmental conference had originally been called to resolve: increased integration in foreign policy and domestic security matters, and institutional reform.[89] Only the second day of the summit was left to overcome the recalcitrant negotiating stance of some smaller countries. Ultimately, institutional reform had to be postponed. This had considerable consequences for German enlargement policy in the run-up to the Luxembourg European Council in December 1997, where the invitation for accession negotiations were issued.

Germany and EU enlargement policy

The discussion on the previous pages has set the scene for the German enlargement policy in the years after the publication of the Schäuble-Lamers paper. We have seen to what extent deepening and widening had become two sides of a coin called Europapolitik. We have also seen that some methods of deepening were more easily compatible with the EU's eastward enlargement than others, and that the fate of EMU had a tremendous indirect effect on the course of enlargement. The following remarks will concentrate more closely on the EU's actual enlargement policy in the same period, and on the German stance within it. They will omit a discussion of the Structured Dialogue and the Association Councils linking Germany's eastern neighbours to the EU, mostly because it is difficult to identify clear national policies in frameworks that were either multilateral or dominated by EU institutions, and because the debate on the relationship between East Central Europe and the EU was at this time no longer about association, but about accession. In deciding on accession German policies had to answer five questions: how to reform EU policies, how much diplomatic initiative to show, what membership criteria to employ, which countries to accept and by what date to do so.

It has already been mentioned that German policy makers were firmly intent on blocking all discussions on policy reform from the agenda of the intergovernmental conference. In a sense, this was understandable. The EU had a sufficient amount of issues to resolve anyway, especially in institutional reform and in foreign policy and domestic security matters. Moreover, the experience of the early 1980s, when heads of government had to negotiate on milk quotas and other trivia, had not been a happy one. One could question, however, whether the German stance was far-sighted. Policy reform in the EU was an extremely intricate process, especially when it came to agriculture and Community finance. Was it not better to address the outstanding issues clearly in order to initiate the process of reform? In an ideal world, that would have been the case. But the Kohl government feared the opposition to enlargement if such a debate were unleashed.

German policy makers duly ignored the wild estimates of the EU's budgetary expenditures in the case of its eastern enlargement, arguing that these relied on the assumption that current policies would not be reformed, and that in any case these estimates did not account for the benefits that EU member states would receive from enlargement. The official German stance was therefore twofold. Enlargement had to be portrayed as a tremendous opportunity for the entire EU. Costs and benefits had to be portrayed as unquantifiable for the time being. That not all other countries were entirely convinced of these two assertions can be deduced from the fact that, for the first time, member states asked the Commission to publish its proposals on financial reform, agricultural reform and the reform of the structural funds together, in a document that came to be known as the Agenda 2000. This had been an important French aim, pursued to ensure that Germany would be unable to devolve its stance on policy and financial reform from the enlargement issue. We will see in the section on Agenda 2000 management below that the distributive side of the enlargement process was not only immensely complicated but also immensely dangerous. A coalition of domestic political actors and sceptical EU member states was an unwelcome thought for any German politician committed to the enlargement process. This coalition would not be dissimilar to that which had been so assertive in the negotiation of the Europe Agreements in the early 1990s. Only this time, it would fight harder, because it had more to lose.

The question of diplomatic initiative was a little easier to answer. As so often in diplomacy, this was a question of balance. If Germany pushed too little, the necessary momentum for enlargement might be lost in the face of opposition from within the EU. If Germany pushed too far, it ran the risk of alienating others – remember the German initiative for the recognition of Slovenia and Croatia in December 1991 – or of at least failing to mobilize the necessary multilateral support. One worry in this context was financial. If enlargement came to be seen as a predominantly German interest, other countries would be less likely to pay for it. German diplomacy, therefore, had to push for momentum without pushing beyond it, and had to be careful not to reveal preferences uncovered by a majority of EU member states.

The question of membership criteria had haunted relations between the EU and the East Central European countries ever since the Copenhagen declaration, because the criteria established there had been vague. Indeed, the specification of criteria was one of the main aims of the East Central European countries, and understandably so, since membership could become a moving target if its conditions were not clear. The German position on this was covered by a consensus within the EU. All assistance was depicted as help for self-help; the burden of adjustment and of catching up, it was argued, had to be carried by the associated countries themselves. The accession of badly prepared countries was ruled out because it was feared that these could destabilize the

EU itself. In this respect the Copenhagen membership criteria were significant, because they determined that new member states would have to be able to fulfil the *acquis*, and to contribute to the advancement of the integration process.

For this reason the Essen European Council had charged the Commission with the preparation of a White Book on the steps the associated East Central European countries would have to undertake in order to prepare for the Single Market. One could argue that the adoption of this White Book at the Cannes summit in June 1995 constituted the point of no return of the enlargement process. In conjunction with the decision taken at the Corfu summit in June 1994 that accession negotiations with Malta and Cyprus could start within six months of the conclusion of the intergovernmental conference, the White Book opened the road for East Central Europe to prepare for accession. It was therefore not surprising that at Madrid in December 1995, the European Council extended the offer of beginning enlargement negotiations to the first countries from East Central Europe. The publication of the White Book advertised once more that the costs of adjustment had to be carried by the associated countries. This was also a German stance. It is significant to evoke the clarity of these German priorities, especially because the debate on deepening and widening has illustrated that German European policy was riddled with tensions. The anchor of stability, from the German perspective, was the EU with its existing structures and policies. Throughout the period under consideration, German policy makers feared nothing more, not even instability in East Central Europe, than the destabilization of that anchor.

The questions of when to enlarge and what countries to accept were, of course, intimately linked. The year 2000, mentioned in the Schäuble-Lamers paper, was endorsed by Kohl when on a state visit to Poland in July 1995. Of course German politicians knew that naming 2000 was ambitious, if not actually misleading. The CDU/CSU publications, more outspoken than ministerial speeches on most matters, did not hesitate to clarify that this date was important especially from a political-psychological point of view. This testified to a German fear of overstretching the East Central European countries' capacity to absorb disappointment. The closer accession to the EU appeared, on the other hand, the easier it was for governments in East Central Europe to defend painful reforms in their countries. The fact that this left aside considerations of the intricacies of Single Market provisions, and of the costs of extending the EU's common policies, was not insurmountable. Hence, German policy makers argued that this enlargement differed from previous ones, and that because of the structural differences between the East Central European and EU economies, transition periods would have to be longer than usual.

Finally, the question of which countries to accept first revealed a clear German priority for Poland, Hungary and the Czech Republic.[90] With the addition of Slovakia, these countries had of course been the first to be associated with the EU. They were also geographically closest to the EU – another way of saying they were closest to Germany – and were generally perceived to be most advanced in their transformation processes. This led to a misperception on the part of some German policy makers, namely that enlargement would only have to deal with these countries, whereas all the other countries of Eastern and South-eastern Europe would not qualify for membership for the foreseeable future. This did not take account of the fact that Eastern Europe had become multi-speed in terms of its transformation processes, with some countries like Slovenia and Estonia overtaking others, like Slovakia. It also did not consider that by 1997, ten East European countries had been associated with the EU, all of them with the expressed desire to become full members. In other words, a small enlargement would no longer suffice. Not only was a first accession wave of five or more countries quite possible, a strategy also had to be devised in order to deal adequately with those countries that were excluded from the first round of negotiations.

In this, no one German position could be identified, either before or after the Commission's *avis* in July 1997 advocated a group of six countries for accession negotiations: Poland, Hungary, the Czech Republic, Estonia, Slovenia and Cyprus. For about a year a debate on 'starting-line', 'stadium', and 'group' models floated freely on the German political scene, linking different models to one another and to similar views expressed in the Commission and in other member states. From this debate only the following two points are significant for the present discussion. First, all contributions crystallized that Poland, Hungary and the Czech Republic would be, or would have to be, in the first round of enlargement. For Germany, an enlargement without Poland in particular was unimaginable and unacceptable. Since this was so, there was a tacit understanding inside the EU and in the Commission that Poland would have to be in the first wave even if it did not quite fulfil all the criteria as well as other countries. Secondly, a difference emerged between the Chancellery and the Foreign Ministry. Whereas Kohl wanted to voice his support for Poland, Hungary and the Czech Republic publicly, the Foreign Ministry, restrained by diplomatic caution and unwilling to face the music from those countries not mentioned by Kohl, urged caution. Not even the Foreign Ministry's restraint, however, could conceal that Germany's priority lay with its immediate eastern neighbours.

This leads to the following concluding observations. First, Germany maintained an absolute commitment to EMU, despite domestic opposition and despite a worsening budgetary situation. Secondly, this was now complemented by a clear and irrevocable commitment to enlargement. Thirdly, German policy makers were cautious not to push the enlargement process too far. Wary of domestic opposition and reticence in other EU member states, German diplomacy concentrated on building up the momentum that would push painful reforms through the political process. This meant, fourthly, that enlargement had to be disentangled from the reform of EU policies – especially on agriculture and finance – and fifthly, that enlargement had to be separated from the EU's institutional reform, if this proved unattainable in the run-up to Amsterdam. Sixthly, in order to ensure that enlargement be seen as a multilateral project, German policy makers had to portray its benefits and opportunities. During all of this, finally, the East Central European countries had to be encouraged to maintain the rate of domestic reform, since they had to carry the main burden of adjustment that would make enlargement possible.

After Amsterdam: Germany as integration widener

The inconclusiveness of the Amsterdam treaty with regard to institutional reform was a resounding failure in preparing the EU for its impending Eastern enlargement. It had been an implicit EU position ever since 1989 to shift the burden of adjustment onto East Central Europe. According to this logic, those countries that wished to join had to ensure that they fulfilled the necessary criteria; the EU would neither question the *acquis communautaire*, nor stop it from expanding. By 1997 at the latest, this position had become partly untenable; it was now up to the EU to reform its decision-making procedures and policies in order to prepare for enlargement. The inconclusiveness of the Amsterdam treaty constituted the failure to do so. This had extensive effects on the debate on enlargement, since, as mentioned above, most member states established a link between enlargement and institutional reform. It is therefore indispensable to probe somewhat further into German responsibility for the failure of the Amsterdam summit.

The present discussion on Germany's policy within the EU's eastern enlargement has so far largely left unconsidered the Efta enlargement that preceded it. Since the Efta enlargement was enormously important for the institutional set-up of the EU in general, and for the nexus between its eastern enlargement and institutional reform in particular, a flash-back to the early to mid-1990s is significant. For the most part, the two enlargements were, of course, quite distinct. On the one hand was a small group of small countries, all of which had a per capita GDP higher than the EU average and which had been linked to the EU through free trade agreements and other arrangements. On the other hand was a large group of countries of varying sizes, low or very low per capita GDP in relation to the EU average, charged with modernizing their domestic political and economic systems at the same time as preparing for membership. In one respect, however, the Northern and Eastern enlargements were similar, namely in the diluting effect they had on EU institutions and decision-making procedures.

German leaders had never made a secret out of their interest in the Efta enlargement. Since the Scandinavian countries and Austria had similar socio-economic models to Germany, their participation in integration was expected to entail many benefits and few costs. An alleviation of German budgetary contributions to the EU was one such benefit. Moreover, Germany has close trading relations with the Efta countries, especially Austria; these were expected to be strengthened by EU enlargement. The most important reason for German policies, however, was the perception of the Efta enlargement as a natural predecessor to the Eastern enlargement, where Germany would then count on support from Austria, Sweden and Finland in particular. This perception emanated from the view of integration inherent in German foreign policy culture. We have seen in Chapter 2 that West Germany's foreign policy culture had been married to the process of integration. In Germany in the 1990s integration was perceived as an ordering model of international relations, one that could be compared to the historical significance of, say, the order that emerged from the Vienna Congress or the Versailles treaty. Though more peaceful and more just, integration was seen as a gospel that had to be spread rather than restricted to a particular geographical area. Integration had a claim to political absoluteness, a claim to the sole legitimate portrayal of Europe's future. This claim manifested itself in German policies in the Efta enlargement concomitantly to the dealings with East Central Europe. In this respect, German designs for the new Europe diverged significantly from those of other countries. One of the reasons, for instance, why Jacques Delors, with French support, proposed the European Economic Area as a link between the EU and the Efta states was to weaken the desire for a proper enlargement. This project failed because the Efta states did apply for membership regardless. But it hints once again at the fundamentally different conceptions France and Germany had about integration between 1989 and 1993. Whereas in France integration was seen as applicable for the close family only, in Germany it was seen as *the* ordering model for relations between European states.

After the enlargement of the Efta states had been decided upon in principle, attention turned to the effects this would have on the EU's existing institutional framework. As this happened in 1992, just after the conclusion of the Maastricht treaty, there seemed to be a general consensus that the necessary institutional adjustment could be made in what was then referred to as the Maastricht review conference and is now known as the Amsterdam treaty. The communiqué of the Edinburgh European Council in December 1992 established in the clearest of terms that institutional reform was no precondition of enlargement.[91] This decision, however, was questioned literally as soon as it had been taken. The combination of events between September 1992 and October 1993 contributed to this dissatisfaction. In this *annus horribilis* of European politics, the general recession, the Danish 'no' in the referendum on the Maastricht treaty, the ejection of Britain and Italy from the ERM, the Bosnian war, the quarrels over the GATT Uruguay round and then the renewed ERM trouble in September 1993 generated an appalling atmosphere for European integration as such. Most of those who had still had high hopes for the Maastricht review conference – in particular its ability to complement monetary union by a genuine political union – quietly came to realize in 1993 that the big institutional feat would be unattainable. And this in turn meant that the Efta enlargement threatened to have diluting effects on the institutional framework of the EU: through the increase in seats in the European Parliament, the number of Commissioners and the Council of Ministers, and secondly through the distribution of votes between small and large member states in the Council of Ministers. Realizing that a simple extension of the distribution of votes practised hitherto would disadvantage large over small member states, France, Britain and Germany presented an initiative at the Brussels European Council in October 1993, the gist of which was a questioning of the decision taken at Edinburgh, according to which no institutional changes needed to precede the Efta enlargement.[92] As the small countries led the rejection of this initiative, the question of institutional reform was in principle solved according to the spirit of Edinburgh. At the same time, however, the question over the blocking minority in the Council of Ministers remained open, and proposals were floated from different corners about how to counteract the potentially diluting effect of the Efta enlargement.

In a paper delivered to a CDU foreign policy seminar, Karl Lamers had demanded as early as August 1993 that institutional reforms should be initiated parallel to enlargement negotiations with the EFTA states.[93] This was a clear rejection of the Edinburgh decision. In detail, Lamers proposed for the Council of Ministers a double majority, the extension of QMV and a larger blocking majority, for the Commission a reduction to ten members, with more powers to the Commission's President, and for the European Parliament the establishment of an upper limit for seats.[94] If institutional reform proved impossible with all 12 – or 16 – member states, Lamers proposed, the necessary consequence would have to be 'variable geometry, i.e. a differentiated density of integration with the formation of a hard core'.[95] This phrase is essential for the enlargement debate in Germany. It illustrates that in Germany the desire to reform the institutions of the EU came prior to the desire to form a hard core. Flexibility was only proposed when institutional reform had turned out to be unattainable.

Since major reforms such as Lamers proposed were improbable after the events of the *annus horribilis* and just prior to the intergovernmental conference convened to address them, institutional adjustments in early 1994 came to concentrate on the blocking majority in the Council of Ministers. As the accession negotiations with Austria, Finland, Norway and Sweden reached their ultimate phase, EU Foreign Ministers were charged at the same time with finding a formula for resolving the dispute about blocking majorities. This in turn had become a highly contentious issue in British domestic politics, used by the leadership of the Conservative party to demonstrate its toughness on European issues, thus rallying support from its Europhobe backbenchers. The British government claimed that lifting the blocking majority from 23 to 27 votes without at the same time reweighing the votes in the Council would seriously disadvantage the larger member states. As indicated by the similar position taken by Germany and France in October 1993, this claim was in principle justified.

By March 1994, however, the British position differed from that of Germany and France in so far as it was less concerned with the work-ability of the system as a whole than with the guarding of apparent British influence. Whereas Germany and France were eager to maintain the efficiency of the Council of Ministers (by increasing the blocking majority), Britain saw the blocking majority as a matter of national pride and power. This view was highly questionable, since even large member states had to block in a coalition with other countries if they wanted to block at all, no matter whether the majority stood at 23 or 27 votes. But in the governing Conservative party in Britain, the issue had assumed a symbolic significance behind which the reality of EU institutions mattered little. This generated a situation where Britain, always one of the chief advocates of the Efta enlargement and instrumental in its promotion during the British presidency in the second half of 1992, threatened to veto this enlargement if the blocking majority in the Council of Ministers was raised to 27 votes. That this position was contradictory, and risked losing sight of aims that were in Britain's long-term strategic interests, is only of marginal significance in this context. What really matters here is that it created a profound challenge for Germany's European diplomacy. For directing the European Union strategically towards a future eastern enlargement was as important as maintaining the workability of EU institutions. To have one without the other, from the German point of view, was not much use. In the event, an increase of blocking majorities from 23 to 27 votes was impossible because of the recalcitrance of Britain and Spain.[96] Under the Greek presidency, Foreign Ministers – under Kinkel's leadership – hammered out a compromise at Ioannina according to which a decision blocked by 23 votes would have to be referred back to the Council for consultation.[97] Though this arrangement was essentially feeble, it had the advantage of guaranteeing that the two German aims – Efta enlargement and institutional workablity – remained in the realm of the possible.

At the same time as they hammered out the institutional adjustments of enlargement, EU Foreign Ministers were deeply involved with the conclusion of the accession negotiations with the four applicant countries. These had to be concluded in March 1994, since the elections to the European Parliament in June, as well as the necessity to ratify the agreements and hold referenda on accession, established structural constraints if accession was to occur on 1 January 1995. It is astonishing that the negotiations with these countries proved so arduous even though the socio-economic model and the level of development were so similar between old and new member states. As negotiations were difficult, and as the stakes were high, the process became political in its final phase and was conducted by the Foreign Ministers, who had gathered in Brussels. While negotiations became increasingly intractable – fishing disputes with Norway, transport disputes with Austria, and so forth – Klaus Kinkel assumed the leadership of the EU negotiators.

Part of Kinkel's ambition surely had to do with the fact that the Greek government, which formally held the EU presidency at the time, was incapable of pulling sufficient weight with either side of the negotiating parties. But part of it also had to do with the fact that the northern enlargement was extremely important for Germany and – in Germany's eyes – for Europe as a whole. In the German scheme of things, these negotiations could not be allowed to fail. They could not fail because this would have undermined the already enfeebled project of integration, because it would have had a disastrous effect on public opinion in the EU, and because it was feared it would have devastating repercussions for the transformation processes in East Central Europe. The uncertainties of Russian politics in the last months of 1993, the return to power of post-communist parties in Hungary and Poland and the ongoing war in Bosnia all reinforced the desire for the web of integration to expand. For Germany, the failure of the Efta enlargement was simply not an option.

The stakes were so high that the final days of negotiations with the Efta states exhibited much of what political scientists and historians look for in their reading of politics. Kinkel had identified Germany as the advocate of the accession countries, especially of Austria. He single-handedly refused to break off the talks – which was a real threat for a time – and brought different disputing sides together in nightly discussions, using all the tools of pressure and persuasion the situation required. Kohl intervened four times by telephone in order to contribute his personal political weight. When the negotiations were finally concluded the German government was unusually forward in identifying both how central this was for German European policy and how decisive a role Germany had played. This was the clearest sign throughout the entire 1990s that when it came to enlargement, German diplomacy was prepared to put its neck on the block. And it is therefore not surprising that some countries resented Kohl's and Kinkel's bloody-mindedness. While the negotiations were still in progress, Kinkel had confidently predicted that Germany would guide these countries into the EU even against the resistance of some EU member states. His constant reiteration that Germany was on the side of the applicant countries and that Bonn would play the role of the advocate called forth objection in other countries. Though criticism came under the guise of the point that Kinkel had made all-too generous offers on behalf of the EU, resentment really focused on the declaration that Bonn was closer to the applicant countries than to some of the EU states on whose behalf it negotiated.[98] In his speech after the conclusion of negotiations, Kinkel explained in the Bundestag that the German government had been guided by the desire to increase the stability of Europe as a whole, and that in this respect 'German and European interests are congruent'. Germany had never identified with a 'Western Union or a South-western Union' in the first instance, the Efta enlargement would send a signal to the reform democracies in East Central Europe, and this enlargement 'constituted a substantial gain for Germany in its central position'.[99] This view was affirmed by Kohl:

> There were a few voices abroad relating to the accusation that the Germans looked after these accessions with particular intensity. I think it corresponds to our common policy that we want the enlargement of the Community. So far it is quite correct that the Foreign Minister – on the instruction of the federal government and naturally of mine – has committed himself especially to it.[100]

As we have seen, German policy did correspond to EU decisions which had welcomed enlargement, and in the form of the Edinburgh communiqué had established that institutional reform was no precondition to enlargement. It is also true that Germany's mediating position pursued the greater European good much more convincingly than those Spanish negotiators who risked the failure of the entire negotiations for a few thousand tons of Norwegian fish. But as the criticisms of other EU member states cascaded around Klaus Kinkel after the negotiations had been concluded, it emerged quite clearly that these could be distinguished into two different kinds. One was from those who resented the style of German diplomacy and the self-assuredness with which Germany had pursued this enlargement. The second was from those who were concerned not just about style, but also about substance. For the Efta states enlargement had entailed a weakening of the institutional system of the EU by compromising the Council of Ministers, and Germany had been central not only in the negotiations with the Efta states but also in the attainment of this particular institutional compromise. In this sense Kohl's speech above omits the central point, namely that the opposition to the Efta enlargement had not just been one of principle, but also one of conditionality.

In sum the institutional provisions of the Efta enlargement led to considerable disappointment in some quarters, notably in France, where concerns about the reliability of German European policy were raised, and in the European Parliament, which threatened to block the Efta enlargement in case deepening was not forthcoming.[101] Indeed, the episode triggered one of the worst diplomatic rows of Franco-German relations since unification. After the French ambassador in Bonn, François Scheer, had deplored the lack of understanding between France and Germany on the enlargement question, he was ordered to the Foreign Ministry in Bonn and asked to explain himself. To be sure, French and German policy makers were committed to overcoming the crisis and to addressing the outstanding issues. The Franco-German effort at a common Eastern policy, for instance, that was agreed in preparation for the two presidencies in 1994/95, has to be seen in this light. The Kohl government tuned down its plans for elevating East Central Europe to central status in its forthcoming EU presidency and pursued a common policy with France again.[102] But the imbroglio over institutional reform testified to the fact that Germany had defined enlargement as a clear priority and expected its partners to follow. The sooner the Efta enlargement was accomplished, the sooner eastward enlargement could be tackled. This reveals that regardless of its continuing absolute commitment to EMU, Germany already had an interest in enlargement that dominated its interest in promoting institutional reform.

In evaluating German policy one cannot stress enough that the support for rapid enlargement was covered by the EU's common policy, that Germany felt bound by that commitment, and that in addition the recalcitrance of Britain (and Spain) made any hopes illusory that a grand sweep of institutional reform was in the realm of the possible. Was it not sensible to await the 1996 intergovernmental conference before attempting to adjust the Union's entire institutional framework? The answer to this question is largely academic. What mattered from the legacy of the Efta enlargement was a lingering doubt in some countries, especially in France, about the commitment Germany felt towards institutional deepening. This doubt resurfaced when the Amsterdam summit failed to resolve the issue with a view to the Union's eastern enlargement. Since it went right to the heart of the widening–deepening dilemma, it is essential for the evaluation of Germany's enlargement policy.

It is often asserted that France has had an at best marginal interest in the EU's eastern enlargement. In this view, France's strategic aim after 1989 was tying Germany into a deepened EU that restricted its room to manoeuvre; since enlargement would dilute integration, France had to be opposed to it.[103] Evidence for this view is Mitterrand's preoccupation with the Maastricht process until the treaty's coming into force in 1993, and his 1991 proposal of a European Confederation, which was widely perceived as establishing a substitute organization for the East Central European countries. This is not the view taken here. Although Mitterrand did have a clear preference for deepened integration, it would be false to assume that this equated to a complete lack of interest in the eastern half of the continent. In addition, French European policy underwent considerable changes between 1990 and 1997. Due to the special circumstances of cohabitation, the Balladur government after May 1993 enjoyed more freedom in foreign policy than the Chirac government had between 1986 and 1988, and tried to make up for Mitterrand's neglect of East Central Europe. Alain Juppé, the new Foreign Minister, was more active in the Weimar triangle – remember the WEU association agreed in November 1993 – and Balladur himself organized a stability conference in Paris between May 1994 and April 1995, which re-established French diplomatic momentum towards East Central Europe. One of the main aims of Balladur and Juppé in this period was a strong EU commitment to stability in the Mediterranean, which was approved at Essen and implemented in the EU Mediterranean conference in Barcelona in 1995.

The reason for this shift in French policy was threefold. It was helped by the affinity Gaullist thinking had for a *Europe des patries*, which sat uneasily with the tight integration engineered at Maastricht, let alone the 'hard core' proposed in the Schäuble-Lamers paper. Secondly, since de Gaulle had prominently spoken of a Europe from the Atlantic to the Urals, his political heirs had a more natural interest in East Central Europe than the Socialists. Finally, a disinclination to grant Nato (and thus the United States) exclusive rights to affect the post-Cold War order in East Central Europe was accompanied by the realization that EU enlargement was dear to Germany and that a persistent French recalcitrance on the subject would not only undermine French diplomatic leverage in the region, but would also damage Franco-German relations. When Chirac assumed the French Presidency in May 1995, this shift in French European policy was confirmed at the highest level.

On a visit to Poland in September 1996, Chirac mentioned the year 2000 as the date of Poland's EU accession; he later said the same in Prague and Budapest. Though this may have been cynical in the light of the plethora of obstacles involved, and motivated diplomatically because Kohl had named the same date in the same place a year earlier, it illustrated clearly that a shift had occurred.[104] By the time the Parti Socialiste came back to office in June 1997, it had come to terms with the EU's eastern enlargement. At the Amsterdam summit, however, the supreme importance of EMU in the preceding election campaign pressurized the Jospin government to focus almost exclusively on the inclusion of employment and the *gouvernement économique* in the treaty.

When it came to the crunch, heads of government had neither the time, the energy nor the political will to reach a consensus on institutional reform. Upon German pressure, a significant extension of qualified majority voting in justice and home affairs was blocked. The treaty established that large member states would have to dispense with one of their two Commissioners if new countries joined. Should the Commission grow to more than 20 members a new intergovernmental conference attempting the reform of the entire institutional framework would be necessary. Hence, the treaty remained inconclusive on one of the main points for which it had originally been drafted. It did not effect a political union. It did not establish the institutional set-up for enlargement. Like a bad essay, it did not answer the question.

This was the stuff of which the tragedy was made. The Jospin government recalled not only how Germany had pushed for rapid enlargement to the Efta states in the spring of 1994, but also that Kohl clearly preferred a small enlargement towards the East. A small enlargement, however, would mean that the Amsterdam treaty's clause on institutional reform would not work. The ultimate French *cauchemar* of a Germany untied from its institutional constraints drifting off eastwards revived. Jack Lang, the chairman of the National Assembly's foreign affairs committee, declared that he for one would not ratify a treaty that did not prepare the EU's institutional system for the Eastern enlargement.[105] Realizing its *faux pas*, the Jospin government cooperated with Italy and Belgium on a declaration noting that the Amsterdam treaty did not 'respond to the necessity for substantial progress on the way to strengthening our institutions'. In this declaration, institutional deepening became a precondition of enlargement. It was presented to the General Affairs Council in Brussels in September and was attached to the Amsterdam treaty as an appendix in order to ensure that the treaty would be ratified in the signatory states. It was, however, unacceptable to Germany. Not only was 'one of the reasons for the failure of the Amsterdam treaty undoubtedly the fact that the Franco-German pair, divided over the principal aspects of institutional reform ... was incapable of producing the impetus that in the past has often been indispensable for the deepening of the Union', but the couple also seemed to be completely divided over how to link this deepening to the forthcoming eastern enlargement.[106] This was the only unambiguous sign over the seven years under discussion here that Germany had left its traditional role of *integration deepener* in order to pursue the new role as *integration widener*. Had German politicians finally seen the light, ridding themselves of institutional constraints in the West in order to pursue a more active policy vis-à-vis the East? Was it true, as the Secretary of State in the German Foreign Ministry, Hartmut von Ploetz, said, that German European policy was becoming more 'British'?[107]

This is only partly correct. First, German leaders, above all Kohl, stuck to EMU and its concomitant deepening. Their rationale for doing so was not simply in the economic benefits it would entail, but in its political consequences. 'EMU is the first step to Political Union' was the chorus of German European policy from 1992 right until 1997. This had important ramifications for the domestic debate on European integration. Germany's political elite attempted to persuade the population to give up the Deutsche Mark not for short-term economic benefits, but for long-term political gains. This logic was remarkable. First and foremost, political benefits were vague and intangible in exchange for the revered Deutsche Mark. Moreover, political union had already been unattainable at Maastricht. If no one else wanted it, one could ask, why should the Germans give up their currency to bring it about? That EMU was sold domestically not as an economic initiative but as a foreign policy necessity undermined its popularity, but hinted at the priorities of German leaders. It also followed the principles of West German foreign policy culture. Deepening through EMU remained the top priority of German European policy; enlargement did not change this.

Secondly, part of the German reluctance to agree to the French initiative for institutional deepening was simple mistrust. Although German politicians shared the French fear that the EU could lose its capacity to act, they did not share the view that institutional deepening should be made a condition of enlargement. Lamers said in November 1997 that a 'real danger' existed that the demand for institutional reform be used 'as a blockade of enlargement'.[108] It was perhaps not France directly that was meant here and French politicians did not accept the charge that their proposal for institutional deepening was an attempt at decelerating enlargement.[109] Whether the Mediterranean countries would not attempt to stop enlargement, however, was less clear. According to an anecdote, Helmut Kohl said in a secret meeting that the European Council would not produce a majority in favour of enlargement. This mistrust, in conjunction with the conviction that the Union must maintain its ability to act, led to the German demand that enlargement be used as a lever for institutional deepening. That at least was Lamers' proposal.

Thirdly, there was a wariness in Germany that too much integration could generate a domestic backlash. The CSU was of particular importance here because it had re-established a specific Euro-sceptic sentiment with Stoiber's coming to office in 1993. In the first months of 1997 Stoiber had positioned himself as the Chancellor's main critic on EMU, arguing that Bavaria would appeal to the Constitutional Court in case the deficit criteria were not adhered to. It is therefore not surprising that Kohl was hesitant to push too far with policies uncovered by a permissive consensus at home. Once EMU was firmly in the saddle, he let it be known, further steps towards integration could be taken.[110] These three factors, the absolute commitment to EMU, the fear that enlargement could be blocked, and the eye to domestic opposition, qualify the German reluctance to sign up to the French–Belgian–Italian initiative. They testify to the fact that Germany enacted its role as *integration widener* and *integration deepener* simultaneously. Since the strategy of role merger had failed, role conflict persisted. Though for the most part this was a latent and subtle conflict, on the question of institutional deepening the different roles clashed. Enlargement had become a *raison d'état* for Germany by about 1995, in the same way that EMU had become a *raison d'état* in 1992. While EMU took clear precedence, enlargement had not only affected German policies towards East Central Europe, but also German European policy as a whole.

These priorities tied Germany intimately to France, and made enlargement dependent upon progress on EMU. Although it is difficult todistinguish phases in Germany's enlargement policy from 1994 onwards, since, in contrast to France, there was greater continuity in office, one can identify three distinct periods. The first is the attempt at role merger, which lasted from September 1994 to the summer of 1995. It witnessed the elevation of enlargement as a top priority of German policy. The second, from the summer of 1995 onwards, witnessed the establishment of EMU and enlargement as clear priorities, but in contrast to the previous phase, featured only modest proposals for institutional reform. Both phases were also characterized by the determination to keep the reform of EU policies off the agenda. The third phase from July 1997 onwards (that is, after the Amsterdam summit and the publication of the Agenda 2000) witnessed a German refusal to accept a strict conditionality between enlargement and institutional reform, and illustrated the contradictions of the German stance on policy reform.

Policy reform

Because of the conclusion of the intergovernmental conference and the publication of the Commission's *opinions* and the Agenda 2000, the enlargement debate in the second half of 1997 was devoted to policy reform.[111] In this debate, the German stance was complex. It had to balance Germany's commitment to enlargement with the demand for a reduction in its net contributions to the budget, moderate change in agricultural policy and structural funds. The debate over Germany's contributions to the EU budget, the *Nettozahlerdebatte*, was in fact an old friend. Having first emerged under Helmut Schmidt in the late 1970s and early 1980s, it had resurfaced in 1992 but was quashed because of Kohl's decision at the Edinburgh summit to agree to a 50 per cent increase in the Cohesion Fund. Then, in 1995, similar criticisms voiced by Finance Minister Theo Waigel were downplayed by the government, due to fears of a popular backlash against EMU and enlargement. By 1994 a German household with four members paid more into the EU than it did in terms of the special solidarity tax levied for the Eastern Länder.[112] In the summer of 1997, the debate erupted again. By now Germany's net budgetary contributions had increased to 60 per cent of the EU total, while its domestic fiscal situation, exacerbated by high transfers to the Eastern Länder, towering unemployment and the attempt to comply with the Maastricht criteria, was exceptionally tense.

As in 1995, Waigel was the prime mover in bringing the debate back into the public domain. As finance minister, he was under severe pressure to rein in government expenditure in preparation for EMU. In addition, the contributions issue was important for the CSU electorally, as it faced the Bavarian election in September 1998, close to the introduction of EMU. Waigel needed to boost his standing as party chairman vis-à-vis his rival, the CSU Minister President of Bavaria Edmund Stoiber, who had repeatedly put forward visions on the EU that differed from the government's. Given that the Bavarian electorate and the CSU are prone to eurosceptical views, and that Waigel as finance minister was one of the main architects of EMU, the budgetary contributions issue was for him a welcome opportunity to elicit domestic support.

Furthermore, the FDP had pushed for reductions in Germany's EU budgetary contributions as early as October 1994, when the coalition agreement between CDU, CSU and FDP was signed to prepare for the fifth Kohl government. The FDP sought to emphasize its role as a tax-cutting neo-liberal party, an image which it had tried to build up especially since 1995. Moreover, neither the FDP nor Kinkel, the FDP's most prominent member of government, had significant influence over European policy, which was dominated by Kohl. Coalition agreements are important documents in German politics, and to recall the 1994 agreement was an ideal means by which the FDP could assert a profile distinct from the CDU/CSU ahead of the federal elections in September 1998.

The Commission's proposals for agricultural reform were one of the main conditions that could make an eastward enlargement affordable and thus possible. However, the EU agriculture minister most vehemently opposed to the proposals was Germany's Jochen Borchert. Neither the next WTO round in 1999 nor the eastern enlargement, Borchert said, made a reversal of the CAP's price support mechanisms necessary. With this logic he did not address the fact that high internal prices were the very reason that the EU's agricultural policy had come under pressure.[113]

In a way reminiscent of the negotiation of the Europe Agreements in 1991, Borchert asserted German agricultural interests in the absence of a guideline from the Chancellor that subordinated them to Germany's overall political interests in enlargement. The reasons were electoral. The CDU/CSU depend on agricultural votes, and Borchert, as a member of the DBV, was sensitive to agricultural interests. This was exacerbated by the fact that the government faced an election in September 1998 and that the CDU/CSU/FDP coalition had won by a mere 147 000 votes in October 1994; it simply could not afford to lose any votes in the run-up to the next election. Although some members of government, like Kinkel, welcomed the Commission's proposals, it was generally agreed and accepted that Germany would resist reform until after the election.[114]

The Commission proposals for reform of the structural funds met a similarly intricate constellation of German interests. On the one hand, German politicians welcomed the Commission's proposal that expenditure should be limited to 0.46 per cent of EU GDP. In this respect, Germany spoke in the name of fiscal prudence. On the other hand, German politicians maintained that long transition periods were needed, and that some deserving regions, for instance the old industrial regions of the Ruhr and the Saar and the agricultural regions on the coast, must not be spared from the funds. In this respect, Germany spoke in the interest of domestic constituencies. How these positions linked to enlargement was less clear. It was, of course, in Germany's interest to limit the structural funds to 0.46 per cent of EU GDP for the period between 2000 and 2006 as the Commission had proposed, simply because this would also limit the transfer payments to the East Central European countries in the event of their accession. Most notably, it was in Germany's interest to support the Commission's assertion that, even with enlargement, the EU's expenditure should not, and would not, rise above 1.27 per cent of EU GDP. For Germany, these absolute figures were good news. They made enlargement defensible vis-à-vis a sceptical domestic audience, and vis-à-vis countries like France, who feared that enlargement would become considerably more expensive than the German government was prepared to admit.

This illustrates a highly contradictory set of German positions on the issue of policy reform. First, Germany continued to support enlargement, and was more adamant about this than most other countries. Secondly, it displayed a remarkable degree of policy conservatism in agricultural reform, where only change could lay the necessary foundations for enlargement. Thirdly, Germany had an ambiguous view of the proposed structural funds, consenting to the principles of budgetary prudence while questioning the criteria governing the distribution of the funds. Finally, German politicians were vociferous in their claims that Germany got an unfair deal on its budgetary contributions and that this should be accounted for in the new financing round commencing in 2000. The problem was that for every German argument in favour of a budget rebate or a new financing code, other EU member states, especially Britain, had a powerful counter-argument demanding that Germany agree to agricultural reform. This, in principle, was the link that made Germany's stance on policy reform precarious and contradictory.

As noted in the discussion of the Europe Agreements, the congruence of overall political interests between Germany and its eastern neighbours was not always matched by a congruence of sectoral interests. This constellation was only exacerbated by the fact that German domestic interests can be translated to the European level without having passed a domestic clearing agency beforehand. Although this is does not make Germany particular, it can impede the implementation of the Civilian Power ethos. In the debate on the Agenda 2000, this institutional weakness was exacerbated by the unusual electoral importance of the farming vote for the CDU/CSU, the unusually strong interest Germany had in enlargement, and its unusually strong demands for budgetary reductions in the next financing round. Similar to the German legalism that affected bilateral relations and the domestic interests that shaped Germany's negotiating position on the Europe Agreements, the domestic institutions that were the preconditions of Civilian Power hampered the application of Civilian Power abroad.

Conclusion

At the Luxembourg European Council in December 1997, the EU invited five East Central European countries and Cyprus to commence enlargement negotiations in the first half of 1998. This was not an exclusive German achievement. But it crowned the German effort to put enlargement on the agenda and to keep it there even in the face of adversity. Despite this overall success, however, it has emerged from the previous discussion that German enlargement policy was affected by two grave miscalculations. The first was the misconception that EMU would be implemented without much ado. Indeed, it is probably difficult to comprehend with hindsight the euphoria that prevailed in the government, especially in the circles around Kohl, in the period between 1989 and 1992. Still on the high of German unification, German decision makers felt that a real unification of Europe was within reach. The tremors in the monetary system, the shocks of unification and the depths of recession had brought these high hopes to an end by 1995 at the latest. These complications crowded the European agenda; they contributed to domestic political instability in France and to a debate on EMU in Germany that became increasingly strained and nervous. The trough in Franco-German relations after August 1993 (the de facto collapse of the EMS) was primarily about EMU. The insecurities surrounding the EU's eastward enlargement fell on futile ground; they were exacerbated out of proportion because of already existing fears and misunderstandings.

Secondly, German policy makers underestimated the pace of developments in East Central Europe. They therefore continued to pursue a small enlargement towards the immediate eastern neighbours at a time when Eastern Europe had already become multi-speed. Ironically, this often went hand in hand with the assertion that France thought 'geopolitically' about enlargement questions, because it favoured the inclusion of countries of the south-eastern flank like Slovenia and Romania.[115] In particular the Chancellor either did not realize or did not care that by 1997 at the very latest, clinging to Poland, Hungary and the Czech Republic was neither up-to-date nor likely to induce French confidence. As South-eastern Europe was not seen in the context of European integration, German policy towards this region was really rather ill-defined. In 1996 and 1997, German policy makers were hazy for far too long about the mechanisms by which those countries unlikely to accede to the EU in the first wave should be tied into the process at large. Although Germany increasingly acted as an *integration widener*, the geographical extent to which this role stretched was actually limited. Evidently, German policy makers feared a dilution of integration should the EU expand too far too fast. Even in its role as *integration widener* towards its immediate eastern neighbours, Germany remained wedded to its role as *integration deepener*.

The German stance on how to combine enlargement with institutional reform underwent considerable change throughout the period of discussion. Whereas 1990 and 1991 were marked by the denial of role conflict, the growing importance of East Central Europe led to role alternation, between deepening and widening, until 1994. The attempted role merger between the end of 1994 and the summer of 1995, which witnessed the introduction of concepts of flexibility, testified to the significance EU enlargement had by now assumed for German policy. The fourth phase, between 1995 and 1997, witnessed a German determination to keep the reform of EU policies off the agenda, and was marked by modest German proposals for institutional change in the run-up to the Amsterdam summit. The final phase, the last six months of 1997, illustrated not only the contradictions of German demands on policy reform, but also the fact that Germany was committed not to let institutional deepening be elevated to a precondition of enlargement.

The crucial point in time, then, is around 1994/95, because it was at this juncture that German policy makers disentangled the role of the integration deepener into two separate roles. One consisted of deepening through EMU, the other of deepening through institutional reform. Their priorities then became deepening through EMU first, enlargement to East Central Europe second and institutional reform third. That priorities were arranged in this order was partly a reaction to external circumstances. The fact that the Efta enlargement had been pushed through without institutional reform was not primarily due to German reluctance but because other countries had opposed it. In this situation, the Kohl government opted for an acceleration of the Efta enlargement, not least because of the positive implications this would have for an enlargement towards East Central Europe. This meant, however, that a window of opportunity for institutional deepening was missed in 1993/94. The 'hard core' proposal of the Schäuble-Lamers paper was the culmination of this, the last German offer for institutional deepening before enlargement. At the time, this was not taken up by France, in part perhaps because Gaullist thinking had come to dominate French European policy. The paradox was that the change in positions surfaced after the Amsterdam summit, when the French offer of institutional deepening was discarded by Germany. The reasons for the French turnaround were the changes in government; the reasons for the German turnaround lay in a fear that institutional deepening could block enlargement.

This has to be made crystal clear. The failure of the Amsterdam treaty to prepare EU institutions for enlargement was not primarily due to

Germany, and Germany had not turned against institutional deepening as a matter of principle. On the contrary, Germany was in favour of an extension of majority voting in matters concerned with foreign policy. It was also in favour of a smaller Commission and a reweighting of votes in the Council of Ministers that would reduce the blocking majority and thereby increase the efficiency of decision making. But the endeavours after Amsterdam to turn institutional deepening into a precondition for enlargement were unacceptable to Germany, because it was feared that they would be instrumentalized by those who did not favour enlargement in the first instance. The German proposal was to use enlargement in order to secure institutional deepening.

This means that the deepening–widening dilemma was never satisfactorily solved. The last chance to do so through the strategy of a genuine role merger was through the proposals of the Schäuble-Lamers paper. Once this opportunity was missed, the role conflict haunting German enlargement policy was likely to be exacerbated. In fact German policy persisted with its strategy of role alternation, promising deepening to the West and widening to the East, until these conflicting aims actually clashed.

This relates to an observation mentioned throughout this chapter, namely the extent to which German European policy was wedded to the *process* of European integration. In the Kohl government's European policy, conflicting aims and irreconcilable interests – between East and West, between domestic interest and European interests, and between different domestic interests – were not overcome by architecture or design. Instead they were pursued simultaneously in the hope – or the conviction – that they would be solved by time. It has often been noted that Kohl's system of government has a tendency to ignore problems until the storm is over – *aussitzen* is the German term. But in European policy this tendency is not something typical for the Kohl Chancellorship alone.

We have seen that German foreign policy culture had a strong emphasis on the notions of *process* and *progress* in its European policy. Until Joschka Fischer's speech in May 2000, few German politicians had elaborated an end state of European integration. Though the CDU did want a real European federation as late as the 1980s and early 1990s, it was quite unclear what this federation was supposed to consist of. Instead of promoting conceptual clarity, German European policy traditionally stands out by banking on the process of integration. This explains a great deal of German enlargement policy towards East Central Europe. Since time was charged with solving the dilemma between deepening and widening, the dilemma was first denied and ignored before both options were pursued simultaneously. A similar reliance on the *process* of integration has governed the Kohl government's stance vis-à-vis the sectoral domestic interests that hampered enlargement. It seems that the German policy-making machinery is only capable of overcoming these, especially when electorally significant, when a considerable amount of momentum has been built up at the European level. Agricultural reform can serve as a perfect example, since the next WTO round, the Agenda 2000 and enlargement had to coincide in order to push for reform. Although it was clear as early as 1991 that reform was badly overdue, a pre-crisis situation was necessary in order to attain the necessary momentum.

The strategy German policy makers pursued was therefore one of division between 'high politics', that is enlargement, and 'low politics', that is policy reform inside the EU. Instead of the old argument, propounded by Stanley Hoffmann, that states would not wish to integrate in 'high politics', German policy was actually characterized by a growing commitment to enlargement. Yet German policy makers realized that enlargement could be derailed by entrenched interests inside the EU. In order to make it possible, therefore, 'low politics' revolving around policy reform had to be appeased at first, and then ignored. Only when sufficient energy had been built up in 'high politics' could the intricacies of 'low politics' be overcome. The entrenched nature of inner EU interests, such as the agricultural lobby or the southern member states, made the orchestration of tremendous momentum necessary to push enlargement through the EU institutional framework. This meant that other member states had to be on board. Enlargement would either be a multilateral endeavour, or it would not be at all. With regard to other member states, this involved the classical tools of diplomacy: pressure, persuasion and incentives, while ensuring that the German position was covered by a majority.

The priorities set by Germany in its enlargement policies were compatible with the Civilian Power ideal type. These were stabilization, democratization and multilateralization. More specifically, German policies were closely in line with the principles of West German foreign policy culture identified in Chapter 2: the adherence to the Franco-German partnership, a turn away from balance-of-power politics, a view of state interests in terms of absolute gains, the benefits of integration, its nature as a process and, finally, the notion that integration represented progress and was therefore desirable in itself. Alas, this overall conclusion has to be qualified by two observations.

First, European policy has developed into a true mixture of classical foreign policy and domestic policy issues. Although one aspect of German Civilian Power, the interest in free trade, propelled German policy makers towards the opening of East Central European markets for German business, other interests, especially in the labour unions and the agricultural sector, sought to prevent or at least postpone enlargement. The decentralization of the German policy-making process, faced with centrally organized socio-economic interests, ensured that the assertion of overall political interests was an uphill struggle. The test of German foreign policy culture against the background of domestic decision-making processes thus points to the conclusion that the nature of the German policy-making process allows a considerable degree of flexibility and interpretation of the Civilian Power ethos. It also points to the tension within the ideal type, where decision makers, in their pursuit of Civilian Power objectives, were tripped up by the institutional constraints put in place in the early years of the Federal Republic.

Secondly, the Civilian Power ideal type suggests that German policy makers were correct in the early 1990s in their decision to privilege the deepening of European integration over its extension to East Central Europe. The doubts over Germany's European intentions were sufficiently grave as it was; a rapid turn to East Central Europe might have robbed Germany of the credibility and diplomatic leverage that it needed. This is not to justify all German policies in retrospect. We have seen that German policy makers relied on the East Central European countries to achieve stabilization and transformation by themselves. Although they reiterated the magnetic effect of Western institutional frameworks, their actual support for East Central Europe, diplomatically and financially, was not on the level of American support for Western Europe after the Second World War, for instance. In the early 1990s, Germany relied on East Central Europe to help itself; in the mid-1990s, it provided considerable diplomatic support. By that stage, however, the transformation processes had reached their second phase; instability was by now improbable. Admittedly, German caution had to do with doubts over Germany's European policy at large. In Western Europe, a highly active German policy towards the Eastern neighbours would have triggered fears and insecurities; in East Central Europe, it would have exacerbated already existing fears of Germanization. As Ingo Kolboom said in defence of Mitterrand's stance at the time, 'stability is a precious commodity, and must not be gambled away carelessly.'[116] Thus the Civilian Power ideal type ends up as an agnostic in evaluating German policy in the deepening–widening dilemma. It is imperative for a Civilian Power to maintain the core of stability *and* to expand it. But the precise relation between the two, which, as has been demonstrated, can be extremely difficult to establish, is not addressed by the ideal type.

5
Germany and Nato Enlargement

Introduction

Although it might at first sight appear peculiar to devote an entire chapter to the discussion of military security in a book that deals with Civilian Power, there are two particular reasons for doing so. First, as noted above, Civilian Power is by no means pacifistic. It organizes its military security in collective security arrangements if possible, and in collective defence arrangements if necessary.[1] Secondly, unified Germany is a product of the end of the Cold War in the same way that the Federal Republic was a product of the Cold War itself. Since military confrontation had dominated West Germany's relationship with the East Central European countries during the Cold War, the military security arrangements that succeeded confrontation merit discussion. Both theory and practice, therefore, necessitate an analysis of how military security was organized in Central Europe in general, and between Germany and its immediate eastern neighbours in particular.

Like the persistence of the European Community, the persistence of Nato was an essential element of continuity from the Cold War to the post-Cold War world. There are several reasons why Nato survived and became the main vehicle for the organization of security between Germany and its Eastern neighbours. During the course of 1990, American and West German foreign policy makers attached considerable significance to Nato in the process of German unification. Next, Nato underwent considerable changes in ethos and organization in order to adapt to the new circumstances after 1989/90. It survived, despite tensions, because it worked. An important element was its ability to adapt to the demands of East Central European countries, to which it responded with the North Atlantic Cooperation Council (NACC), the Partnership for Peace programme and, of course, the prospect of enlargement. Finally, Nato persisted because of the absence of credible alternatives. The simple mechanisms of institutional immobilism might have played a part in this. But it is also true that the relevant policy makers at no point saw a strengthened CSCE or a European defence organization as reliable alternatives to Nato.

By and large, therefore, the politics of military security in East Central Europe became the politics of Nato enlargement. This leads to the question of whether the enlargement of a defence alliance can at all be reconciled with the exercise of Civilian Power. One might argue, for instance, that Civilian Power has the duty to overcome, not sustain, military blocs and defence alliances, and that instead of Nato, German policy makers should have promoted collective security arrangements in the form of the CSCE or the UN. And it is true that at first sight Nato enlargement seems to sit a little more uneasily with Civilian Power principles than EU enlargement and the general mending of fences that occurred after 1989/90. We will see, however, that on the whole German policy within the enlargement of Nato was broadly compatible with the principles of Civilian Power. This view rests on four arguments. First, the functions Nato fulfils for its members are congruent with Civilian Power; a dissolution of Nato would undermine Civilian Power principles. It follows that an extension of Nato to Germany's immediate eastern neighbours was an extension of Civilian Power, at least for the countries likely to accede. Secondly, Nato underwent significant changes after 1990, and in line with these, its enlargement was not legitimized as extended defence but as the 'transfer of stability'. Thirdly, Nato enlargement has to be seen in its own right, and not merely in terms of its effects on other states. The argument that the extension of Nato to Poland, Hungary and the Czech Republic leaves, say, Romania unconsidered does not invalidate the argument that Nato enlargement is the exercise of Civilian Power. It is merely a reminder that this is an imperfect world in which even Civilian Powers face difficult choices.

This is also true for the position of Russia. One of the most frequently used arguments in Germany against Nato enlargement was that it would ostracize Russia. This presented German policy makers with a conflict between the *Muscovite* and the *Warshaviste* roles. However, as we will see, only a merger of these roles was compatible with Civilian Power. The fourth reason, then, is that German policy in the mid-1990s constituted a merger of the two roles; this merger, that is a consideration of East Central Europe *and* for Russia, allowed Germany to enact its Civilian Power ethos. This also explains the distinction in phases. Whereas the initial period was marked by *Muscovite* considerations that neglected East Central European security needs, the first enlargement phase in 1993 left unclarified how enlargement would sit with Russia's position, and whereas the second enlargement phase in 1994 represented an attempt to reconcile the *Muscovite* and *Warshaviste* positions conceptually – and therefore witnessed the most notorious public disputes – the final enlargement phase from 1995 onwards was an attempt to reconcile these different priorities in practice.

This points to the differences and similarities between Germany's enlargement policy within the EU and Nato. Whereas EU enlargement was backed by consensus and shaped by social and economic interests, Nato enlargement was driven by a small number of officials. Historical circumstance and diplomatic contingencies mattered more than they did for the European Union. Next, the American factor was a crucial variable for Germany's Nato calculations, but for the EU it mattered only marginally. This affected Germany's policies differently in different phases. Ultimately, however, Germany was successful because it managed to establish a congruence between American and German priorities. Thirdly, the extension of Nato was more contested within Germany's foreign policy elite. Whereas the enlargement of the EU was backed by an overall consensus, regardless of disagreements about costs and modalities, Nato enlargement was hotly debated within the CDU, between the coalition partners and between government and opposition. Although German policies were characterized by role conflicts in both enlargement processes, the role conflicts over Nato enlargement not only set different groups up against one another, but also existed within the beliefs of some policy makers. The government itself was a good example of this. Whereas Volker Rühe clearly favoured enlargement and Klaus Kinkel was clearly hesitant, Helmut Kohl seemed to embody both support and scepticism and the role conflict this entailed. Though the modalities of Nato enlargement constituted a role merger, the roles of the *Atlanticist* and the *Warshaviste* ultimately dominated the roles of the *Gaullist* and the *Muscovite*. This domination affected not only the policies Germany pursued within the enlargement process, but also the way policies were debated and legitimated at the domestic level. Nato enlargement, therefore, reflects the contested nature of foreign policy culture, and elucidates the view that culture is linked to legitimation and power.

The discussion begins with an analysis of the effects of German unification on the nature of European security as a whole, especially for the relationship between unified Germany and the United States, and the persistence and subsequent extension of Nato. It then looks at the emerging role conflict between the *Muscovite* and the *Warshaviste* positions. German security policies towards East Central Europe between 1990 and 1993 were marked by a domination of *Muscovite* considerations and a neglect of East Central Europe. This was addressed in the first steps of the Nato enlargement process in the course of 1993, which are discussed in the fourth section. The fifth section is an analysis of the time of decision during the course of 1994, which witnessed the establishment of a conceptual merger between *Muscovite* and *Warshaviste* priorities. The sixth section is a discussion of the domestic debate on enlargement in general, and the link between German foreign policy culture and German policies in the enlargement process in particular. The final section features an analysis of German policies between 1995 and 1997, when the enlargement process was already under way and heavily dominated by American policy.

European security and German unification

If the relationship between the Federal Republic and the United States had been the linchpin of the Atlantic Alliance during the Cold War, the diplomacy of German unification ensured that the same held true for the relationship between unified Germany and the United States in the post-Cold War world. Because the Bush Administration made its support for unification conditional upon Germany's continuing Nato membership, it set the course for the entire security architecture of post-Cold War Europe. It ensured a continued American presence in Europe, invented the principle of institutional extension as opposed to institutional inception, subverted the attraction of alternative security arrangements, and provided an overall framework of continuity within which change could occur.

The close relationship between the Bush administration and the Kohl government went back to 1982/83, when the CDU/CSU/FDP coalition came to power with the promise of deploying Pershing and Cruise missiles in West Germany. Helmut Kohl's resolve to go ahead with the deployment despite fierce domestic opposition reaffirmed the functioning of the Alliance. Indeed, the immensely contested circumstances of the deployment forced Kohl to identify with crystal clarity the basic principles of West Germany's foreign policy culture:

> The Alliance . . . is the core of the German *raison d'état* . . . It combines
> the basic values of our liberal constitution, for which we stand, the
> socio-economic order, in which we live, and the security, which we
> need.[2]

And for those who argued that the term 'German *raison d'état*' conflated
the national interest of the German people with the state interest of the
Federal Republic, Kohl clarified that it was significant to recognize that

> the decision of the Federal Republic in favour of Europe and the
> Atlantic Alliance is *irreversible* . . . and that it contains a realisation
> for us Germans, which is as important as it is bitter: the realisation
> that freedom takes precedence over unity, that it is no use to the
> people in Leipzig to be reunited in a communist Germany, if the
> larger part of the Germans in the Federal Republic lose their freedom
> in the process.[3]

Kohl's firmness earned him enormous credibility from the Reagan Administration, which, in the persons of George Bush and James Baker,
was still in office in 1989. Upon this credibility Kohl could capitalize
when the issue of unification was at stake. The security compact between the Federal Republic and the United States, which had been an
integral element of West Germany's foreign policy culture, was therefore
lubricated by personal relationships. Though it would be difficult to
argue that these personal relationships caused specific outcomes, we
can assume that they facilitated them.

Bush had elevated German–American relations to new heights with the
'partners in leadership' speech in Mainz as early as May 1989.[4] That this
was not just useful support for a domestically embattled chancellor but
reflected the policy priorities of the new administration became evident
in December 1989, when Bush and Baker established a set of criteria upon
which their support for unification hinged.[5] These were self-determination, the membership of a united Germany in Nato and the European
Community, the peaceful and incremental progress of unification and
the adherence to the Helsinki Charter on the question of borders. The
principles of self-determination, in particular in conjunction with Nato
membership, was hotly contested, not only within Germany, but also
between Bonn and Washington on the one hand, and Moscow on the
other. The clarity of these principles, however, determined their success.
They also established Washington as the one reliable Western partner
that Bonn could count on in its hour of need.

Although Bush and Baker were supportive of unification, the price they asked, full Nato membership, appeared to be high, perhaps too high, in the first weeks of 1990. As the Soviet Union was strictly opposed to Nato membership for a unified Germany, the American demand seemed to risk gambling away the historic opportunity. What was needed to grasp the *Mantel der Geschichte* (the coat of history), some argued, was to compromise on Nato membership in order to achieve unification as a whole. Indeed, it seemed nothing short of audacious to expect the Soviet Union not only to withdraw its 300 000 troops from East German territory, but also to expect it to accept that the territory cleared be integrated into Nato straightaway.[6] This view was operationalized in the so-called *Deutschland-Plan* proposed by Hans-Dietrich Genscher on 31 January 1990.[7] In order to assuage Soviet fears, Genscher proposed that East Germany's territory be demilitarized and neutralized after the removal of Soviet troops. Although West Germany would remain part of Nato, both Nato and the Warsaw Pact would become components of a collective security structure headed by the CSCE. There would, in Genscher's plan, be no eastward extension of Nato territory. In a press interview published on 28 January Genscher clarified why: 'Whoever wants the border of NATO to extend to the Oder and Neisse...is closing the door to a united Germany.'[8]

Genscher's proposals caused consternation in the CDU/CSU in general, and in the Chancellery in particular. Gerhard Stoltenberg, the Defence Minister, openly criticized Genscher and rejected the demilitarization of East Germany. Kohl then intervened in the dispute in order to pacify Genscher and in order to prevent the issue from provoking a backlash in the forthcoming East German elections. His compromise declaration omitted the formula that Nato territory would not be extended eastwards, and included the assurance that 'no formations and institutions' belonging to the Western Alliance be moved into East Germany.[9] He had thus gone a long way to accommodate Genscher. In Moscow a week later, Kohl obtained Gorbachev's assent to unification on the principle of self-determination. Although the Soviets were reluctant to equate this with an agreement to Nato membership, Kohl's caution seemed to have been rewarded. 'This', the Chancellor said to the German press in Moscow, 'is a good day for Germany and a happy day for me personally.'[10] With the tempting proximity of unification, and in the face of domestic and international opposition to the American demand, even Helmut Kohl, the staunch Atlanticist, had been tempted to compromise.

It follows that the tough stance of the Bush Administration on Nato membership during Kohl's visit to Camp David on 24 February was crucial in defining the outcome of the saga. American policy makers had come up with the simple diplomatic calculation that the Soviet Union could by now do little to stop the process. Although East Germany would have a special military status after unification, Bush and Kohl agreed, the unified Germany would remain in Nato and in Nato's military structures. American troops would remain in Germany. That Kohl got Gorbachev to agree with these principles on his trip to the Caucasus in July was perhaps his greatest single success during the diplomacy of German unification. But the pegs to make it possible had originally been rammed in by the Bush Administration, first in December 1989 and then again in February 1990. These pegs maintained the Atlantic Alliance and re-established the German–American security compact as the main parameters of European security, establishing the framework for an eventual Nato enlargement.

Nato enlargement was not yet on the agenda, to be sure. And Nato membership for a unified Germany was not the only issue that tied the negotiations over German unification to questions of European security at large. First, Germany accepted limitations to its military power as part of the 2 + 4 agreement. Most important among these were the renunciation of nuclear, biological and chemical weapons, and the agreement to reduce German troop levels to a maximum of 370 000. Secondly, Germany promoted the strengthening of the consultative mechanisms of the CSCE in order to make German unification more palatable to the Soviet Union. In its Foreign Minister Hans-Dietrich Genscher, Germany provided one of the main architects of the drive to invigorate the CSCE, and to equip it with its own institutional structure, which was agreed upon in November 1990. Thirdly, Western countries pushed, within the CFE treaty, to reduce the overall level of conventional forces in Europe, and to conclude the START talks on the elimination of short-range nuclear weapons in Europe – a particular German concern – following the INF treaty of 1987.[11]

Fourthly, and perhaps most importantly, Nato heads of government agreed to change the ethos of the Alliance and bring it into line with the post-Cold War world. This was above all an outcome of improved relations between the two blocs in general, if indeed blocs still existed. It was also expressly designed to ease the Soviet acceptance of Nato membership for a unified Germany. Again, close cooperation between Bonn and Washington was instrumental in framing reform. Whereas the Kohl government had been eager to change the alliance ethos in order to facilitate Soviet acquiescence to Germany's Nato membership, the mobilization of diplomatic support was primarily engineered by Bush.[12] At the London meeting in July 1990, Bush overcame Margaret Thatcher's recalcitrance, generating agreement for a change of Nato's self-conception. The Warsaw Pact, the London meeting agreed, was no longer an enemy, the doctrine of flexible response had to be modified, and Nato and the Warsaw Pact were to sign a joint declaration on European security. These changes equipped Kohl with considerable leverage when in the Caucasus only days later he was trying to persuade Gorbachev that a unified Germany should be a member of Nato. The changes agreed in London were the first in a series of alterations Nato underwent in order to adapt to the post-Cold War world. They determined that, despite the continuity of Nato's existence, European security experienced a metamorphosis. It is one of the recurrent themes of this chapter that Nato enlargement has to be seen in the light of these changes and that German policies within the enlargement process would have been unimaginable without them.

Thus the close rapport between Bonn and Washington in 1989 and 1990 meant that German unification constituted a small eastern enlargement of Nato and the EU. It determined that in post-Cold War Europe, institutional extension would be more successful than institutional inception. The institutions that had given security and prosperity to Western Europe had to be adapted before they could be extended eastwards, to be sure. This was especially so for Nato, where adaptation became a precondition for eastern enlargement. But the principle had been established through the modalities of German unification, and this came to affect the German debate on Nato enlargement in the years to come. In a debate in the Bundestag in 1997, one of the CDU's main thinkers on foreign policy asked: 'With what argument should we tell Poles, Czechs and Hungarians: what we demanded for ourselves, you cannot have?'[13]

The modalities of German unification thus had three main consequences for European security after 1990. It guaranteed a continued American involvement, for without the intention to remain committed to Europe, the American insistence on Nato membership for unified Germany would have been a curious diplomatic exercise. Next, the American commitment to Europe established the pattern for a possible future Nato enlargement. As German unification had established that the United States were in Europe to stay, it also established that the East Central European countries would mainly look to the United States for protection, and that ultimately only the United States could guarantee their security. Any European state interested in Nato enlargement, regardless of whether it had formerly been on the East or the West of the Iron Curtain, or both, had to convince American policy makers of the attraction of Nato enlargement. Finally, the modalities of German unification reinforced the role of the *Atlanticist*. This entailed the persistence of the German–American security compact, in which Germany was a *security consumer*, though the extent to which it consumed security had declined because it was no longer a front-line state the way the Federal Republic had been, and because non-nuclear security issues became increasingly important. It transpired over the following years that this persistence of the *security consumer* was compatible with Nato enlargement and thus the role of the *Warshaviste*, but sat uneasily with the alternative roles of the *Gaullist* and the *Muscovite*.

The vindication of the role of the *Atlanticist* determined that Bonn continued the balancing act between Washington and Paris that had characterized its foreign policy since the 1960s. It also determined that the American security shield continued to have a paradoxical effect on European integration. On the one hand, the American pledge to remain committed to Europe provided reassurance. Without it, the disquiet of some West European countries over German unification might have erupted in a much more damaging form at the end of 1989 and the beginning of 1990. On the other hand, the affirmation of Atlanticism weakened the incentive for West European states to organize their security through the 'Community method', that is to say independently of the United States, and involving pooled sovereignty and supranational institutions. The failure of the Maastricht treaty to establish a genuinely *common* foreign policy has to be seen in this light. The incentives for it to succeed were limited as long as Nato did the job.

Since unification occurred on Western terms, national and democratic values were reconciled successfully for the first time in German history. The Western orientation that Kohl had described as Germany's *raison d'état* had, in the end, not contradicted the ambition of unification. Success vindicated German foreign policy culture, and this explains why after unification its principles remained largely unchanged. To be sure, the tumultuous months of early 1990 had challenged the firmness of these principles, in particular Nato membership. When push came to shove, however, the principles held. They held because of power structures, that is because the Kohl government was in office and because it could count on the benefits of American influence. They also held because they worked: unification and Western integration had in the end not contradicted one another. But perhaps most significantly in the context of the present discussion, they held because, by and large, they were backed by a consensus that included almost the entire political establishment.[14]

Of course, the modalities of unification also contributed to change in German foreign policy culture after 1990. Germany was suddenly much larger than it had been, and, because of the removal of the Berlin and East German vulnerabilities, much less threatened and therefore less dependent on the American security guarantee. In addition, the confirmation of Atlanticism through unification crystallized the security compact between Germany and the United States as the most important relationship within Nato, and therefore elevated Germany to a higher status than Britain and France. As discussed throughout this book, this had been a slow process that can be traced back to the 1950s, but it was accelerated by unification. As Wolfram Hanrieder observed:

> ... who (if not the Federal Republic) should assume the task of the transatlantic mediator. Britain and France had, over the years, disqualified themselves. Britain had a viable relationship with the United States, but none with Europe; France had a viable relationship with Europe, but none with the United States; and both had no viable relationship with one another, mostly because of the distance that had grown through the opposing, uni-dimensional orientation of their respective alliance diplomacy.[15]

In addition, the decline of the Soviet Union's position in East Central Europe triggered an increasing need to combine the role of the *Atlanticist* with the desire to provide stability and security for Germany's eastern neighbours. It was this combination which over the following years drove change within the overall framework of continuity, and which came to dominate the politics of Nato enlargement.

Security before enlargement: Atlanticists, Muscovites, Gaullists

In the first years after unification, it could not have been predicted that German security policy towards East Central Europe would become the politics of Nato enlargement. True, the inception of the North Atlantic Cooperation Council (NACC) in December 1991 underscored Nato's increasingly political nature and its interest in cooperative security structures.[16] This forum opened Nato's consultative and political mechanisms to the former Warsaw Pact countries, including the Soviet Union and the by now independent Baltic states. The cooperation council was a German–American idea. It had been proposed tentatively in the spring of 1991 at the Nato foreign minister's meeting in Copenhagen, but was then developed further by Hans-Dietrich Genscher's and James Baker's respective aides, Frank Elbe and Robert Zoellick. By the time the two foreign ministers presented the new concept on the first anniversary of German unification, it featured regular consultations between foreign ministers and civil servants, and envisaged the development of closer military cooperation.

The inception of NACC was regarded as a German success. Hans-Dietrich Genscher saw it as a means to involve the United States in the larger issues of European security, which, he hoped, could counteract the isolationist tendencies that had started to spread with the arrival of recession and the implosion of the Soviet Union. Moreover, with their agreement to NACC, American policy makers recognized the value of Nato's political role. This recognition played into German hands, because it combined the American military commitment to Germany with the German interest in forging structures of cooperative security in post-Cold War Europe. This combination was vindicated by the resolutions of the December 1991 Nato Council, where Nato offered to foster a new, closer relationship with the CSCE.[17] At the same time, however, it was clear that neither Germany nor the United States saw NACC as the first step to Nato enlargement.

This was so for a variety of reasons. Above all, the existence of the Warsaw Pact, which was dissolved in July 1991, convinced Western policy makers of the wisdom of exercising caution. Ever since 1989, the Bush Administration had been eager to avoid demonstrations of triumphalism at the Soviet Union's loss of influence in East Central Europe. The prospect of Nato enlargement, in this situation, would have added insult to injury. In addition, the rise of the hard-liners who eventually plotted against Gorbachev in August 1991 proceeded rapidly throughout the second half of 1990. This manifested itself most clearly in the resignation of Eduard Shevardnadze in December 1990, and in the shootings in Lithuania in January 1991. For German policy makers, it was clear that this was not the time to weaken Gorbachev's already besieged position vis-à-vis conservative domestic critics, especially not since 300 000 Red Army troops were still stationed on German soil.

Alas, calculations of power and influence do not tell the whole story. It would be misleading to assume that Western countries merely postponed enlargement until the Soviet Union's position in East Central Europe was further weakened, that in their overall quest for power and influence they waited for the moment when the weak had to accept what the strong had decided. On the contrary, one has to consider at least two further reasons – one general, one specific – why Nato enlargement was not an issue until 1993. The first was tradition. Moscow had been the main addressee of Germany's eastern policies since the late eighteenth century. The role of the *Muscovite* had been a strong influence in German foreign policy culture well before the foundation of the Federal Republic, and it had traditionally taken precedence over concerns for Germany's smaller Eastern neighbours. More specifically, the *Muscovite* experienced new legitimation and popularity in the immediate wake of unification because of widespread gratitude towards the Soviet Union. In the eyes of German policy makers, it had been the Soviet turnaround that had made unification possible. Without the renunciation of its territorial status in East Central Europe, it was argued, the end of the Cold War and the peaceful nature of unification would have been unattainable. This gratitude was focused on Mikhail Gorbachev in particular. Although the summer of 1991 did not experience the same 'Gorbymania' as the previous two summers had, the Soviet President continued to enjoy tremendous popularity in Germany.

It has sometimes been speculated that the German reluctance to advance Nato into East Central Europe was a consequence of a promise made by Helmut Kohl to Gorbachev in the Caucasus in July 1990, to the effect that Nato territory would not be extended further than the Oder–Neisse line if Gorbachev agreed to Nato membership for the unified Germany.[18] There is no evidence to substantiate these rumours. The Russian side has produced no written record, Kohl has denied categorically that this was talked about at all, and the Russian side has since argued that Nato enlargement violated the spirit, rather than the letter, of the 2 + 4 agreement. Regardless of whether a promise was made, however, it appears as though German policy makers had to overcome a mental hurdle in their treatment of Nato's position in East Central Europe.

In the absence of a role for Nato, German policy makers exhibited a strong focus on the CSCE.[19] Although, ultimately, this policy came under pressure because it ignored the security aspirations of Germany's East Central European neighbours, it was easily compatible with the principles of Civilian Power, with multilateralism and cooperative security. The focus on the CSCE conformed to Germany's foreign policy culture because it sat easily with the roles of the *Atlanticist* and the *Muscovite*, by remaining in Nato while establishing special relations with Moscow. It also conformed to the personal preferences of the

Foreign Minister. Genscher had come into office during the final stages of the Helsinki negotiations in 1974; his self-conception and electoral appeal since 1982 had emanated from balancing the Atlanticism of Helmut Kohl and the CDU/CSU. Genscher subscribed to the principles of Atlanticism, to be sure. But as proposed in his *Deutschland-Plan* in January 1990, his conception of European security left Nato west of the former Iron Curtain, the Warsaw Pact east of it, and proposed a collective security umbrella in the form of the CSCE in order to connect the two. Krysztof Skubiszewski related in an interview with the author that Genscher never even mentioned the possibility of Nato enlargement to him, whereas the strengthening of the CSCE process was discussed regularly.[20] Genscher's view manifested itself in the German promotion of an institutionalization of the CSCE and its links to the operational structures of Nato.

On top of lending support to a reinforced CSCE, German policy makers emphasized the security functions of the EU. The security problems of East Central Europe, they argued, were no longer problems of military security. What mattered, instead, were market access and trade to stabilize the East Central European economies, environmental agreements to clear the ecological damage of socialism, and a more active migration policy in order to protect Western Europe from floods of immigrants. These new 'soft' security problems could not be addressed by Nato enlargement. 'A European answer to these dangers', Helmut Kohl opined, 'can only mean leading the states of Central, Eastern and South-eastern Europe into the European Community.'[21] The German pledge of support for EU accession in the bilateral treaties with Poland, Hungary and Czechoslovakia has to be seen against this background, as do the considerable payments of direct bilateral assistance. 'Our state aid for Eastern Europe', the junior minister in the Defence Ministry clarified, 'is by no means only altruistically or charitably motivated. That would be noble, but it would not attack the problems fundamentally. Our aid for Eastern Europe is also part of our liberal-democratic stabilisation strategy for *this part of the continent*' (my italics).[22]

What is most noticeable about this period is that German policy makers failed to propose a coherent project through which the military security of its eastern neighbours could be tied to Germany's own. In the absence of such a project, they proposed a multiple level of institutionalized cooperation, which could address security problems old and new, and would accommodate the already existing Euro-Atlantic institutions. According to Hans-Dietrich Genscher, 'The decisive feature of the new understanding of security is that security is no longer sought against or from the other.' Therefore, 'security and stability should over the next years be organised on three levels: the European level, consisting of the European Community...and the WEU, the transatlantic level, consisting of the Atlantic Alliance, and of the overall European level that are the CSCE and the Council of Europe.'[23] Which of these would actually address the security needs of Germany's eastern neighbours, however, remained unclear.

The conceptual incertitude was exacerbated by the failure of the Maastricht treaty to establish the genuinely *common* foreign and security policy to which Germany had aspired. Had such a common policy come into force, the enlargement of the EU would at the same time have had stronger security-political connotations. When proposing an intergovernmental conference on political union alongside that on EMU in 1990, Helmut Kohl had hoped that a common foreign policy could finally be achieved.[24] Yet the differences of opinion between Germany and France – not to mention the other member states – about what a common foreign policy should look like meant that only an intergovernmental mechanism was agreed upon at Maastricht, not only because Britain and the Netherlands resisted a merger of the WEU with the EU, but also because the level of supranationalism, that is Commission involvement and majority voting in the Council of Ministers, acceptable to France turned out to be minimal.[25]

This leads to the conclusion that the role of the *Gaullist* in German foreign policy culture was dealt two blows in 1990 and 1991. The first blow was the affirmation of Atlanticism, as opposed to Europeanism, in the process of German unification. The second was the inability of EU member states to agree on a genuinely common foreign and security policy. Although the process of European integration had accelerated with the calling of two intergovernmental conferences in 1990, the Maastricht treaty failed to deliver the promise of a political union. Despite EMU, therefore, the European strut of the Atlantic bridge remained unstable. This did not affect German security policies towards East Central Europe directly. But it predetermined that the foundations on which these policies were to rest after 1993 would be the structures of a rejuvenated and extended Atlanticism. At the same time the military security needs of Germany's eastern neighbours were strangely absent from Germany's deliberations on European security immediately after unification. Between the United States, France and the Soviet Union, it seems, there was little thought about East Central Europe. The roles of the *Atlanticist*, the *Gaullist* and the *Muscovite* dominated the still feeble role of the *Warshaviste*.

Enter the *Warshaviste*

Although German security policy in the two years after unification was marked by a neglect of East Central Europe, it was also marked by growing signs that this neglect would not be sustainable. The security environment in Eastern Europe as it presented itself to German policy makers in early 1993 looked considerably different from the way it had done on the eve of unification: the Warsaw Pact had been dissolved; the Soviet Union had imploded, leaving the Baltic States, Belarus and the Ukraine as completely new entities in Germany's proximity and Russia a lingering giant just behind them; Czechoslovakia had separated peacefully; and Yugoslavia had broken up violently, exposing the inadequacies of German and EU foreign policy. In addition, the role expectations from East Central Europe came to concentrate more narrowly on Germany and on Nato.

Next, the bilateral treaties that Germany signed with its Eastern neighbours in 1991 and 1992 cleared the road for multilateral cooperation. Skubiszewski's Polish–German community of interests now truly came into its own. Out of all countries in East Central Europe, Poland experienced the most dramatic elevation of status in the security conceptions of German policy makers. Part of this had to do with Poland's size and proximity, which distinguish it from the Czech Republic, Slovakia and Hungary. Part of it has to do with geography. Although the Czech–German border is longer than the Polish–German border, Poland's location between Germany and Russia augments its significance for both sides. Germany's interest in Poland also increased because of the instability in Poland's environment: in the beginning of 1993, Poland no longer shared a single border with any of the states it had bordered on in September 1990. Thus, Poland's Western integration became more desirable for both Germany *and* Poland.

The East Central European countries had paid homage to Nato ever since their domestic liberalization had begun. This was especially true for Poland and Hungary; for Czechoslovakia it became true during 1991, when the concentration on Nato replaced a more idealistic conception of security that revolved around the CSCE.[26] Although it had been Nato policy to discourage public applications for membership from the countries of East Central Europe – in order not to provoke the Soviet Union – disclosures of intent became increasingly common throughout 1991 and 1992. On a visit to Nato's headquarters in March 1991, Vaclav Havel reminded his listeners that 'an alliance of free and democratic states cannot close itself off from like-minded neighbouring states for ever'.[27]

Poland's new Defence Minister, Jan Parys, forced the pace in the direction of Nato when he assumed office in January 1992, at that time against the explicit resistance of the military establishment.[28] When on a visit to Warsaw in March 1992, Nato's Secretary-General Manfred Wörner was informed in the clearest of terms that Poland sought Nato protection because of its anxieties about Russia.[29] At the end of March, the Polish newspaper *Observator* welcomed Gerhard Stoltenberg, the German Defence Minister, with the headline 'Through Germany into Nato'.[30] When he devised the new Polish military doctrine in August 1992, Janusz Onyszkiewicz, the new Defence Minister, included Nato accession as a prime objective. In the same document, cooperation with Germany was described as 'one of the most important paths to integration into Western Europe'.[31]

With all these advances, Rüdiger Moniac observed, it 'would be good if Nato itself understood...with what immense force it attracts the emerging democracies in Eastern Europe'.[32] The strong role expectations from East Central Europe, to Nato in general and Germany in particular, rendered the absence of a coherent German conception for military security in East Central Europe increasingly untenable. In particular, the argument that Nato enlargement was dangerous because it might upset Russia was by now contentious. At the Polish–German forum in December 1992 Bronislaw Geremek remarked pithily: 'I do not understand that argument: does it mean that Russia receives a veto over Nato's elementary questions?'[33] A popular German line of reasoning was that Nato's stability in Western Europe would also radiate into Eastern Europe and thereby render enlargement obsolete.[34] Such logic might have been persuasive in 1990. By the end of 1992, however, the East Central Europeans received it with growing impatience and resentment. Germany was expected to behave like a *Warshaviste*.

What precisely motivated the East Central European striving for Nato membership? Strategically, there was the insurance against Russia and the insurance against Germany. The two were perceived differently, to be sure. Whereas Germany had been a stable and prosperous democracy for decades, and was tied to European and Atlantic structures, Russia was not. But East Central European views of Germany were also affected by residual doubts. These were only exacerbated by the stark differences that existed between Germany and its eastern neighbours in terms of wealth, size and power. Belonging to the same military club, therefore, promised that the East Central Europeans would be able to deal with Germany on a par in the same way that it had allowed the Federal Republic to deal formally on a par with the vastly more powerful United

States in the 1950s. It was therefore not only an underlying insecurity about Germany that motivated East Central Europe's Atlanticism. Its Atlanticism was also motivated by the principles of *de jure* equality and alliance solidarity, which had made Nato vastly more attractive than the Warsaw Pact, and which promised the smaller members a say in what the larger members did. Though none of the East Central Europeans expected to be as powerful as the United States, Nato's principle of diffusing power in favour of common objectives signified an empowerment, and provided a strong incentive to partake.[35]

In addition to these political and strategic incentives, the East Central European countries strove towards Nato membership for symbolic reasons. The argument that belonging to the Euro-Atlantic institutions advertised their 'return to Europe' – as Vaclav Havel phrased it – is a familiar one that does not need to be reiterated. In some cases, for instance for the Czech Republic and Hungary, this symbolic aspect of Nato membership was much more important than any practical benefits Nato membership might hold.[36] In Poland's case, this was different. As we have seen, there was at times a very real perception of the threat of instability emanating from the former Soviet Union.

What is significant for the present discussion is that this affected the self-conception of German policy makers and strengthened the role of the *Warshaviste* in Germany's foreign policy culture. Initially, German policy makers affirmed with increasing regularity that Cracow and Budapest were as European as cities like Madrid or Edinburgh. This rendered it much more problematical to defend the status of East Central Europe outside those West European institutions that had unduly claimed the title 'European' in the 1950s. When East Central European politicians spoke about Europe, therefore, they implicitly reminded their Western listeners that their expectations remained unfulfilled. This rendered it much more difficult for German policy makers to speak of Europe – a favourite pastime – without referring to East Central Europe. Bismarck's dictum that Europe was nothing but a *notion géographique* had always been exaggerated. But especially for the countries that had previously belonged to the Soviet orbit, the notion of 'Europe' after the Cold War expressed much more than a label. It referred to a set of values for which they had fought – democracy, liberty, human rights, to their past as independent states, and to a future that merited the bearing of hardships in the present.

These expectations, in conjunction with the fact that the values at the heart of Nato were now the same as those in East Central Europe, reinforced the *Warshaviste* in Germany's foreign policy culture. Vaclav

Havel was correct in pointing out that an alliance of free and democratic states could not for ever close itself off from neighbouring states who shared their values. This would cause a problem of legitimacy. It would not only undermine democratic values in the rejected countries, but would call into question the very legitimacy of the Western institutions. The process of redefinition, which Nato had started in July 1990, advertised its link to the values of post-Cold War Europe. This made Nato attractive to the East Central European countries. It also made it increasingly difficult to deny Nato membership to them. The problem of legitimacy remained: if there was any reason why Nato should still exist, there was no reason why the East Central European countries should not be admitted. These arguments, for German policy makers, were difficult to counter. In a Bundestag debate on Nato enlargement Günther Verheugen, then one of the SPD's leading foreign policy experts, quoted the Polish Foreign Minister, Dariusz Rosati, who had told the SPD's Bundestag caucus quite simply: 'We want to join Nato for precisely the same reason that Germany does not want to leave it.' Asserting the pro-enlargement position against the sceptics within the Greens, the FDP's Ulrich Irmer said: 'He who struggles against the opening of Nato . . . basically favours the dissolution of this organisation. He who denies the Poles, Czechs and Hungarians accession to Nato ought to ask himself: why should they not come in, if we are in it?'[37]

The role of the *Warshaviste* in Germany's foreign policy culture was, therefore, critically shaped by external role expectations. This generated two separate role conflicts. First, the role of the *Warshaviste* contradicted the role of the *Muscovite*, because Nato enlargement was interpreted as being directed against Russia, and, later, because Moscow was opposed to it. Secondly, it contradicted the role of the *Gaullist* because it addressed East Central Europe's security needs through the mechanisms of Atlanticism. France had reacted negatively to the German–American NACC initiative in 1991, for instance. It saw the CSCE and WEU as more adequate instruments to address the security questions at hand, and, some said, to exert French diplomatic influence.[38] Nato enlargement was, however, obviously compatible with Atlanticism. As it found a new role for Nato, it infused the Atlantic partnership with new vigour. This constellation of preferences meant that the German debate on Nato enlargement was dominated by two role conflicts. On the one hand stood an evident role conflict – that between the *Warshaviste* and the *Muscovite*; on the other stood a latent role conflict – that between the *Atlanticist* and the *Gaullist*. The only two roles that were reconcilable effortlessly were those of the *Warshaviste* and the *Atlanticist*.

At this juncture it is high time to discuss the conceptual issues in-volved in the roles of the *Warshaviste* and the *Muscovite*. It would be misleading to argue that these roles stood for alternative choices of alliance partners alone, that Germany wanted to gang up with Moscow against Warsaw, or, in the event, with Warsaw against Moscow. Of course, such calculations cannot be discarded completely. Every propon-ent of Nato enlargement knew that if Poland were a Nato member, an attack on its territory would be treated as an attack on the alliance as a whole. This was laid down in Article 5 of the Washington treaty. It could, potentially, involve Germany in an armed conflict with Poland against Russia. In this extreme case, the choice of the *Warshaviste* was therefore alliance-building. Corresponding to the realist concept of the balance of power, two or more weaker states collaborated in order to offset the power of a stronger state. This view, however, does not ac-count fully for German policies towards East Central Europe, not least because it cannot explain the pro-Russian policies that Germany pur-sued as soon as Nato enlargement was firmly under way. On the con-trary, one has to pay attention to the nature of the role conflict that afflicted Germany's security policy towards East Central Europe. At heart, this was about the different conceptions of security and integra-tion that separated the *Warshaviste* and the *Muscovite*.

Those German policy makers that represented the *Muscovite* role would reject vehemently the view that they were motivated by consider-ations of power politics, or that they confronted the East Central Euro-pean states with the traditional 'about you without you' between Germany and Russia. Their conception of European security was one of collective security in which no state was ostracized, and in which military cooperation and collective decision making would replace the anachronistic division into blocs. The vehicle for collective security was the CSCE, which approximated closely the ideal type of collective secur-ity. The CSCE had the additional benefit of strengthening Russia, which as a newly democratizing state rightly objected to being ostracized, and without which security in East Central Europe would be impossible anyway. This view was reinforced by an emphasis on disarmament made possible by the end of superpower antagonism. The INF and START treaties had eliminated all American and Soviet intermediate range missiles from Europe, and had turned Europe into a virtually nuclear-free zone. The CFE treaty had not only reduced overall conven-tional capabilities in Europe but had also established parity between the formerly opposing blocs. This favoured defence because a three to one majority is conventionally seen as necessary for a successful attack. It was disarmament and transparency, Michael Mandelbaum argued, which symbolized 'the dawn of peace in Europe'.[39] Nato enlargement, because it estranged Russia, would put the very foundations of this peace at risk.[40]

In contrast, the *Warshaviste* view promoted a conception of security that was directly linked to integration. It has already been pointed out that the functioning of the Atlantic Alliance entails benefits for weaker states because it equips them with the opportunity to influence alliance leaders. That this is so emanates from a sense of community, which holds together the Atlantic Alliance and which rests on shared democratic values. As these link domestic politics and foreign policy, they made the *Warshavistes* considerably more reluctant to accept Russia as an equal member in the security framework, not because Russia posed an imminent threat, but because it was not seen as a democracy and therefore seemed unstable and unpredictable. Whereas *Muscovites* defined security without a reference to these values, that is inclusively – remember Genscher's dictum that security could no longer be sought against or from another state – *Warshavistes* established a link between security and integration.

These different views of security were at the heart of the role conflict in Germany's enlargement policy. It is highly significant for the present discussion that both views were compatible with Civilian Power principles, and that neither side could claim these principles completely for itself. The *Muscovite* view might not have repeated the traditional 'about you without you' between Germany and Russia, but risked subjecting the East Central European countries to second status. The *Warshaviste* view responded to the security needs of Germany's immediate eastern neighbours, but risked ignoring the larger picture. Evidently, any European security architecture needed to establish a place for Russia, and it was unclear how this could be achieved as long as Russia was opposed to Nato enlargement. These calculations continued to inform the discussion about security in East Central Europe for most of the 1990s.

That Nato enlargement would succeed was difficult to predict at the end of 1992. The recession of the early 1990s forced American policy makers to turn their attention to domestic politics and contributed to Bill Clinton's election victory on a ticket emphasizing domestic social and economic issues. The disappearance of the Soviet Union posed the question of what the United States were in Europe for. The serious differences that separated the United States from its European Allies over the war in Bosnia reinforced already existing doubts about the

Atlantic Alliance. After the Cold War, the Atlantic Ocean appeared to have widened. Indeed, Nato seemed to need the infusion of new energy in the same way that older couples sometimes need a common project when the children have left home.

The first enlargement phase

The older couple's project became Nato's eastern enlargement. It was put on the agenda in March 1993 with a speech delivered in London by Germany's new Defence Minister, Volker Rühe.[41] The starting point of Rühe's analysis was that the Atlantic Alliance had to reconsider fundamentally what it was about and how it could adapt to the post-Cold War world. If it wanted to preserve the essential, Rühe argued, it had to change the peripheral. Starting from this basic premise, Rühe identified three areas for change: strengthening Nato's European pillar (hardly a new issue but significant because of Europe's failure in the Yugoslav conflicts), developing a military capability beyond territiorial defence (which did not lend itself to German leadership because of domestic constraints) and opening Nato to East Central Europe. In contrast to the first two issues, Nato enlargement was an issue where Rühe could talk plainly.[42] After elaborating on the exigency of economic assistance to East Central Europe, Rühe argued that Western Europe had to devote more security-political assistance to the eastern half of the continent. Eastern Europe could not be allowed to remain a 'conceptual no man's land'. In Rühe's words, Nato had to develop a conceptual approach that satisfied two demands:

> First, it has to consider the vital security interests of our Eastern neighbours, as well as the fact that these states have always belonged to the community of European nations. Secondly, this conception has to consider the impact of enlarged membership on the Euro-Atlantic space as a whole. We need a balanced approach.[43]

With these sentences alone, Volker Rühe outed himself as the *Warshaviste* personified. Although it is true that he called for a balanced approach that took into consideration Russia's importance for overall strategic questions, Rühe's starting point was the recognition that East Central European security interests existed and had to be addressed in their own right. Only then, he said, could they be accommodated as part of an overall strategy. This was not the way German policy makers had hitherto argued.

At its most basic level, therefore, Rühe's argument saw democracy, stability and security in East Central Europe as inextricably linked.[44] It was no new proposition that without democracy both stability and security in East Central Europe would remain unattainable. But previously, the Western contribution to democratization had primarily been seen in terms of technical assistance, trade and political association with the European Union. Without discarding these contributions as insignificant, Rühe proposed that the importance of military security had hitherto been neglected. The crux of his argument lay in inverting the conventional logic: without military security, stability and democracy in East Central Europe would be unattainable.

Since Eastern Europe seemed increasingly endangered by instability – ethnic strife, nationalism, fragmentation – Rühe argued that it was high time to extend Western Europe's institutions eastwards: 'We cannot afford to postpone the necessary decisions until perfect plans for a new Europe have been devised.'[45] The conventional view that EU enlargement should precede Nato enlargement, or quite possibly render it unnecessary, could therefore no longer hold. Though both enlargements were intimately related to one another, they had to be decided upon in independent processes:

> The Atlantic Alliance must not be a 'private party'. I can see no valid reason to withhold Nato membership from the future members of the European Union. I also ask myself whether membership in the European Union necessarily has to precede the accession to Nato... When developing criteria for Nato membership, we should therefore avoid automatisms and rigid rules. We need a clear analysis of common interests, values, and political aims.[46]

The force of Rühe's argument lay in the clarity with which it prioritized the different roles of Germany's foreign policy culture. Above all, it ranked the *Atlanticist* over the *Gaullist* and the *Warshaviste* over the *Muscovite*. It thereby terminated the both-the-one-and-the-other style of diplomacy that had sometimes marked the foreign policy culture of the Federal Republic and that had continued to affect German policies towards East Central Europe in the first two years after unification. It is true that Rühe softened the clarity of his priorities by proposing a balanced arrangement, that is a European pillar in Nato to appease the *Gaullists* and consideration for Russia to appease the *Muscovites*. He made plain, however, that these balancing arrangements could only be functions of the priorities he had established. In addition, his argument featured a compelling logic because the two roles it promoted were mutually reinforcing. The compatibility with Atlanticism bolstered the still feeble priority given to East Central Europe. The concentration on Nato enlargement, on the other hand, rejuvenated the gaunt fundamentals of Atlanticism. *Atlanticism* and *Warshavism* became two sides of the same coin.

Rühe's proposals, then, were ground-breaking. But were they compatible with Civilian Power? One can argue that they were, in principle, for four reasons. We have already seen that Nato had undergone important changes, and that Rühe had proposed its enlargement in line with these changes, that is as a 'transfer of stability'. Similarly, the role expectations from East Central Europe were effective precisely because they appealed to the values that held the Atlantic Alliance together. These values were those of Civilian Power. Next, the relationship of weaker and stronger Nato members made the Alliance attractive to the East Central European countries. The advantage of Nato enlargement was that it constrained the stronger states and empowered the weaker ones. It constrained the stronger states because it prevented them from doing what they said they did not want to do in the first instance: it prevented Russia from establishing a sphere of influence in East Central Europe, it prevented the United States from withdrawing from Europe, and it prevented Germany from pursuing bilateral Eastern policies. It empowered the smaller East Central European countries because it handed them leverage not only over Russian, and Western, policies towards themselves, but also over Western policy towards Russia. 'About us without us' was East Central Europe's historical trauma. No other arrangement promised to make it impossible in the post-Cold War world in the same way that Nato enlargement did.

Thirdly, the fact that a small Nato enlargement left other countries unconsidered, the Baltics and the Balkans for instance, does not invalidate the assertion that Nato enlargement per se corresponded to the principles of Civilian Power. Neglecting one's friends does not invalidate the love towards one's spouse. The exercise of Civilian Power, in this case, becomes a question of perspective. But although it is true that from Tallinn or Skopje German policies appeared too neglectful for a Civilian Power, from Prague or Warsaw they did not. On the contrary, only Nato enlargement enabled Germany to consider its eastern neighbours appropriately.

The position of Russia, finally, has to be seen in a similar light. On the one hand, omitting Russia completely from all calculations around Nato enlargement would have been incompatible with Civilian Power prin-

ciples, because it would have failed to install cooperative security structures. Hence although Rühe mentioned 'a balanced approach' to compensate Russia for enlargement, his early speeches did not develop this
theme sufficiently to make them entirely compatible with Civilian
Power. On the other hand, Nato enlargement did not violate Civilian
Power principles per se. All too often, the argument that pan-European
security structures had to be found was merely a way of privileging
Russia over East Central Europe. 'I have repeated endlessly', Bronsilaw
Geremek said, 'that there might be good reasons to hesitate with the
enlargement of Nato. But if the real reason is consideration for Russia,
then that is simply unbearable for us Central Europeans.'[47] Talking
about Europe when meaning Russia was no longer feasible for Germany,
not only because of concerns for its own security and prosperity, but also
for its self-conception as a Civilian Power. Only a merger between
Muscovite and *Warshaviste* priorities allowed Germany to conduct Civilian Power policies. Until 1994, this merger was insufficiently developed.
If the *Muscovite* policies before 1993 had neglected East Central Europe,
Rühe's *Warshavism* neglected Russia.

There was a further reason why Rühe's speech was ground-breaking.
His mentioning of 'the vital security interests of our Eastern neighbours'
contained an ambiguity. Who did Rühe refer to when speaking of *our*
eastern neighbours? Was it Western Europe as a whole? Or was it Germany in particular? It was at least doubtful whether Portugal or Britain
shared a sufficiently acute interest in East Central Europe to convince
them of the charms of Nato enlargement. The call for enlargement was
therefore also a cautious reminder that Germany had national security
interests in East Central Europe that were not addressed by current
arrangements. To be sure, Rühe phrased this reminder in the most
cautious of terms. He merely pointed out that the forces of integration
in Western Europe were offset by the forces of fragmentation in Eastern
Europe, and that Nato enlargement could assist in the stabilization of
East Central Europe. But the gist of his argument was clear, reminding
Nato allies and the German domestic audience of Germany's vital security interests in East Central Europe.

If it seemed evident by the late 1990s that the main aim of Germany's
foreign policy had become to surround itself with stable market democracies, this had not been quite so evident in the immediate period after
unification. Only with Rühe's speech was enlargement elevated to the
same status that Western integration had traditionally enjoyed in the
Federal Republic's foreign policy culture: that of Germany's *raison d'état*.
According to this reasoning, Germany's national interests were security,

liberty and prosperity. These were unattainable without security, liberty and prosperity in East Central Europe. Since it was impossible for Germany to guarantee security, liberty and prosperity in East Central Europe by itself, the double enlargement of Nato and the EU was imperative. It was this reasoning that had already influenced Rühe's previous thinking and that came to the fore with crystal clarity in the London speech. In the previous two years, numerous questions were asked and few answers were given about the future of East Central Europe's security. Those answers that were given were tentative at best and ill-conceived at worst. Only with Rühe's speech was a project proposed that addressed the question clearly and that had a strategic use to it.

Support and opposition for the *Warshaviste*

The reception in Germany and the other Nato countries of this speech, however, was far from enthusiastic. It was met with a thundering silence from Kohl, who simply refused to comment on the issue, and with a hefty dose of scepticism from Kinkel and the Foreign Ministry. This was hardly surprising, since Rühe had violated the domestic consensus, and thereby, at least implicitly, criticized the 'Russia first' policy promoted by Kohl and Kinkel. Only six weeks before Rühe's London speech, Kohl had reasserted the hitherto cautious German approach:

> We know that some of our immediate Eastern neighbours want more – including the accession to Nato. I realise that there is no easy answer to this question, but that a cautiously formative policy is imperative, which takes into account the stability in this region and the justified security needs of all our Eastern neighbours.[48]

This was a somewhat convoluted way of saying that Nato enlargement was unfeasible because it offended the 'justified security interests' of Russia. What is noteworthy here is that the Chancellor used exactly the same formulation in a speech at the end of June.[49] Surely, had he wanted to, he could have endorsed Rühe's proposals, or rejected them straightaway. But Kohl chose to do neither, letting Rühe and Kinkel fight over the issue instead. This remained the case until the autumn of 1994, when the constant quarrel between Rühe and Kinkel threatened to endanger the coalition's electoral fortunes. Kohl's activism in the enlargement of the European Union contrasted starkly with his passivism over Nato enlargement. If Kohl was a visionary over EU enlargement, over Nato enlargement he remained an agnostic, at least in the most important phase.

It is true that Klaus Kinkel had signalled his readiness to consider closer links between Nato and the East Central European countries even before Rühe's London speech. In a newspaper interview in early March 1993, he had contemplated a half-way approach between full membership and the NACC.[50] Kinkel's views differed significantly from Rühe's on two points, however. First, Kinkel paid more attention to Russia, which is why he considered a proper enlargement of Nato unfeasible. Secondly, he professed to think only 'conceptually' about the issue, with no direct plan of action or reason for pushing ahead quickly. Rühe on the other hand was pressed for time. In a number of speeches throughout the summer of 1993 he elaborated the ideas originally developed in his London speech. This included the assertion that a viable arrangement had to be found for relations between Nato and Russia, while maintaining that Russian doubts must not be allowed to obstruct enlargement itself. Confidently, Rühe now opined that 'accession is not so much a question of Whether, but of How and When.'[51]

This confidence was remarkable considering the reception of the enlargement proposals within the Alliance at large. Neither France nor Britain had been encouraging. France placed emphasis on the CSCE especially, since American influence was diluted in this forum, and since France, not being an integrated member of Nato militarily, pulled little weight in Nato.[52] Britain, initially hesitant, feared a weakening of Nato's functions as a defence alliance in the case of its widening, and in any case seemed to gain few tangible benefits from an enlargement.[53] Most significantly, the new Clinton Administration was dominated by proponents of a 'Russia first' policy, which had been devised by the influential Deputy Secretary of State Strobe Talbott. As Clinton was inexperienced in foreign policy, and Secretary of State Warren Christopher still cautious, 'Russia first' guided the Administration's policy towards Eastern Europe for most of its first year in office.[54] In retrospect it is remarkable how isolated the German Defence Minister was in these early days of the enlargement debate and how vigorously he pursued his objective in spite of his isolation.

If Rühe had a weak hand, he played it rather well. Above all, as we have seen, he had a compelling logic on his side. But this alone did not carry the day. It was helped by a set of other factors. One of these was the timing of the London speech. Although 'Russia first' remained the official policy of all Nato countries, especially the United States, throughout 1993, there was an obvious search for ways to rejuvenate the alliance and to adapt it to the post-Cold War world. Furthermore, Rühe managed to acquire some powerful allies. The most obvious candidates were Germany's East Central European neighbours, who came to see the German Defence Minister rather like a knight in shining armour. Their support became important because it appealed to Nato's new self-conception as a *community of values*.

A further ally in Rühe's quest for Nato enlargement was Manfred Wörner, Rühe's predecessor bar two in the German Defence Ministry and Nato's Secretary-General since 1988. Although sceptical initially, Wörner had come to see Nato enlargement as an important project during the course of 1993, not least because he sought a big issue for the Nato summit in January 1994, which was Clinton's first. In a speech in London in September, Wörner said:

> In my view, it is time to offer a concrete perspective to those countries of Central and Eastern Europe that want to accede to Nato and that we can see as possible candidates for a future membership. This should also be one of the main subjects of the coming Nato summit.[55]

The last ally Rühe found was Richard Holbrooke, the new American ambassador to Bonn. Holbrooke returned to Washington in the summer of 1994 as Assistant Secretary of State for Central Europe, firmly convinced by the benefits of enlargement.

Despite the lacklustre reception of Rühe's speeches initially, the cause of Nato enlargement experienced a sudden and unexpected boost in August 1993 from the corner of a most unlikely candidate, Russia's President Boris Yeltsin. On a state visit to Warsaw, Yeltsin – reportedly infused by the surplus energy of Polish vodka – conceded publicly that Poland was free to choose which alliance it wanted to belong to.[56] Since this was a scarcely veiled admission that Russia no longer opposed Poland's Nato membership, the ball of enlargement now seemed to be in Nato's court – at least this was how the two Foreign Ministers, Andrej Kozyrev and Krzysztof Skubiszewski, summarized the summit for the press.[57] It is hard to overestimate the boost this gave to Poland's efforts to achieve full membership and the pressures this exerted on the Atlantic Alliance to respond, regardless of how much vodka the Russian president had consumed prior to his statement. Until 1997, Polish politicians quoted Yeltsin's original consent in order to put Russia's resistance to Nato enlargement into perspective.

The euphoria, however, was short lived. Yeltsin retracted his statement within a month. Though the retraction was moderate compared to the warnings the Kremlin was going to issue in the future, Western efforts to push Nato enlargement had experienced a setback.[58] Furthermore, the Defense Department in Washington devised a plan that promised to address the security concerns of Germany and its East Central European neighbours while giving Nato time to consider the pros and cons of a possible enlargement. This plan, which came to be known as the 'Partnership for Peace' programme, was first presented at the meeting of Nato Defence Ministers in Travemünde, Germany, in October 1993. Its essence was the conclusion of bilateral treaties between Nato and the former Warsaw Pact countries. These entailed provisions for military cooperation but no security guarantees from Nato.[59] 'Partnership for Peace' improved on the association policy of NACC in two ways. It was open to all CSCE countries, rather than just the former Warsaw Pact countries, and thereby included the former neutrals in Scandinavia and the Yugoslav successor republics. It also created the mechanisms for practical military cooperation rather than yet another talking shop.

'Partnership for Peace' obliged the signatory states to adhere to democratic values and the principles of peaceful conflict resolution.[60] These were general principles of Civilian Power that were endorsed, but by no means initiated, by Germany. The programme also obligated its signatories to make their defence spending transparent and to establish civil and democratic control over the armed forces, which even in a country like Poland had not been achieved. A further important element was the attainment of 'interoperability', that is the restructuring of non-Nato armed forces to facilitate their military cooperation with Nato troops. Bearing in mind the in part pitiful state of many armed forces in East Central Europe, the opportunity of military cooperation created an immense pressure for reform. It opened up a more realistic way for restructuring than that of a Polish joke at the time, which proposed the declaration of war on the United States followed by instantaneous surrender as the cheapest way of military reform. 'Interoperability' played into the hands of those who favoured enlargement because it allowed them to create facts. This was especially true for Volker Rühe, whose push for military cooperation with Germany's East Central European neighbours created considerable pressure for enlargement in the years to come.

Initially, however, the Partnership for Peace programme was seen as a victory for the opponents of enlargement, especially as it entailed no Nato security guarantee for East Central Europe. The then Polish Foreign Minister Andrzej Olechowski related in an interview with the author that he initially saw 'Partnership for Peace' as a substitute for enlargement, a view which he had come to due to signals from the Clinton

Administration.[61] The United States seemed to have taken the initiative with a few paragraphs of a still vague proposal, the *Süddeutsche Zeitung* wrote, and concluded: 'It is sensible to see Volker Rühe as the loser of the enlargement debate.'[62] Some observers complained that PFP did not stand for Partnership for Peace but for Policy for Postponement. Yet although these reactions testify to the initial shock of rejection, the crux of Partnership for Peace was its ambiguity. It was by no means clear whether the programme would actually facilitate or postpone enlargement. Whereas opponents of enlargement, like the British Secretary of Defence Malcolm Rifkind, saw it as a deferment, enlargement promoters, like Rühe, interpreted it as a first step in the right direction. In the event, the programme served the purposes of enlargement rather well. That it would do so, however, became evident only in 1994 and 1995; in the autumn of 1993, it seemed, indeed, as though enlargement had come to a halt.

The last months of 1993 witnessed an increasingly passionate debate about enlargement within the German government. The tensions exposed the different roles inherent in German foreign policy culture and were exacerbated by events in Russia. At the end of September, Karl Lamers wrote a newspaper contribution urging caution in the enlargement debate. Contradicting Rühe, Lamers asserted that realistically Germany's allies were not yet prepared to extend Nato's security guarantee to any East Central European state. The security of Germany's East, therefore, had to be linked to the WEU, which was an obvious choice because of its link to the European Union, which would render it more palatable to Russia.[63] Though Lamers appeared to unite the roles of the *Gaullist* and the *Muscovite* in this question, his real concern lay with European integration and the creation of a truly common foreign and security policy. Just as Rühe's enlargement policy strengthened Germany's Atlantic ties, Lamers hoped that the incorporation of East Central Europe into the WEU would strengthen this organization, lead to a stronger foreign policy mechanism within the EU, and liberate Europe (and Germany) from American tutelage. As if in response, Rühe used a joint newspaper interview with Manfred Wörner only days later to call the old Nato 'obsolete' and to reassert his position that it was time to push ahead with enlargement.[64]

In the first days of October, the putsch against Boris Yeltsin in Moscow and the subsequent bombardment of the Russian parliament heightened insecurities in East Central Europe, especially since this went hand in hand with Yeltsin's retraction of his Warsaw statement Germany's eastern neighbours were concerned by the sympathy with which Western countries accepted the retraction. Justifiably or not, this led to fears that the West continued to regard East Central Europe as a Russian sphere of influence. Yet the events in Moscow had an ambiguous effect on Germany's Nato enlargement policy. It was used by those who were opposed to enlargement as an argument for its postponement. Hans-Dietrich Genscher advocated 'absolute reticence' in the enlargement question with a view to the situation in Russia.[65] Klaus Kinkel, on the other hand, professed to be 'in favour at heart, but opposed in mind'.[66]

Indeed, it seems difficult in retrospect to determine what precisely Kinkel's position was in this early period of the enlargement debate. As he warned against Rühe's impetuous insistence, Kinkel did seem to hold a deeply felt belief that Russia must not be alienated. Yet Kinkel said at no time that he was opposed to enlargement in principle. This distinguished his position from Genscher, who consistently argued in favour of Moscow and the CSCE. Genscher's position was also shared by key diplomats in the Foreign Ministry.[67] In order to limit public damage, the Chancellery issued a consensus formula to the effect that 'the Western institutions had to be extended *incrementally* towards the East'.[68] Though this was used by Kinkel and Rühe for a while, it could scarcely mask the underlying difference of opinion. This difference did not only bear the pungent question as to who in year two after Genscher was, as Herbert Kremp put it, 'the real existing German Foreign Minister'.[69] It also bore the question as to which security policy the German government actually pursued vis-à-vis its eastern neighbours.

From the evidence presented here, it seems justified to argue that there was at this time no such thing as a *German* policy. Rühe pushed ahead, but did not represent a consensus view either in his party or in the government. Although Rühe lobbied the Chancellor, he did not speak for him. Kinkel urged caution, but seemed to have no clear project of his own. The Chancellor, finally, stood out through a near-total public silence on the issue. On 1 December Kohl crowned his government's decision-making mumbo-jumbo by rejecting enlargement, arguing with obvious reference to Russia that this 'would not contribute to a good development' in the current situation.[70] On enlargement, the voices of the German choir did not only sing different tunes, they sang from entirely different hymn sheets.

The confusion of the debate was only exacerbated by rifts within the CDU/CSU foreign policy establishment and by the elections to the Russian Duma in December 1993. We have already seen that the CDU/CSU's most prominent foreign policy spokesman, Karl Lamers, objected to Nato enlargement primarily because he feared that it would weaken the incentives for a common EU foreign and security policy. Since the Maastricht review conference, which was to reconsider the possibility of a genuine political union, was little more than two years away, Lamers thought it imprudent to remove the incentives by strengthening Atlantic ties. Within the CDU/CSU Bundestag caucus, Lamers' view was complemented by the CDU's chairman of the foreign affairs committee, Karl-Heinz Hornhues, who was reticent about enlargement on the grounds that it might alienate Russia.[71] The CDU was thus by no means a party of *Atlanticists* and *Warshavistes* only.

As the Nato Council's autumn meeting approached in early December, it seemed as though the proposals for enlargement had failed. None of the European allies supported enlargement, the American policy remained 'Russia first', and 'Partnership for Peace' was widely seen as a substitute programme. Rühe, however, did not take this for a no. At the Nato Defence Ministers' meeting a week later, he criticized Nato publicly for being 'too defensive about enlargement', proclaimed that Germany and the United States were 'marching in step', and combined a proposition for a 'deepened integration' between Nato and Russia with the assertion that no third state could be granted a 'veto' on enlargement.[72] The assertion that Germany and the United States were by now marching in step in endorsing enlargement was at least exaggerated, if not plainly false. There is no reason to assume that Washington, in the first half of December, planned to include a reference to enlargement in the communiqué of the January 1994 summit.[73] And after Kohl's confession on 1 December that he was opposed to enlargement in the present circumstances, there is no reason to assume that he did either.

This changed with the elections to the Duma in Russia and the success of the ultra-right 'liberal' party under Vladimir Zhirinovsky. As German newspapers produced headlines like 'New Hitler wins' and 'Yeltsin's opponent: Vladimir the terrible', CDU politicians of the second tier voiced increasing concerns about the cautious approach the Alliance was set to adopt at its January summit. If Rühe had seemed isolated vis-à-vis Kinkel and Kohl in previous weeks, he was now supported by a sound number of politicians who were critical of the Foreign Minister and thus, by extension, the Chancellor. 'The election in Russia has demonstrated what imponderabilities go along with the collapse of the Soviet Empire,' Jürgen Rüttgers, one of the CDU caucus leaders, argued and concluded: 'Nato must act immediately and initiate concrete steps to guarantee the security of our East European neighbours.'[74] Meanwhile, the disquiet about Russia was not only caused by the election results, but also by a general shift in Russia's policy towards an apparently anti-Western stance. The new Russian military doctrine had proclaimed the former republics of the CIS as 'near abroad' and special Russian sphere of influence. In a speech on Nato enlargement, Friedbert Pflüger, one of the CDU's rising foreign policy specialists stated:

> The formula for the coming years has to be: the more the forces of reform have the upper hand in Russia, the more relaxed and long-term we can work on Nato enlargement. But the more the nationalists win the upper hand, the more threats come out of the Kremlin, the more rapidly and decisively we have to push for Nato membership. In any case, one thing is clear: the key to Nato enlargement must not lie in Moscow, neither today nor in the future.[75]

It is almost impossible to establish a clear causal connection between instability in Russia on the one hand and the push for Nato enlargement on the other. The original push for Nato enlargement not only preceded instability in Russia, but was phrased in terms of a stability transfer and shared values, which appealed to Nato's political role much more strongly than to its defence mechanisms. Yet the insecurity that the events in Russia generated in East Central Europe, and in Germany, complicated this line of argument. Suddenly, what had always been true for the countries of East Central Europe became true for some German politicians, like Rüttgers and Pflüger, too: that despite all shared values, Nato was at heart a military alliance which could defend the countries of East Central Europe in the unlikely event of a Russian attack. This meant that German politicians could promote Nato enlargement for very different reasons. It also meant that they could promote it for different reasons than they publicly proclaimed. There is no reason to assume, however, that Nato enlargement was ever conceived of in terms of defending East Central Europe against Russia. The threat was instability, not a military attack.[76]

This leads to the observation that the role of the *Warshaviste*, which had been feeble until March 1993 and embattled afterwards, experienced a push towards the very end of 1993, just prior to the Nato summit in Brussels in January 1994. This is not to suggest that the Duma elections had an exclusive causal effect on enlargement. As we have seen, the ground had been conscientiously prepared by Rühe. But the Duma elections crystallized some of the arguments that proponents of enlargement had put forward, and it is therefore difficult to discount them. They affected the public debate in Germany considerably, and they were the only event between the beginning of December, when it seemed as though no perspective for enlargement would be given, and the Brussels summit, when a perspective was opened up. If nothing else, the events in Russia in the last four months of 1993 might have crystallized the fact that the turmoil in the Eastern half of Europe was not yet over. As Volker Rühe put it: 'The lava is still running.'[77]

Nato enlargement: the time of decision

Just prior to the Nato summit in January 1994 all sides, Russian and East Central European, American and West European, reiterated their points of view and voiced their demands for the summit. Whereas Boris Yeltsin warned only days before the summit that Nato enlargement would destabilize Russia, the Baltic states, with a view to the Duma elections in December, enunciated their interest in close cooperation with Nato, and in the case of Lithuania even applied for Nato membership.[78] Jiri Dienstbier, the former Czechoslovak Foreign Minister, evoked the analogy of Munich to remind Western leaders that cowardice would not pay off in the face of adversity, and implicitly, that the Western powers owed the Czech Republic for the betrayal of Munich. The Partnership for Peace programme, Dienstbier warned, must not become an *Ersatzzuckerl* (a substitute sweet) for proper enlargement.[79] The Clinton Administration endorsed 'Partnership for Peace' just prior to the summit. Clinton himself stated that Nato must not create new dividing lines in Europe, that Russia must not be ostracized and, quite plainly, that there was no consensus about enlargement within Nato.[80]

For the Kohl government, these conflicting signals generated a difficult set of external role expectations. Since the government lacked a coherent line, its internal tensions were exacerbated. Just as Klaus Kinkel asserted that Nato enlargement was a long-term process, Volker Rühe continued to push for rapid progress. Interestingly, Kohl's attempt to mediate between the two positions and establish a coherent governmental line led to a situation in which the Chancellor himself made the biggest U-turn. Whereas he had ruled out enlargement at his meeting with President Mitterrand in early December, Kohl was now suddenly in favour of enlargement. Two days before the summit, Kohl demanded a 'clear perspective for accession' from the summit for Germany's eastern neighbours. At the same time, he proposed that Nato 'expand its security relationship with Russia to the closest possible level.'[81] Thus, although differences about timing and the relationship with Russia remained, the German position before the summit was now clearly in favour of enlargement.

The Brussels summit decided on more issues than the question of enlargement. The crisis in the alliance over Yugoslavia had deteriorated to such an extent that some German politicians quietly doubted whether the United States were prepared to stay in Europe at all. That they were was one of the significant outcomes of the summit. Equally, Nato leaders decided that Nato would be prepared to use military force in defence of UN, that is mostly British and French, forces in Bosnia. This paved the way for the American involvement in the conflict that culminated in the Dayton peace agreement and the deployment of Nato troops in Bosnia. Finally, the summit brokered a deal between the United States and France over the Europeanization of Nato, which France had demanded as a condition for its return to Nato's military structure.

The relationship with the countries of East Central Europe, however, remained the summit's main agenda. As expected, Nato leaders agreed on the Partnership for Peace programme. At the same time, and this was perhaps more surprising, the invitation to the programme contained a reference to a future enlargement:

> We expect and would welcome if a Nato enlargement included democratic states to our East, as part of an evolutionary process, and considering political and security-political developments in the whole of Europe.[82]

This sentence contained the essence of the new Nato approach. On the one hand, it opened consultative and cooperative mechanisms to all non-Nato countries in Europe, on the other, it differentiated between countries by opening up the prospect of membership, which clearly favoured some over others. The ingenuity of Partnership for Peace as agreed at Brussels was therefore its combination of cooperation and differentiation. Although in a formal way it treated all non-Nato members equally, the reference to enlargement advertised that some were more equal than others. This ingenuity was one of default rather than design. As we have seen, the original motivation for the development of Partnership for Peace was to take the steam out of German and East Central European demands for Nato enlargement. By the sceptics of enlargement, it was hailed as a programme that would avoid 'new dividing lines' in Europe. By proponents of enlargement, it was feared to be an *Ersatzzuckerl*.

It transpired over the following months, however, that Partnership for Peace utilized cooperation in order to foster differentiation. The possibility of military cooperation assisted those who were most willing to accede to Nato. Thus, the Partnership for Peace programme, which had originally been designed as a clamp-down on enlargement, was hijacked by the proponents of enlargement and turned into a vehicle for their purposes. The possibility of 'creating facts' favoured Germany's East Central European neighbours, since for them military cooperation with Nato was easiest. It also favoured the German Defence Minister over his rival in the Foreign Ministry.

Volker Rühe had initiated preparations for military cooperation with Germany's eastern neighbours since his arrival in office. It was partly due to his initiative that Poland and Germany concluded an agreement on military cooperation in January 1993. Actual cooperation had been postponed repeatedly because of legal and constitutional reservations in Germany. By early 1994, preparations involved joint manoeuvres with Poland, preferably with the participation of troops from another Nato country like Britain or Denmark. Within days of the Brussels summit Rühe made these plans public, and in addition announced the preparation of joint planning for peacekeeping missions and joint training schemes.[83] After Poland had joined Partnership for Peace in early February, and had presented its 'wish list' to the Nato headquarters in Brussels at the end of April, the road was cleared for military cooperation as envisaged by the Polish–German agreement. Poland did everything it could as soon as it could. If it has been one of the arguments of this book that civilianization is in part a demand-led strategy, Polish policy on military cooperation can serve as an example.

Rühe's attention to military cooperation was illustrated by his considerable personal involvement. He had already proposed the replication of the Weimar meetings of Foreign Ministers to his colleagues from Poland and France in 1993. He suggested regular trilateral meetings on the same model to his Polish and Danish colleagues in 1996. When in May 1994, Boris Yeltsin came to Germany on the occasion of the fiftieth anniversary of the end of the Second World War, Rühe declined the company of the Russian Defence Minister, Pavel Grachev, in favour of meeting his Polish and Danish colleagues in Warnemünde. At this meeting, the plans for the first trilateral manoeuvres in September and October 1994 were announced, the latter involving Polish participation in the Nato exercise 'Chinese Eye'. In the spring of 1994, one of Germany's and Nato's most senior generals, Henning von Odarza, was appointed adviser to the Polish Defence Minister. Von Odarza's special responsibility was Poland's relationship with Nato, that is with Partnership for Peace questions in general, and Nato accession in particular.[84]

Over the following years, military cooperation between Germany and the countries in Eastern Europe grew exponentially.[85] In 20 out of 22 countries, this cooperation was systematized in annual programmes by 1997. These programmes included: first, cross-border contacts (featuring informal activities like concerts, sporting events and open door happenings); secondly, military consultancy (whereby German experts advised on military reorganization, often with a view to the *Bundeswehr*'s own experience after unification); and thirdly, military education and language training (offering officers' 'scholarships' to the institutions of *Bundeswehr* education). In addition, the annual programmes involved participation in Partnership for Peace activities, which were coordinated from the Nato headquarters, and participation in activities 'in the spirit of Partnership for Peace', which were compatible with Nato schemes, but were planned and executed independently of it. In 1996, for instance, Germany participated in 10 out of 25 Partnership for Peace exercises, and organized 16 activities 'in the spirit of Partnership for Peace'.

It is perhaps no longer surprising to reveal that Germany's military cooperation with its immediate eastern neighbours was far more active than with other Partnership for Peace countries. In 1996 the *Bundeswehr* was engaged in 95 activities with Poland, 94 with the Czech Republic and 66 with Hungary; with Slovakia, only 41 activities were pursued, with Bulgaria 32, with Romania 31. It is true that not all of these activities were strictly military and that they were facilitated by simple geographical proximity. It is much easier to send a *Bundeswehr* football team to Slubice than to Sofia, for instance. Although one might chuckle at the thought of German soldiers spending much time with their Polish colleagues at barbecues and on football pitches, the features of the *Bundeswehr*'s cooperation does also reveal German priorities. One of the reasons for engaging in non-military exchanges and activities was to show the civilian side of the *Bundeswehr* to countries that had suffered from German occupation. As in European integration, Slovakia was not left behind by Germany or by the Western institutions, but by the Meciar government. Slovakia was included in all conceptions of enlargement until, in about 1995, it became clear that the Meciar government was unwilling to implement the necessary domestic reforms to make possible the accession to either Nato or the European Union. It is part of civilianization that, as a demand-led strategy, it does not force countries to respond to it. Prodigal sons have to return out of their own free will.

The *Bundeswehr*'s active cooperation with Poland, Hungary and the Czech Republic was planned from above. In official documents, these countries were clearly identified as Germany's top priority, whereas Albania, Bulgaria, the Baltic States, Macedonia, Romania, Russia, Slovakia and Slovenia were allocated second rank.[86] These facts indicate, perhaps more clearly than lofty political rhetoric, that by the mid-1990s it had become Germany's explicit aim to be surrounded by stable market democracies. Although German politicians, especially the Foreign Minister, proclaimed Germany to be the advocate of all of East European countries vis-à-vis the Western institutions, it was by now evident that some countries were more equal than others. In the dispute within the German government about the timing of Nato enlargement, military cooperation played a significant part. By creating bare facts, it underlined the readiness of Germany's East Central European neighbours to take up membership. By bolstering the role of the *Warshaviste* in practice, it rendered it difficult to escape it in rhetoric.

In the six months following the Brussels summit, this rhetoric left unclear what precisely the position of the German government as a whole was. In Kohl's governmental declaration on the summit on 13 January the *Warshaviste* and the *Muscovite* seemed to speak with equal force:

> In the face of the desire for membership from our Eastern neighbours, Nato is confronted with a difficult question. We understand the desire for security and the fears of people in these countries. They stem from tragic experiences in this century. In addition, people in Central and Eastern Europe longed for freedom and democracy during the Cold War... But at the same time there are historically grown fears of isolation or encirclement in Russia. These fears we have to take seriously, too. Nato therefore seeks a comprehensive and deepened partnership with Russia and Ukraine in security-political and military matters.[87]

The Chancellor's admission that Nato was confronted with a difficult question revealed the nature of his government's uncertainty. It clarified that Germany could no longer ignore the security needs of its East Central European neighbours, especially not with vague references to a pan-European security architecture that they regarded as oblivious to their interest. After the Brussels summit had established the perspective for membership, the German uncertainty was no longer about Nato enlargement per se.[88] Within the overall consensus that Nato would enlarge, the uncertainty in Kohl's government now focused on what to do with Russia, and at what time precisely to enlarge. This was the essence of role merger.

With regard to the first point, there was, almost, a consensus on the need to build a special relationship with Russia. What Kohl had called 'comprehensive and deepened integration' was later called 'strategic partnership' by Rühe and 'security partnership' by Kinkel. The genuine confusion within the government's ranks was illustrated by the fact that it remained largely unclear what these 'partnerships' would actually consist of. Neither Germany nor any other Nato country had yet found a way to operationalize the enlargement process with regard to Russia. This had been the weakness of Rühe's concept ever since the London speech in March 1993. Although the proposition to enlarge Nato addressed the security concerns of Germany's immediate eastern neighbours, it left undefined how it would affect those countries that did not join. This was not just a concern about Russia and Ukraine; it also held for Romania and Slovenia, and perhaps most importantly for the Baltic States.

The debate surrounding Nato enlargement ever since 1993 was precisely about this factor, or to put it differently, about the role conflict between the *Warshaviste* and the *Muscovite*. No German politician managed to escape this role conflict completely. Even Volker Rühe, clearly a *Warshaviste par excellence*, was responsive to concerns about Russia. This had formed part of his London speech as much as all his subsequent speeches. The weakness of his enlargement concept, however, was that it had not proposed a clearly thought out, operationalized mechanism through which to attempt a role merger. It was unacceptable because it left unconsidered one of the fundamental roles of German foreign policy culture, namely the *Muscovite*. This was what Kohl's and Kinkel's scepticism was about. For much of 1993, both Kohl and Kinkel had continued to give priority to Russia over East Central Europe. With the emergent strength of *Warshaviste* role expectations, however, they had started to alternate between roles. The Chancellor's defence of the Partnership for Peace programme in the Bundestag can therefore be interpreted as role alternation. It recognized the conflict, testified to uncertainty about how to solve it, and pursued both roles at once.

The first six months of 1994 are significant in this context because they witnessed the gradual emergence of a tender consensus about how to reconcile *Muscovite* and *Warshaviste* priorities. The catchwords of this consensus were 'cooperation' and 'integration': the former with regard to Russia, the latter with regard to East Central Europe. This formula originated from a memorandum drafted by the planning staff of the Foreign Ministry in the spring.[89] Depending on their personal views, ministers differed in their respective treatment of 'integration' and 'co-operation'. Yet the formula served the demonstration of governmental unity rather well. Volker Rühe, recognizing that his apparent neglect of Russia had weakened his stance, explored the concept of 'security co-operation' with Russia in a series of speeches in the spring. In May 1994, he argued:

> If we do not 'export' stability now, we will sooner or later be seized by instability. We therefore have to enforce the concept of the stability transfer, which consists of two core elements: integration and cooperation. Especially in this time of transition it is essential to consider everyone's interests adequately. We have to advance cooperation with Russia as intensively as we prepare the integration of new members into our institutions.[90]

Although Kinkel continued to place even more emphasis on Russia than Rühe did, reiterating the need to support Russian reformers and the danger of excluding Russia from European security affairs, he did not question the basic consensus on enlargement.[91] Much of the German consensus, it is true, was part of a larger Nato charm offensive designed to persuade Russia to participate in the Partnership for Peace programme.

Since 'integration' and 'cooperation' have remained the foundations of Germany's security policy towards the East ever since 1994, it is worth discussing their relationship in more detail. Evidently 'integration' corresponded to the role of the *Warshaviste*, 'cooperation' to the *Muscovite*. Was it possible, however, to solve the role conflict by simply mixing these priorities? In a sense, it was. An intensified cooperation with Russia was likely to reduce Russian fears about Nato enlargement. The very fact that the East Central European countries were admitted to Nato, in turn, would calm their fears about close German–Russian relations. As per usual, the contradictions of German foreign policy would be solved in a both-the-one-and-the-other fashion. On the other hand, however, the strategy of integration and cooperation solved the role conflict in favour of the *Warshaviste*. Not least due to Article 5 of the Nato treaty, Germany would be closer politically and strategically to Poland inside Nato than to Russia outside Nato. In this respect, all mechanisms fostering Nato–Russian cooperation were mere diplomatic decoration. It is therefore true that although 'integration' and 'cooperation' attempted a role merger, the *Warshaviste* became the dominant role in Germany's Eastern policy. The preference of security integration over security cooperation is only reconcilable with Civilian Power, however, because it also incorporates elements of security cooperation.

This reinforces the view that judging Germany's Eastern policies as a whole turns the question of Civilian Power into a question of perspective. From Warsaw, Budapest or Prague, Germany's Nato enlargement policy might have appeared as an exercise in Civilian Power. But from Moscow, it might have appeared threatening, and from Riga, neglectful. Equally, a refusal to promote Nato enlargement might have seemed perfectly compatible with the Civilian Power ideal type from the perspective of Moscow, but from Warsaw, it might not only have appeared neglectful and ignorant, but threatening. As this study has chosen to test the ideal type against German policies towards Poland, Hungary, Slovakia and the Czech Republic, it arrives at the view that Germany did act like a Civilian Power. It is an open question whether one would arrive at the same conclusion when judging German security policies towards the Baltic states.

The carefully crafted consensus of 'integration' and 'cooperation', despite its achievements in masking latent disputes over substance, could not mask repeated disputes over timing. These disagreements erupted with new force in the autumn of 1994 in preparation for the Nato Council meeting in December. Rühe had initiated the dispute when he announced in Warsaw in July that Poland was likely to accede to Nato by the end of the decade.[92] Considering that the Alliance had at this juncture not even decided on the formal mechanisms of enlargement, this was a provocative claim. After the summer break, Rühe renewed his push for rapid progress. At the Nato Defence Ministers' meeting in Spain at the end of September, he demanded that Nato name the candidates for the first round of enlargement soon, and by naming Poland, Hungary, Slovakia and the Czech Republic, let it be known which countries he favoured.[93]

Within a week, Kinkel had publicly dismissed 'those who push for Nato enlargement too quickly' without mentioning Rühe by name, and the German press was full of reports about new rifts between Rühe and Kinkel.[94] Whereas Rühe pushed for a small, rapid enlargement, balanced by close cooperation with Russia, Kinkel favoured accession in the long-term, with more countries in the first round. It is significant to remember that Kinkel's caution was in principle related to timing. It focused on the adverse effects a rushed enlargement could have not only on Russia, but also on those states that were not admitted to Nato, like Bulgaria,

Romania and the Baltic states. This caution was justified. It sometimes seemed from Rühe's utterances on enlargement as though Germany's East consisted only of East Central Europe and Russia. Before an answer to the security of these countries was found, Kinkel argued, enlargement would have to wait.

The inter-ministerial dispute was brought to an end by the Chancellor, who, without revealing on whose side he stood, terminated the argument abruptly in the first week of October. The fact that Germany was only three weeks away from a general election almost definitely played a part in this, as did the publicity of the dispute, which seemed to undermine Kohl's authority. No single factor stands out to explain why Kohl had been quiet for such a long time. Part of it might have been the attempt to place a lid on his Defence Minister's personal ambition, part a reluctance to get caught up by the imbroglio of security policy, part, finally, an attempt to insulate his various close personal contacts, through which he conducted much of his diplomacy, from the disputes over practical policy. The coalition agreement of the CDU/CSU/FDP, negotiated after the October 1994 election, is so cautiously phrased that one may interpret it as a victory of Kinkel over Rühe. The governing parties, one reads there, agree to pursue 'the incremental enlargement of Nato, which has to be seen in close relation with the enlargement of the European Union and the WEU'. In addition, 'integration and cooperation' have to complement one another 'so that no new dividing lines emerge'.[95] No time-frame is envisaged, no group of countries named.

In the event, the commitment to the balancing of integration and cooperation resulted in active German support for the further institutionalization of the CSCE and its transformation into the OSCE, which became one of Germany's main priorities in the last months of 1994. By this time, however, the external environment of Germany's enlargement policy had changed considerably, because the Clinton Administration had placed the United States at the forefront of the process. As early as February 1994, the new American Defence Minister William Perry had stated at a conference in Munich that 'Partnership for Peace' would eventually lead to Nato enlargement – the first time a high ranking member of the Administration had been so unequivocal about the topic.[96] In the summer of 1994, the American ambassador to Bonn, Richard Holbrooke, was recalled to the State Department to prepare enlargement with a specially constituted task force. It is noteworthy that with Holbrooke's transfer to the State Department, we can identify with reasonable certainty the moment in the enlargement process when leadership changed from Germany to the United States. Testimony to this was a Clinton speech in July 1994. To the surprise of his Alliance partners, the American President announced on a visit to Warsaw that enlargement was no longer a question of 'whether', but of 'how' and 'when'.[97] Although evidence is fragmentary, we can assume that this was a reaction to the individual Partnership for Peace agreement which Nato had negotiated with Russia at the end of June. 'Integration' could be advanced if 'cooperation' succeeded.

Clinton's announcement was a milestone in the enlargement process because it indicated that the United States had by now taken the initiative. Pushed from within by Richard Holbrooke's dynamism in the State Department, the Clinton Administration soon started irritating its European partners with its activism. By November, Nato's European members, including Germany, voiced concern about American impatience on the subject. A letter by Germany's ambassador to Nato, Hermann von Richthofen, was leaked to the press, suggesting that the unrestrained American push for enlargement caused great damage to the Alliance.[98] It seemed that within less than 12 months, the roles of Germany and the United States had changed completely. Because of deep rifts over enlargement and over the Bosnian war, Nato had plunged into its worst crisis since the early 1980s.

In a sense, Germany could relax its campaign for enlargement precisely because the United States had now taken over the torch. This was particularly true for Volker Rühe, who had fought more vigorously for enlargement than any other Nato official, and who could now afford to share the responsibility for the project with others. Chief among those were the members of the Clinton Administration, especially Richard Holbrooke. But the American leadership had also persuaded the British government to espouse the project, if not for East Central Europe, or for Germany, or for nationally calculated reasons, then at least for the sake of the special relationship with the United States. France had also shed its earlier hesitancy in favour of tentative support for enlargement, not least because it was difficult to be out of touch with Germany for so long over Eastern Europe. That the general mood had shifted towards enlargement manifested itself in the decision of the Nato Council in December to commission the Nato administration with drafting a study on the 'how' and 'when' of enlargement, to be presented in the second half of 1995.

At the CSCE summit in Budapest in the first week of December, Kohl mediated between Clinton and Yeltsin, who presented himself as unusually irate about the prospect of enlargement. Germany could now be popular with everyone: with Russia because it appeared restrained on

enlargement, with Poland because it was seen as an enlargement promoter, with the United States because it remained the loyal ally, and
with France because it emphasized the WEU and the CSCE. Germany
could hide behind the more forcefully promoted American interests,
which were in fact its own, though with different nuances. Hiding
behind American diplomacy took the edge off German enlargement
policy. It concealed the latent role conflict between the *Muscovite* and
Warshaviste elements of German foreign policy culture, which had
earlier been in evident conflict. In summary, then, 1994 was the year
of decision in the process of Nato enlargement.

Nato enlargement and German foreign policy culture

Considering how contested Nato enlargement was within Germany's
political establishment, including the government and the major
governing party, one wonders about the reasons for its success. Was it
merely an outcome of the constellation of officials who were in the right
place at the right time? Or was it also affected by the longer trends in
Germany's foreign policy culture, which ultimately disposed Germany
towards the role of the *Warshaviste*? We have already seen that the
constellation of policy makers originally in favour of enlargement was
astonishingly small. In Germany, these were: above all, Volker Rühe,
Ulrich Weisser, head of the planning staff at the Defence Ministry,
Karsten Voigt, the foreign policy spokesmen of the SPD Bundestag
caucus, and Friedbert Pflüger, who, though by no means a senior parlia-
mentarian, was one of the CDU's Young Turks and vociferous on the
topic in his function as chairman of the Polish–German Society in Bonn.

At the Nato headquarters, the most influential figure was Secretary-
General Manfred Wörner, assisted by his policy adviser Klaus Scharioth
and supported by one of Wörner's deputies, the German diplomat Gebhard von Moltke. In the United States, Richard Holbrooke was the main
supporter of enlargement, assisted by the public relations talents of
Senator Richard Lugar. Interestingly, Holbrooke had been Ambassador
to Bonn until the middle of 1994 and therefore knew the German
officials well; he achieved the Administration's turnaround on enlargement, but then left the project in 1995 because of his involvement in
the Bosnian peace process.[99]

This mix of early supporters had a distinctly German flavour. By late
1993 one would have been very hard-pressed to find a promoter of
enlargement in Nato who was neither German nor based in Germany,
a fact that led Stephen Szabo to conclude that Nato enlargement was a

project *made in Germany.*[100] In this light one might doubt James Gold-geier's analysis, according to which Nato enlargement was almost exclusively a project of the Clinton Administration even at this early stage.[101] While the public relations genius of the Clinton Administration, in conjunction with the sheer weight of the United States within the Atlantic Alliance, were decisive at a later stage in convincing both a sceptical domestic audience in the United States and recalcitrant partners in the Atlantic Alliance, the initial push was a German one.

The small number of initial supporters suggests that Nato enlargement was affected by historical circumstance and personal relationships. But Germany's foreign policy culture shaped the debate on Nato enlargement and delimited its boundaries. Though these boundaries were far wider than those on EU enlargement, they existed nevertheless and affected the way German policy makers reasoned, both with one another and with those outside Germany. In the following section we consider this debate, which stretched for the better part of four years, and which cut across the dividing lines between political parties, government and opposition, executive and legislature. We will see that, although the debate was blurred, the CDU/CSU was a more natural *Atlanticist* and therefore found the adoption of the new role of the *Warshaviste* easier.

This is not to say that the role of the *Warshaviste* was uncontested in the CDU. As we have seen, its foreign policy spokesman in the Bundestag, Karl Lamers, was sceptical about enlargement on *Gaullist* grounds. The chairman of the foreign affairs committee, Karl-Heinz Hornhues, had reservations about the effects of enlargement on Russia, and in this respect, was close to the Chancellor. It is significant for the argument on foreign policy culture that the *Muscovite* persuasion was strong even in the political party that came to be most closely associated with the *Warshaviste*. Incidentally, this was less true for Friedbert Pflüger. Though hesitant in the very beginning, Pflüger came to argue more forcefully than anyone else in favour of enlargement from the end of 1993, often reiterating the threat perceptions that existed in Poland. Though these different perspectives are remarkable because they expose a considerable variety within the CDU, they are also remarkable because they delineate the boundaries of the debate.

Most importantly, few contributions advocated the renationalization of German security policy, but instead supported the concept of security integration. Although the *Gaullists* preferred this to occur in a Europeanized context, they did not question the principle as such. Furthermore, no contribution advocated enlargement as directed against Russia. Though Pflüger evoked the danger of Russian instability more readily than others, he too shared the conviction that cooperative security measures with Russia were imperative. This leads to the observation that, within the CDU, Civilian Power principles affected the debate on enlargement strongly. First, enlargement was not portrayed as the extension of a military alliance but as a transfer of stability. Secondly, the doubts expressed questioned not whether Germany adhered too much to Civilian Power principles, but whether it adhered to them too little. Thus, the Chancellor only supported enlargement when he had convinced himself that it did not undermine cooperative security relations with Russia.

It would also be misleading to argue that the dividing lines on Nato enlargement ran between government and opposition. Some SPD foreign policy experts supported enlargement from a very early stage. Most important among these was Karsten Voigt, the party's foreign policy spokesman in the Bundestag, who had called for a future enlargement as early as February 1992.[102] If anything Voigt's role in the debate has been neglected in the present discussion. Until the first half of 1994, Voigt was Rühe's only major ally on Germany's political scene. By lending enlargement his timely and unequivocal support, Voigt not only pressurized his own party – which was resistant – but also the government. Although Voigt's position was elevated to greater prominence when he was elected as the chairman of the North Atlantic Assembly – the Nato parliamentarians' club – one should not underestimate his significance in the early period. After the election in 1994, Voigt was supported by Günther Verheugen, another foreign policy expert, and by Rudolf Scharping, who was the SPD's party leader and chancellor candidate, and became its parliamentary leader in November 1994.

The proponents of enlargement were isolated within the SPD for a long time. Specifically, one can identify three lines of opposition. The first was proposed by the veteran foreign policy expert Egon Bahr, and objected to enlargement because this was set to tie Germany's hands. Without proposing equidistance between Russia and the United States, Bahr advocated a more independent, cooperative German security policy.[103] Incidentally, this argument was not just a fringe view inside the SPD, but also received some support from the national-conservatives in the CDU. It testified to the consensus around Germany's foreign policy culture that these fringe views never entered the mainstream policies of either party. Secondly, SPD politicians objected to Nato enlargement on *Muscovite* grounds. This promoted a stronger focus on Moscow, and, in the tradition of the Helsinki process, cooperative security. This view was not directed against Nato as such, but against Nato's exclusiveness. For the continent as a whole, a security architecture had to be constructed, which encompassed the eastern neighbours and especially Russia. This view was also not exclusive to the SPD. It was closely associated with Hans- Dietrich Genscher and the Genscherist legacy in the Foreign Ministry and, as we have seen, it commanded considerable support in the CDU too.

Thirdly, however, there existed a strand of SPD opposition that was directed against Nato enlargement not out of consideration for Russia, but out of hostility towards Nato. This strand, which belonged to the party's left and was also prominent with the Greens, objected to Nato out of a long-standing ideological opposition to Nato in general, and the role of the United States in Europe in particular.[104] Much of this emanated from the peace movement of the early 1980s, and, in the mid-1990s, seemed strangely antiquated. 'The source of left- wing opposition to Nato enlargement', Karsten Voigt said in an interview with the author, 'is the complete inability to come to terms with the changes since 1989/90. The German left wing has neither understood the changes to the ideological climate, nor the changes to Nato, nor the changes Germany has undergone and will have to undergo in the future.'[105]

We may recall from Chapter 1 that the view of foreign policy culture inherent in our argument is a political one. This means that culture has to be contested and compromised before it is legitimated. It also means that culture is related to the formal institutions of government, and therefore to political power. The discussion in this chapter elucidates this argument. Above all, those who favoured the renationalization of German security policy were so far removed from the levers of power in their respective parties that their opinions were irrelevant for practical policy. If anything, they served as additional arguments to push ahead with enlargement in order to make renationalization impossible. Moreover, because of opposition from the Greens and the party's left wing, an SPD-led government would have had to struggle to elevate Nato to the prime mechanism of a European security order. Karsten Voigt recalled in an interview with the author that the CDU/CSU managed this 'in a cool and calculated way', and that the SPD would have found the turnaround much more difficult.[106] It follows that Nato enlargement was critically affected by the outcome of the Bundestag elections in December 1990. Although the outcome of the elections in 1994 was important, too, leadership on the enlargement issue had already been assumed by the United States, and we can at least assume that this would have forced an SPD-led government to adjust.

A consensus on enlargement emerged within Germany after the Clinton Administration had placed itself at the head of the enlargement train in the second half of 1994. This was true for the government and the governing parties, but it was also true for large parts of the SPD and the 'mainstream' wing of the Greens. This convergence was partly a grudging acceptance of the inevitable. But partly, it was also a conscious decision by the centre-left to earn foreign policy respectability. One of the engineers of this turnaround was Günther Verheugen. 'Kohl had said before the elections in 1994 that no social-democratic party wanted the SPD to win in Germany,' Verheugen recalled in a conversation with the author, 'and regardless of whether or not he was right, this undermined us and cost us a number of votes.'[107] In the 1998 Bundestag debate on the ratification of the new, extended version of the North Atlantic Treaty, Verheugen said:

> Whoever governs or wants to govern in Germany must never forget that no European country depends on the trust of its neighbours as much as Germany. For our country, it is particularly true that its foreign policy has to be reliable and predictable. A *national consensus* in the fundamental questions of our foreign policy orientation is therefore not only enormously important for domestic politics, but also an enormous achievement in foreign policy.[108]

When the votes were cast, the SPD voted in favour. The Greens either abstained or partly voted in favour, too: out of 620 votes, 553 were ayes, 37 noes, and 30 abstentions.[109] Nato enlargement and the role of the *Warshaviste* had entered German foreign policy culture as a matter of virtual consensus.

Now, in many respects the change of position on the centre left was not only an attempt to gain electoral respectability. It was also the attempt to convince itself, as the governing parties had successfully demonstrated, that the mechanisms of Nato enlargement did not contradict the Civilian Power ethos, that the roles of *Muscovite* and *Warshaviste* could be reconciled and that cooperation and integration did not contradict one another. But it illustrates nevertheless that foreign policy culture is affected by power and the formal institutions of government. The power of government had established the *Warshaviste* as a new element of Germany's foreign policy culture. Therefore, just as the SPD had swung around to support Western integration in the late 1950s and the CDU had come to advocate Ostpolitik in the late 1970s, the SPD now adjusted its foreign policy in order to stay in line with the thrust of Germany's foreign policy culture.

Enacting role merger

If the last months of 1993 had heightened fears in East Central Europe about the future of Russian foreign policy, the war in Chechnya, which broke out in December 1994, had a similar effect. These fears were exacerbated by Yeltsin's threat at the OSCE summit in Budapest in December 1994 that if Nato enlarged, a 'Cold Peace' would follow the Cold War.[110] The first months of 1995 were thus marked by common deliberations about how the impending enlargement could be made palatable to Russia. Volker Rühe belonged to those who first spoke of a legal structure for the new relationship between Nato and Russia; William Perry added the idea of a standing consultative commission.[111] This became especially important as Russian recalcitrance to Nato enlargement increased and as it became even clearer than before that Poland was the peg on which Russia's opposition to Nato enlargement hung.[112]

In principle, the year 1995 brought little progress. The hopes, nurtured in both Germany and the United States, that Russia would accept enlargement if one came to an agreement about a new security relationship, proved ill-founded. In May, the German foreign policy scene was in considerable disarray over a rumour that President Clinton had offered Nato membership to Russia.[113] Though it was never entirely clear whether this had actually been an American offer, it is noteworthy that all members of the German government objected to it on principle. Kinkel noted cautiously that 'in this respect, most Nato states do not share the opinion of the United States'; his junior minister Werner Hoyer warned that 'one cannot expect too much of the states in Central and Eastern Europe,' adding that 'Germany is the advocate of the legitimate security interests of its neighbours.'[114] It seemed from these reactions, as indeed from much of the period under discussion, that Bonn could afford to play whatever card Washington kept close to its chest. Bonn appeared to push enlargement when Washington followed its 'Russia first' instincts; when Washington pushed the enlargement processes, Bonn warned that Moscow must not be alienated.

In September 1995, Nato's new Secretary-General Willy Claes presented the Nato study charged with exploring the 'why' and 'how' of enlargement. Justifying Nato's opening with the need for stability, the study proposed that already existing European institutions be incorporated in a larger security framework, involving both integration and cooperation. Once the study had been approved by the Nato Council in December 1995, the Alliance had answered the three most important questions surrounding enlargement: 'whether', 'why' and 'how'. At the same time, it established a moratorium on decision making for 1996, for fear that enlargement would be unduly politicized in the Russian and American presidential elections.

Although the debate on enlargement continued throughout 1996, it witnessed few new arguments: the East Central European countries jostled, Russia resisted and Nato countries endeavoured to appease both sides. The debate only opened anew in late 1996 and the first half of 1997, now not so much about 'when' – as it became clear that the decisive meeting would be in June 1997 – but about 'who'. Before jumping to that debate, however, it is worth looking at German policies throughout 1995, in particular with regard to a topic which has been neglected so far, namely the relationship between the EU and Nato enlargement. This relationship points to three arguments about the Civilian Power nature of Germany's eastward policies.

That the two enlargement processes were intrinsically related had been a German argument ever since Nato enlargement was first proposed. We may recall from Chapter 4 that Volker Rühe had been one of the first German politicians to criticize the government's deepening–widening atrophy in 1992. Then, in 1993, Rühe argued that EU enlargement by itself was insufficient for the stabilization of East Central Europe and had to be complemented by the enlargement of Nato. This argument in itself elucidates the Civilian Power ethos of German policies towards East Central Europe. The objective was the stabilization of Germany's eastern neighbours; the instrument was the extension of the Western institutions. The extension of Nato was justified as a transfer of stability, was only pursued when EU enlargement appeared insufficient and was balanced by a reinforced cooperation with Russia. This argument was supplemented by the view that it would be difficult to prevent future members of the European Union from becoming members of Nato, too. Over the following years, German policy makers expressed this in the catchphrase that 'there must not be zones of different security' in the EU. This argument illustrates that Civilian Powers cannot afford to ignore matters of military security, but have to find a cooperative, if not collective, mechanism for managing it.

The arguments of 'stability transfer' and 'one zone of security' were directed at Russia and the *Muscovite* audience in Germany and other Nato countries. Their purpose was to underline the Civilian Power nature of Nato's eastward enlargement. They were complemented by the argument – directed at opponents within Nato itself – that Germany's eastern border must not be the eastern border of the EU and Nato. As the following quotation from one of Helmut Kohl's speeches in February 1994 illustrates, this was at times phrased in undiplomatically plain language:

> The German–Polish border must not permanently be the Eastern border of Nato and the European Union. Whoever sees this differently has to know he would pre-programme conflicts. This conviction is an elementary component of German policy.[115]

Earlier in this study, this 'elementary component of German policy' has been described as a *raison d'état*, perceived as fundamental for the maintenance of freedom, security and prosperity in Germany itself.

The civilianization of East Central Europe, then, was not philanthropic, it was a basic German interest. As such it did not contradict Civilian Power. We noted in Chapter 1 that it would be false to assume that Civilian Powers have no interests, only ideals, and we have seen in the discussion of Germany's EU enlargement policy that Maull's ideal type leaves considerable room for the interpretation and application of the Civilian Power ethos, including the pursuit of more narrowly defined national interests. The term 'national interest' is thus not necessarily incompatible with Civilian Power policies. The question is not whether a policy is in the national interest, but whether it is compatible with the Civilian Power ideal type.

The three basic arguments in favour of enlargement – stability transfer, one security zone, national interest – had been made by 1995; although they were repeated, they no longer moved the debate. In contrast, the discussion now moved on to the question of timing, including the question of whether the two enlargement processes would have to occur concomitantly. In this discussion, Volker Rühe repeated his old argument that future EU members had to be members of Nato, that the two enlargement processes therefore stood in 'an inseparable, logical relation to one another', and that Nato enlargement should precede EU enlargement because it was easier to implement.[116] Klaus Kinkel argued along similar lines, pointing out that the two enlargement processes had to be part of a coherent concept. He warned, however – implicitly against Rühe – that they could 'not be achieved through the stroke of a pen', but had to be longer-term processes.[117]

This discussion was both provoked and enriched by a publication of the Rand Corporation, an American think-tank, which analysed the different methods of enlargement.[118] Nato could either enlarge concomitantly with the EU, or in reaction to instability in Russia, or on its own terms, the Rand authors argued. Whereas the first option would leave the timing to the Europeans, the second option would leave it to the Russians. Only the third option would allow the United States to determine the timing, and therefore also the modalities, of its security commitment to East Central Europe. Bearing in mind that the Clinton Administration did in the event press for accession as early as June 1997, it seems reasonable to assume that it took at least some cues from the Rand study.

The Rand study suggested that Washington was now by and large in charge of the process, leaving Bonn to concentrate on other matters. Secondly, it established that Nato would enlarge much earlier than the European Union. Volker Rühe was therefore not mistaken when he reiterated his call for enlargement 'before the end of the century'.[119] Precisely because Nato enlargement now seemed to be on track, a remark by the Chancellor prior to his visit to Poland in July 1995 caused noticeable confusion. Kohl, perhaps without bad intent, had said that Nato and EU enlargement could not be separated. In Poland this was received with concern because it was interpreted as a formal link, a *Junktim*, established to delay the enlargement processes.[120] Perhaps it was due to this dramatic prologue that Kohl's visit to Poland became a resounding success. Speaking in front of the Sejm, the lower house of the Polish parliament, Kohl announced that he hoped to see Poland inside the EU and Nato by the year 2000.[121] Of course, this was precisely what his audience wanted to hear. Equally, it was not entirely truthful, at least not with regard to the European Union. And eventually, Kohl's promise caused bad blood, because it was not kept. But at the time his words established the grand declaration for which Poland – as much as Hungary and the Czech Republic – had been waiting. It signalized to East Central Europe as much as to Western Europe that Germany stood by its unequivocal support for both enlargements.

Although 1996 was no year of decision, it produced three results that were significant for the enlargement process as a whole. The first was that Slovakia's accession to Nato, or, for that matter, the European Union, seemed increasingly improbable. The second was that it initiated the debate on the financial costs of enlargement. Whereas this became a source of controversy for the domestic debate in the United States over the following months, German policy makers were silent on the issue.

This suggests that the question of finance was seen as a potential obstacle to enlargement, which, for fear that it could derail the process, was best discussed in private or after enlargement had been formally agreed upon. Thirdly, President Clinton announced in an election speech – incidentally in the Polish-American hometown of Detroit – that he hoped Nato would enlarge by the summer of 1999.[122] This implied that invitations to the new members would be issued by the summer of 1997.

As indicated above, German diplomacy could focus on making Nato enlargement palatable to Russia in 1996 and 1997 precisely because the key decisions on enlargement had been taken. Kohl and Kinkel, especially, slipped into the role of the *Muscovite* as soon as the substance of their policies had favoured the *Warshaviste*. This *Muscovite* diplomatic activity took three forms in particular. The first was an increased frequency of meetings. Kinkel met the new Russian Foreign Minister Yevgeni Primakov ten times in 1996 alone. Kohl visited Russia seven times in 1996 and 1997. These visits seemed to indicate that German priorities immediately prior to enlargement lay with Russia. This is true, yet only one part of the story. Diplomatic activity concealed that the essence of Germany's security policy towards Eastern Europe consisted of Nato enlargement. Although the personalized diplomacy between Kohl and Yeltsin, Kinkel and Primakov facilitated Germany's objective of balancing integration with cooperation, Germany's security relationship with East Central Europe had become closer than that with Russia.

Secondly, Germany was instrumental in negotiating the new Russian security partnership with Nato. In the summer of 1996, it had emerged that Russia would accept such a partnership although it continued to object vehemently to Nato enlargement. It was not least a German achievement that the Nato Council decided in December 1996 to equip the new Secretary-General Javier Solana with a mandate to negotiate the partnership. The United States, in particular, had been reluctant to consent to this. As the Secretary-General was seen as a more acceptable negotiating partner to Moscow than any national representative, however, Kinkel had insisted on his nomination. In the months between the December 1996 Council and the conclusions of negotiations in May, Kinkel and the German Foreign Ministry were centrally involved in the drafting of the Nato–Russia Charter. This was helped by the return of Klaus Scharioth, previously at the Nato headquarters, to head the Nato division in the German Foreign Ministry, and by the influence of Gebhard von Moltke, who was charged with the drafting of the document in Nato's headquarters. Partly due to Scharioth's return, partly because the process had now moved into the realm of diplomacy, the Foreign Ministry managed to retrieve from the Defence Ministry the authority over Germany's enlargement policy.

Thirdly, Germany interceded with its Western partners on Russia's behalf. Despite tremendous doubts in many member states, Russia acceded to the Council of Europe in February 1996, supported by Germany. Although the Russian economy was actually shrinking, Russia acceded to the so-called G7 club of the largest industrialized nations, again as a result of German lobbying. A cooperation agreement between Russia and the European Union came into force in February 1996, and three months later, the EU decided on an 'action plan' that intensified cooperation with Russia even further. At the same time, we must not forget that German financial aid to Russia had been and continued to be substantial. According to one calculation, Germany had already paid over 90 billion dollars to Russia by the time the Russian troops had left Germany.[123]

The debate over Nato enlargement that mushroomed in Germany in the first half of 1997 was a bifurcated one. It was conducted by scholars and publicists evaluating the pros and cons of enlargement on the one hand, and the community of policy makers pondering about which countries should accede on the other. That this was so was unfortunate in many respects. A real debate over enlargement would have benefited the arena of politics. But this should have occurred in 1993 and 1994, not in the first half of 1997. At this juncture, all important decisions had already been taken and the debate in the arena of published opinion seemed strangely removed from the arena of decision making. Interestingly, no clear German negotiating position for who should be included in the first wave of enlargement existed in early 1997. Germany's position was delineated by a minimum (namely Poland, the Czech Republic and Hungary) and a maximum (which also included Slovenia and Romania). This negotiating position was therefore clear on two counts: it included Poland, the Czech Republic and Hungary, and excluded the Baltic states. Both have important ramifications for the evaluation of Germany's enlargement policy against the background of Civilian Power.

The debate on which countries should be included in the first round of enlargement sheds a rather different light on Germany's exercise of Civilian Power. Germany had never promised that it would support the Baltic States' accession to Nato in the first round of enlargement. There were valid reasons for this. Some Baltic states had border disputes with Russia, for instance. Others contained sizeable proportions of Russian minorities. Not all issues related to these minorities – citizenship, language, education – had yet been solved. Enlargement would thus be premature. But these were not the real reasons against the Baltic states' accession to Nato. The real reason was that their accession was completely unacceptable to Russia, and that Nato knew this and accepted it. This sheds a different light on the arguments put forward by the proponents of enlargement towards East Central Europe, especially by Volker Rühe. Enlargement, Rühe had always said, was not directed against Russia but was a transfer of stability. If this was so, no objection should have prevented enlargement from including the Baltic states, since they, because of their exposed position, were much more in need of the stability provided by Nato membership. Rühe had also reiterated ad infinitum, and had been echoed by Kinkel and Kohl in this, that the choice of alliance was the autonomous decision of any state, and that Russia could not be granted a veto over it. If this was true for Poland, why was it not true for the Baltic states? Furthermore, Rühe, as much as the other members of the German government, had claimed that no 'zones of different security' must exist within the European Union. By early 1997 at the very latest, however, it was clear that Estonia had performed miraculously in the first phase of administrative and economic transformation, and was well qualified to join the EU in its first round of enlargement. Curiously, different zones of security no longer seemed an insurmountable problem.

None of these arguments contradicts the view that German policies towards East Central Europe were those of a Civilian Power. A sensible policy vis-à-vis Poland does not become less sensible because it is not pursued vis-à-vis Estonia, too. But the arguments do reinforce the view that deciding on whether or not Germany acted like a Civilian Power is a question of perspective. At times even a Civilian Power has to choose from a complex set of ideals and interests. In its policies towards East Central Europe, the ideals and interests of German Civilian Power coincided. In its policies towards the Baltics, they did not. For the inclusion of the Baltics in the first round of enlargement would have provoked an even fiercer Russian resistance, jeopardizing enlargement towards East Central Europe and rendering a close security relationship with Russia all but impossible. In the case of the Baltics, therefore, Civilian Power ideals failed against Civilian Power interests. Although this does not contradict the overall argument, it is a reminder that this is an imperfect world where all states, even Civilian Powers, face difficult choices. Especially because Civilian Powers have a highly normative approach to foreign policy, this reminder can be a frustrating one.

The complexity of choices is also illustrated by German policies to-wards Slovenia and Romania in the period immediately prior to enlarge-ment. Volker Rühe had argued in the autumn of 1996 that he preferred a small enlargement, evidently because this would have a better chance of meeting the approval of both Russia and the American Senate. Though Rühe did not specify what a small enlargement meant, it was assumed that it included only Poland, Hungary and the Czech Republic. In the first half of 1997, however, Slovenia and Romania became increasingly popular candidates. Romania's case was strengthened by the reform measures introduced by the Ciorbea government, by a vigorous diplo-matic campaign in Western capitals and by support from European countries, especially Italy and France.[124] In addition, Hungary sup-ported Romania's accession, not only for foreign policy reasons, but also because it expected assurances over the Hungarian minority in Romania. Although Romania's application to the Nato cause was followed with benevolence in Bonn, however, the German government was never a real supporter of Romanian accession in the first round of enlargement.

This was at least partly different with respect to Slovenia, whose membership enjoyed popularity especially in the German Foreign Office.[125] There were a number of reasons why Slovenia became a popular candidate. The speed of transformation was one. Geography was another, because Slovenia could establish a Nato bridge to Hungary, which, because of Austria's neutrality, would otherwise be an island inside Nato territory. The radiation of Nato stability into the Balkans was a further reason, put forward by the Foreign Ministry in particular. Since the Balkans were the most unstable region in Europe even after the Dayton peace agreement, this seemed a sensible argument. Yet Roma-nia's and Slovenia's accession in the first round was unfeasible because of the difficult situation of the Baltics. It had hitherto been Bonn's, especially Rühe's, position that enlargement would be a continuous process that could include the Baltics in the second wave. By leaving out a likely candidate like Slovenia, the Baltics would be reassured that they, too, would be considered in a future round of enlargement. In the event, therefore, Bonn was agnostic about Slovenia. Though the Foreign Ministry would have liked to include it in the first round, the Defence Ministry objected, as did the Chancellery.

This echoes the tendency in Bonn's policies, already observed in Chapter 4, to stake its hopes on the *process* of enlargement. Often the tensions of its policies only seemed soluble through the passage of time. At times, this worked. The rapid economic progress of the East Central

European countries, for instance, reduced the tensions between deepening and widening in Bonn's EU enlargement policy. But at other times it failed, as it did, for instance, in the Amsterdam treaty's institutional provisions. In Bonn's Nato enlargement policy, a similar approach can be observed. The first steps of the process of security integration were regarded as far more significant than a clear idea of where the process would lead. To recall Volker Rühe's London speech: 'We cannot afford to postpone the necessary decisions until perfect plans for a new Europe have been devised.'[126] This frequently led to outright contradictions in Bonn's policies. What Bonn really hoped for, and needed, for a successful and finite role merger were modified role expectations from Russia, no longer objecting to the security integration between Nato and East Central Europe. Bonn needed Moscow to accept the *Warshaviste* in the same way that it needed Paris to accept the *integration widener*. This hope was not completely unfounded. There were plenty of voices in Russia who accepted Nato enlargement. But hoping for the future could not always solve the contradictions of the present.

The final part of the story is quickly told. Javier Solana returned from Moscow with an agreement on the Nato-Russia Act on 15 May 1997. It was signed in Paris 12 days later, and was followed by intense speculation about whether the Nato summit in Madrid in the beginning of July would invite three or five countries for membership. Clinton's position was fixed on a small enlargement. This was initially supported by Kohl. As it transpired, however, that eight European Nato allies were in favour of a five-country enlargement, Kohl backtracked from his initial position. Indeed, he brokered the crucial deal between Clinton and Chirac at the Nato summit in Madrid on 8 July, while Kinkel phrased parts of the final communiqué in person. The communiqué invited only Poland, Hungary and the Czech Republic, but portrayed a future enlargement as likely, specifically mentioning Romania, Slovenia and the Baltic states. Although the destination of the enlargement train remained unclear, it had now left the station. On 12 March 1999, Poland, Hungary and the Czech Republic became members of the Atlantic Alliance.

Conclusion

German security policy after 1990 was fundamentally shaped by the modalities of unification, which established *Atlanticism* as the predominant role in Germany's foreign policy culture. If anything, the severity of the tensions that riddled the Atlantic Alliance in the period under discussion have been underplayed in the discussion so far, not just over Nato enlargement, but especially over Yugoslavia. It is not churlish to argue that, had the United States not committed itself to Europe through the modalities of German unification, these tensions would have confronted Nato with the real danger of break-up. That this did not happen influenced European security at large, and Germany's Eastward security policies in particular. It contributed to the compelling logic that underscored the relationship between the *Warshaviste* and the *Atlanticist* and established that Germany's Eastern security policy became the politics of Nato enlargement.

All roles affecting German policy – *Warshaviste, Atlanticist, Muscovite, Gaullist* – were compatible with the Civilian Power ideal type. Though some of these roles conflicted, Germany did not contradict the principles of Civilian Power. In particular with regard to the changes that Nato underwent after 1990, this is an important point. Since Nato manages the security of its members collectively, and the security relationship with non-members cooperatively, it has been interpreted as compatible with Civilian Power. It follows that Germany's Nato enlargement policies were also compatible. This view is reinforced by the fact that enlargement was interpreted as a 'transfer of stability'. It is also reinforced by the fact that the role conflict between *Muscovite* and *Warshaviste* forced German policy makers to devise a role merger between 'integration' and 'cooperation', and thereby approximate the Civilian Power ideal type more closely.

Nato enlargement, in contrast to EU enlargement, was driven by a small number of officials, especially in its initial stages. Personal relationships and constellations of interests were more significant than underlying social and economic forces. Athough this reflects the nature of security policy, it also reflects the fragile consensus that existed on Nato enlargement, especially in Germany, in contrast to the enlargement of the European Union. Although German foreign policy culture provided the parameters and limitations of the debate, it did not make Nato enlargement inevitable.

Finally, judging to what extent Germany exercised Civilian Power is in large part a question of perspective. Germany's tender love and care towards its eastern neighbours was not matched by equal consideration for the rest of Eastern Europe. In Volker Rühe's case, especially, one was sometimes left wondering whether any countries apart from Poland and Russia mattered for his conception of Germany's Eastern policies. What many have accused him of, the exclusion of Russia from European security, seems unjustified. Russia played as important a part for Rühe's conception as early as 1993, though the weakness of his original idea was to propose an action plan for enlargement with East Central Europe, while thinking more conceptually about cooperation with Russia. What would happen to the other countries, to the Baltics and the Balkans especially, however, received insufficient attention. Particularly if one recalls that the Partnership for Peace programme had not formed part of Rühe's initial proposal, one can question whether Rühe had really understood the implications of his proposal for Eastern Europe as a whole.

This argument could, of course, be countered by suggesting that Nato enlargement, like EU enlargement, is a process that could potentially involve all East European countries. This seemed a valid argument, especially when by 1997 a number of realistic applicants were impatient to accede. But the dynamic nature of the process had not been identified by Rühe's initial speeches. It is edifying to conclude with Günther Verheugen's words: 'Nato enlargement is an essential step for Germany and for Europe. But I do not think that anyone knows where it will lead us in the future.'[127]

Conclusion

By September 1998 the Western integration of the East Central European countries, with the exception of Slovakia, was in principle a decided matter. Although Nato enlargement was more specified than EU enlargement in terms of the timing and conditions of accession, both enlargement processes had, in principle, become irrevocable. The velocity with which Western integration had occurred was breathtaking if one remembered 1989–90. The economic turmoil and hyperinflation in Poland in the early 1990s, for instance, suggested a Romanian or Bulgarian future as more likely for the decade to come than the path Poland eventually took. And although the Czech Republic and Hungary enjoyed more stable economic conditions, we must not forget that their average per capita income was equally small compared to that of the EU, and that the transformation from a command to a market economy was no easy ride for them, either. After the Second World War, it had taken ten to twelve years for Western Europe's political economy and military security to settle. In this light the ten to twelve years that it took to extend the principles of Western integration eastwards after the watershed of 1989–90 do not seem extraordinarily long.

Of course, this was above all the achievement of the East Central European countries. But in many respects, it was also a success for German Civilian Power. As we have seen, German policy makers pushed the two enlargement processes in their crucial stages, that is in 1993 and early 1994 for Nato, and throughout 1994 and in late 1995 for the European Union. We have been at pains to emphasize that the coalition of interests pressing for enlargement went beyond Germany. Especially in the early stages, for instance, the Commission appears to have been highly influential in the enlargement of the EU. Even though it was for long common to argue that French policy makers opposed EU enlargement, we have tried to argue that, on the contrary, the key for the success of German policy lay in its gathering support for its Eastern policies from its Western partners. Equally, Nato enlargement was crucially supported and advanced by American diplomatic initiative (without which it could not have succeeded), yet only, as we have seen, once the United States was convinced by the merits of enlargement – which in the beginning they were not. The Western integration of East Central Europe elevated the relations between Germany and its Eastern partners to a new status and resulted in the creation of a new order for the international politics of Europe, nothing more and nothing less. In its pooling of nation-state sovereignty, in the creation of lasting supranational institutions, in the new relationship between large and small European states, in the intimate link between domestic and foreign policy and in its dynamic nature, the historic novelty of this pan-European order was a dramatic one.

Using the term historic, however, reveals a problem. The present study was written about processes that, for all intents and purposes, were still ongoing at the time of writing. Not only was the author not able to base his judgement on archives, he also had to describe the vastness of the historical dimension without a historian's perspective. We have tried to compensate for the lack of historical perspective by adding different geographic angles. Things looked different from Germany than from Britain, and they looked different from Poland altogether. Yet the temporal proximity to events might also have had advantages. It is hard to reconstruct the mood of the time decades after, and we have therefore paid particular attention to this aspect: the concentration on the Soviet Union in 1990–91, the significance of EMU for all other aspects of integration, the importance of Franco-German cooperation for EU enlargement, Volker Rühe's isolation in 1993 and the ramifications of the Yugoslav conflict for the atmosphere of the Atlantic Alliance as a whole. In addition, the Western integration of East Central Europe might in retrospect be interpreted as a rather smooth and logical process. We have therefore also been at pains to point out the wrestling and jostling, the contradictions and compromises that were involved: between countries, within countries, within governments and within political parties. From afar one is tempted to see only the spires of history – and might therefore fall for an optical illusion. 'Time', as W. H. Auden put it, 'will say nothing but I told you so.' As the perception of mediocrity comes with the proximity of the observer, writing about the often mediocre, improvised and conflictual nature of East Central Europe's Western integration can also be seen as a positive outcome of historic proximity.

What did the success of German Civilian Power consist of? Although it is evidently difficult to determine who played what part in any particular outcome, it is possible to judge the success of German policies by comparing the state of play at the end of 1998 with priorities in the early 1990s. In the European Union, the particular combination of deepening and widening that had emerged after the Amsterdam summit was close to what German policy makers advocated in 1990/91. It is true that it had been a German aim to create a proper political union, which in the event proved unattainable. The post-Amsterdam EU, however, was closer to the German idea about the future of integration than to British or French conceptions. For deepening through monetary union went far further than Britain had proposed in 1991, while widening was far more advanced than France had advocated at the same time. In this respect, Germany got its way, and the burden of adjustment lay on Germany's Western partners. In a similar vein, neither the European allies nor the United States at first supported Nato enlargement. Although one may doubt to what extent Rühe's backing for the project could actually be described as German governmental policy in 1993, it is justified to describe it as such by early 1994, because Kohl advocated it at the Brussels summit. It is therefore tempting to argue that Germany got its way again.

With all this in mind, it would nevertheless be churlish to insinuate that Germany had had clear plans for East Central Europe immediately after unification. The countries to Germany's east remained a conceptual no man's land until 1992–93. For the reasons we have explored, German policy makers did not think systematically about the international politics of East Central Europe in 1990–91. This conceptual cluelessness notwithstanding, German policy makers did have the right hunch; their instinct pointed them in the right direction. This direction was a set of medium- to long-term strategic interests focused on the desired centrality of Nato and the European Union for Europe's international politics after the Cold War. The precondition of this desired centrality was the adaptation of these institutions, and it is noteworthy that Germany was at the forefront of change in both the EU and Nato. Though in the German reading adaptation at first meant 'deepening' for the EU (especially in a political union) and 'opening' for Nato (in order to build trust with the former Warsaw Pact) the principle remained the same: both institutions were part of Germany's *raison d'état*, it was the German desire to maintain them amid rapid international change, and in order to maintain them they had to be changed.

In part this was tremendously far-sighted. Free of the quixotism of national grandeur, German policy makers were quick to realize that a deepened EU would provide the necessary stability for Western Europe. In this respect they were partly in line with France. But they also discerned the strong expectations from East Central Europe, first towards the EU, and then towards Nato, and in this respect they were closer to the British position. Realizing the inevitability of an eventual enlargement, German leaders proposed an eastward enlargement in a credible and timely manner. That they did so was a matter of clarity of judgement. *Ducunt volentem fata, nolentem trahunt*: fate leads the willing, it drags the unwilling behind. Though German leaders wanted enlargement, it was not only them, but also fate that dragged the unwilling behind. As Joschka Fischer, the new Foreign Minister in the Schröder government, put it: the 'events of 1989–90 have already decided on the "if" question of Eastern enlargement', only the 'how' and 'when' really needed to be talked about at all.[1] Yet for the entire time under consideration, German policy makers were guided by two principles in the pursuit of their strategic interests: that the key lay in gathering support from the West; and that going too slowly *and* going too fast both risked the failure of the entire process.

These observations raise the question about the nature of German power and link to the theoretical argument of this study. How does Germany attain its objectives? What is specific about the power of a Civilian Power? What can we learn about power in international relations as such? There is considerable evidence in favour of the conclusion that Germany's sheer size makes it difficult for Germany's partners to resist an important German objective. Since the Western integration of East Central Europe had become a German *raison d'état*, those Western states that had originally been reluctant to endorse enlargement were under pressure to reconsider their stance. This was especially true for the United States with respect to the enlargement of Nato and for France with respect to the enlargement of the European Union. Staying out of touch on so important an issue with so important a partner was difficult for both countries. Material power capabilities facilitate the pursuit of normative objectives.

This observation notwithstanding, we have found that normative principles remain the basis of Civilian Power. Though the ability to create and to effect change is important, what matters above all are political priorities and the will to create. As we have argued throughout, a country like Sweden might be much closer to the ideal type Civilian Power than Germany, even though its resources in material power are smaller. The rhetoric by which German policy aims towards East Central Europe were defended, both within Germany and vis-à-vis Germany's

Western partners, revealed a set of values highly indicative of Civilian Power. One important such value was 'Europe'. In German rhetoric, what was good for Germany's eastern neighbours was also good for Europe. This was slightly misleading, since, say, Poland's Western integration was much more clearly in Poland's or Germany's interest than in Portugal's or Ireland's. In a sense, therefore, 'Europe' was a term that clouded more narrowly defined German national interests. In a sense, however, it was also more. For in the rhetoric of German foreign policy, Europe was not only used as a geographical concept, it was often taken to refer to the process of European integration. In this respect, it referred to the way European countries organized their relations among one another, east and West, large and small. Especially after unification, when Germany was faced with a large number of mostly small countries to its east, 'Europe', meaning the process of integration, was an immensely important, fundamental value at the heart of German foreign policy.

The significance of integration for the normative principles of Civilian Power lies in its organization of the relations between large and small countries. The German pursuit of integration is also the pursuit of the rights of small countries, and the legalization of relations with them. Thus, the significance of 'Europe' in German foreign policy stretches beyond the purely geographical concept because it relates to the values at the heart of Civilian Power: democratic rights, justice, multilateralism and, of course, the non-military pursuit of foreign policy objectives. German power, as Civilian Power, is tied to normative principles, and it invokes these principles in order to pursue its interests. In this respect, Germany's support for Poland's Western integration benefited countries like Portugal or Ireland, too. It benefited them economically because it opened up markets and a more sophisticated division of labour. It benefited them politically because it reapplied the successful cooperation of large and small countries that had been such a significant aspect of European integration. And of course, it benefited them in terms of security politics, because it supported the stabilization that, ultimately, all European countries shared an interest in.

The nature of Civilian Power thus relates to the relationship between material and normative factors in international relations. Questions of norms and values cannot be separated completely from questions of legitimation and order. This is a nexus often neglected in the constructivist literature about international relations.[2] It is true that the methodological approach employed in this study is ill equipped to explore this factor further, since it focuses on the definition of interests within

Germany rather than on the effects of German policies outside. We cannot say much more than that the normative foundations of Civilian Power relate to Joseph Nye's 'soft power' or Steven Lukes' 'three-dimensional power', which rely not on coercion, but on influencing other states' conception of their own interests. Yet since the Civilian Power approach points to the nexus between norms and power, by merging the normative concept 'civilian' with the concept of 'power', we can attempt to draw two preliminary theoretical conclusions: one relating to the power effects of the norms that guide Civilian Power, the second relating to the transformative effects of Civilian Power and its ability to effect change in the international environment.

First, the normative principles that Germany invokes in order to defend its interests also tie and tame German power itself. German power remains 'precarious'.[3] The immaterial sources of German power, as Gunther Hellmann argues, are often underestimated in comparison with the material sources. Examples for the immaterial sources of German power can be found in Germany's 'trust capital' and its assumed 'benevolent intentions'. These are vulnerable because of the after-effects of German foreign policy before 1945. In order to be effective the immaterial sources of German power therefore have to be tied to normative principles. German policy was tremendously effective when invoking the principles of Civilian Power that were supported by its trust capital and benevolent intentions. Yet equally, other countries were tremendously effective when linking their particular interests to the normative underpinnings of German foreign policy. The norms of Civilian Power thus did not simply empower the strong at the expense of the weak. On the contrary, they empowered the weak by equipping them with potent argumentative leverage. In this respect, the weak got what they wanted and the strong had to adjust. The normative underpinnings of Civilian Power thus have an ambivalent effect on German foreign policy, because they empower it and constrain it at the same time. We have seen, for instance, that the role expectations from East Central Europe affected Germany's foreign policy culture by strengthening the roles of the *Warshaviste* and *integration widener*. Since 'Europe' remained such an important value in Germany's foreign policy culture, it was the hinge through which the East Central European countries could influence Germany's policies towards them.

Secondly, and related to this, the normative dimension of Civilian Power hints at important transformative effects. Although Civilian Power is also reproductive, for instance in its view of the state as the central unit of decision making, it is transformative in its attempt to overcome the effects of the supposed anarchical nature of international politics. Specifically geared to Germany, Simon Bulmer, Charlie Jeffery and William Paterson have termed this transformative capacity the ability of 'shaping the regional milieu'.[4] In this view German European policy is not simply informed by a narrow perception of losses and gains, but by a view to the international politics of the specific regional environment, the 'milieu', as a whole. This analysis has been supported by the evidence of this study, which found German foreign policy oriented towards long-term, strategic and transformative goals, not only in the direct relationship with Germany's eastern neighbours, but also in its policies towards the international institutions of which Germany was part. This sits uneasily with the neorealist view of 'relative' gains.[5]

Is all well then in the brave new world of Civilian Power? From a theoretical point of view, the Civilian Power concept has stood its ground rather well. It enriches liberal international theory in important respects, for instance in its focus on foreign policy analysis, in its use of constructivist insights and in its broadening of democratic peace theory to non-state actors and non-military issues. The observation about Civilian Power therefore relates less to the theoretical underpinnings of the concept than to the construction of the ideal type, which is normatively highly laden. Elements of Maull's original *Foreign Affairs* article can be interpreted as a criticism of American foreign policy, suggesting an idealized version of German or Japanese foreign policy as a model all states (especially the United States) should emulate.[6] Contrary to the Weberian conception the Civilian Power ideal type was never constructed simply as an analytical tool facilitating the comparison of theory with reality. It was not simply a foreign policy construct, but a normatively biased form of foreign policy advice. This normative bias has come under pressure. By 1996, Maull's version of the ideal type Civilian Power had already changed, allowing for instance for cooperative security structures (Nato) instead of relying on collective security structures (the United Nations).[7] We have, in these contested spheres, adopted the latter version of Civilian Power as the basis of the present discussion, and confess that the present argument about Germany's close compliance with the ideal type in the policies on Nato enlargement have been informed by the latter version of the ideal type rather than the earlier one. With Maull as much as with this author, the use of the ideal type Civilian Power tells us as much about social reality as about the normative predisposition of the analyst. In other words, the sometimes blurred distinction of theoretical inquiry and personal bias –

present in all international relations, even if seemingly absent – is also present in the discussion of Civilian Power.

Not all is well in the world of Civilian Power, then, and this relates to a point about actual German policies. We have seen that although Germany did, by and large, conform to the ideal type Civilian Power in its policies towards East Central Europe, there were also exceptions. One such exception resulted from the domestic constraints on German foreign policy. German policy makers tripped over the institutions that had been created in the early years of the Federal Republic in order to limit the power of the state. In the bilateral relationships with its eastern neighbours, the legalistic nature of Germany's political culture radiated into foreign policy. By continuing to mar Czech–German and Polish–German bilateral relations with the shadows of the past, it prevented Germany from pursuing Civilian Power policies. In the negotiation of the Europe Agreements, sectorally entrenched producer interests asserted themselves over more generally defined political interests, and also prevented the pursuit of Civilian Power. These interests reawakened in the run-up to the opening of enlargement negotiations in 1997 and 1998, when Germany pursued a highly contradictory set of policies consisting of the advocacy of enlargement, conservative positions on policy reform and claims to lower its budgetary contributions. By 1997, the vigour of integration had brought sectoral problems to the fore and had illustrated that the spasms of growing together are more tense when this growing together is forced and rapid.

This leads to the observation that the liberal constitution of Germany's domestic polity, the plethora of interests and institutions, were the basis of Civilian Power, but limited it at the same time. EU enlargement was accompanied by a babble of voices that defied harmonization. The paradox was that this multiplicity of voices was a precondition of Civilian Power on the one hand but was at the same time responsible for the limited success of its external application. Thus, the congruence between German and East Central European interests in general political terms was not matched by congruous sectoral interests. Yet although the Civilian Power ideal type is open to the general criticisms levelled at democracy – short-termism, inertia, party politics – it has to accept these necessary evils in favour of higher principles: an emphasis on individual rights, the limitation of state power through checks and balances, and the emancipation of civil society from the state.

The second exception is German policies towards the Baltic states, Slovenia and Romania. One could argue, as German policy makers did, that Slovakia's inability to accede to either the EU or Nato was of its own making, and one could argue the same in the case of Romania. For Slovenia and the Baltic states (especially Estonia), this was less true, however. We have seen that the very logic with which German policy makers defended Nato enlargement towards East Central Europe as a stability transfer that could not be stopped by a Russian veto faltered when confronted with Russia's intransigence over the Baltic republics. From Tallinn, Vilnius and Riga, it must have seemed as if Germany, regardless of whether or not it exercised Civilian Power in principle, chose not to apply its Civilian Power ethos in its policies towards the Baltic states. Interests and ideals, then, have to coincide, even in the policies of a Civilian Power.

This should conclude our discussion on Civilian Power and bring us to a few final remarks about Germany. One of the most discussed questions about German foreign policy after unification was the question about change and continuity. This was also a question that guided this study. The picture that emerges is one in which the principles of West German foreign policy culture, presented in Chapter 2, have held their ground rather well. Germany's policies within the enlargement of the EU exhibited the special partnership with France, the pursuit of amicable solutions to divergent interests as well as the pursuit of overall positive gains and the shedding of decision-making rights to the European level. Equally, the Western integration of East Central Europe was seen as a process, whose end state was ill defined, and as progress, that is as a good thing in itself, even in the absence of a clearly defined end state. Germany's position in Nato continued to be affected by the principle of indivisible security, by the American security guarantee, and by the paradoxical effects this guarantee had on the nature of European integration.

Only two principles guiding the Federal Republic's foreign policy culture in the 1950s changed noticeably after unification. The first was the declining significance of the American nuclear guarantee. This meant that unified Germany, like the rest of Western Europe, was less vulnerable than the Federal Republic had been, which contributed to the diversification of Nato and the strengthening of the European pillar. Secondly, the supreme significance of the Soviet Union during the Cold War declined in favour of a growing importance of East Central Europe. Part of this was due to the end of Deutschlandpolitik, part because the East Central European countries now had independent governments, and part because the Soviet Union had disintegrated, leaving Russia further from Germany than the Soviet Union had been until 1991.

This explains success and failure of the hypotheses advanced at the end of Chapter 2. Although the commitment to deepening integration dominated the commitment to widening it, it did so in the early 1990s especially. From 1995 onwards, deepening through monetary union remained Germany's top priority, while widening had assumed such importance that it was freed from its attachment to the precondition of a proper political union. It is true that even in its attempt to widen the process of integration geographically, Germany remained wedded to its deepening, not only through EMU, but also through the attempt to limit enlargement to a small group of countries. In short, although the role of *integration widener* strengthened over the period of discussion, the *integration deepener*, at the heart of West German foreign policy culture, persisted. Secondly, the *Atlanticist* continued to dominate the *Gaullist*, because security cooperation in a European context never achieved sufficient support. This was predetermined through the modalities of German unification which enforced Atlanticism. Although initially Atlanticism did not affect the solution of East Central Europe's security problems directly, its success in 1990 set the scene for the decision to enlarge Nato seven years later.

Thirdly, the heightened role conflict between the *Atlanticist* and the *Muscovite* did erupt over Nato enlargement, subjecting the concerns of the *Muscovite* to Atlanticism. This was so not only because Atlanticism had emerged reinforced through the modalities of German unification, but also because the role of the *Warshaviste* achieved significance very quickly. The ingenuity of the plan to enlarge Nato was its combination of the *Warshaviste* and the *Atlanticist*, which were mutually reinforcing. In a sense, of course, the *Warshaviste* was merely a part of Atlanticism. But in a sense, it also marked the dawn of a new Atlanticism, which redefined the function of Nato for security in post-Cold War Europe. Hence, Atlanticism dominated the *Muscovite* in the role conflict over Nato enlargement, but it dominated in a refined form. In addition, through its support for the Nato-Russia Act, *Muscovite* considerations did influence German policy with respect to Nato enlargement. These findings indicate that within the framework of overall continuity, German foreign policy culture did undergo small and incremental change in the first years after unification.

We thus return to the overall argument of the study. German unification and the end of the Cold War were material factors that enabled unified Germany to undertake the geographical extension of the old principles of West German foreign policy culture and explain why the exercise of Civilian Power was possible. Yet material factors find it more difficult to account for the nature of these principles, and the reason for their continuity in the face of large-scale material change. We have therefore argued that material changes have to pass through the prism that is foreign policy culture before affecting foreign policy. By looking at the different roles a foreign policy culture consists of, we can gain insights into why policy makers define their interests in the way they do. The key to understanding the nature of German foreign policy after 1990 is not in Germany's geographical situation, which revokes the 1890s and the 1920s, but in the changes that occurred in West German foreign policy after 1945 and that grew and became institutionalized over the following forty years. It is these changes that led to the construction of Civilian Power, which, in the New Europe after 1990, manifested itself in the Eastern enlargement of Nato and the European Union.

Epilogue

Although Helmut Kohl had lost the Bundestag elections in September 1998 and was now no longer Chancellor of Germany, he was – untarnished yet by scandals of party financing – invited to the December 1998 European Council in Vienna as a guest of honour. The purpose of the invitation was to confer an award. As only the second person after Jean Monnet, Kohl became an 'Honorary Citizen of Europe'. The photo of the heads of government, with Kohl in their midst, came to be seen as a tribute to the man who had dominated Europe's international politics over the previous 15 years. He had not only committed his political capital to the four central undertakings of the European project of his time, the Southern enlargement in 1983–85, the Single Market project in 1985–86, European monetary union in 1989–91 and the Eastern enlargement of the European Union throughout the 1990s, he had, at the same time managed to achieve German unification as part and parcel of European integration. Jürgen Habermas had famously stated that Kohl, who as a leader of a centre-right party had decisively turned against nationalism, was the *personifizierte Entwarnung*: the personified calling-off of the alarm about recurrent German nationalism. To put it differently one might suggest that Kohl had come to be seen as the incarnation of Civilian Power. This begs the question of how influential Kohl had actually been. Was the continuity of German European policy after unification only an outcome of Kohl's remaining in power? Would change manifest itself more clearly now that the old guard had gone? How does the significance of individual decision makers link with the explanatory aspirations of foreign policy culture? To answer this question we will first look at the three central decision makers of the period under discussion, Helmut Kohl, Klaus Kinkel and Volker Rühe, and ask how their individual policies linked to German foreign policy culture and to Civilian Power. Later, we will consider briefly the new Schröder government, with special attention to Gerhard Schröder and Joschka Fischer, the Foreign Minister.

Kohl's position within German policies towards the Western integration of its East Central European neighbours is marked by two phenomena. The first is his sheer importance. Like a spider in the web of the European policy-making process in Germany he dominated through his presence and his absence, created facts by making decisions and by postponing them, by addressing issues and by keeping them off the agenda. The intransigent German negotiating stance on agricultural reform in 1991 (as well as in 1997–98), the decisive push for northern enlargement in 1994, the initiation of the Structured Dialogue in the same year, removing policy reform from the EU's agenda between 1995 and 1997, sticking to the preferred three East Central European countries, all were decisions to which Kohl was central. Under Kohl's leadership, the process of enlargement gained much of its momentum and specific character. Not only was he crucial for the gathering of support from Germany's Western partners for the stabilization and then integration of East Central Europe, he also played a critical part in assembling political momentum strong enough to overcome the resistance of entrenched interests groups within the European Union. Though this means that he can be credited with much of the success of East Central Europe's Western integration, it also means that he shoulders part of the responsibility for the weaker points of enlargement: its conceptual weaknesses, the shortcomings of the Amsterdam treaty, budgetary incertitudes.

Like many great statesmen, Kohl combined an acute sense of what was politically possible with a powerful vision of what was politically desirable. There cannot be any doubt that he was committed to the eastern enlargement of the EU throughout the period under discussion, though, as we have seen, it took longer for Nato enlargement to become a priority. Kohl shared and promoted the absolute belief of West German foreign policy culture that European integration is inherently good and thus *progress*, as well as its belief that integration is a *process* with an undefined end state. These beliefs can partly explain why there was so little emphasis within German European policy on a grand plan for what enlargement would result in. For Germany under Kohl, European integration was not characterized by the essentially static vocabulary of *architecture*, *structure* and *order*, but by the essentially dynamic vocabulary of *process*, *progress* and *development*.

Apart from Kohl's centrality to the process of decision making, the other noteworthy feature of his role was his assumption of the middle ground on any particular policy. There was not a single incident in the period under discussion on which Kohl took a position that could be described as extreme or uncovered by a domestic consensus. Another way of putting this is that Kohl seemed to personify every single role conflict that we have detected: he was both an *integration widener* and an *integration deepener*, he built himself up to be a formidable *Atlanticist* and then a *Warshaviste*, while never letting any doubts arise about his *Gaullist* and *Muscovite* credentials. It was Kohl who staked his personal political capital on the enlargement process by saying to Skubiszewski in 1992 that he would be German Chancellor until Poland had joined the European Union, and who was at the same time seen as the great promoter of the Maastricht treaty. It was Kohl who convinced his French counterparts of the merits of enlargement. It was Kohl who was seen as a knight in shining armour in Poland, while at the same time entertaining the best possible relations with Russia. Precisely because he embodied the role conflicts and role mergers of Germany's enlargement policy, Helmut Kohl also embodied many features of Civilian Power.

This stretched to the incidences where Civilian Power failed. Scholars who have discussed the 'Kohl system' of governance have found that it frequently subjected considerations of foreign policy or public relations to considerations of party politics and coalition cohesion.[1] This was also true for Germany's enlargement policy. As we have seen, bilateral relations with Poland and the Czech Republic recurrently suffered from the need to accommodate divergent strands within the CDU and the CSU. Agricultural policy was deliberately exempted from reform in order to facilitate enlargement, since this would have endangered the CDU/ CSU's electoral prospects. That interest groups at home limited the application of Civilian Power abroad can be most easily identified by scrutinizing the manoeuvres of Helmut Kohl, who, though a Chancellor with a European vision, was also a party leader exhibiting considerable short-termism and nous.

This hints at the differences between Kohl and Kinkel. Though Kinkel was leader of the FDP between 1993 and 1995, the roots of his power lay in his office, not in his party. He was not only inexperienced in foreign policy but also hassled by his failures as party leader. These weaknesses accumulated and became evident, especially in the beginning of his term in 1993 and 1994, while between 1995 and 1998, when he was liberated from the shackles of party management and had collected expertise in the field of foreign policy, he rose to become highly influential in certain fields. While Kohl seemed to have marginalized his Foreign Minister completely from the nuts and bolts of European policy making, Kinkel did become an important actor on Nato matters. In contrast to Kohl, he did at times take extreme positions, most notably on Nato enlargement. This really mattered only in 1993, however. Come 1994 the Alliance consensus had proceeded far enough to render any serious opposition to Nato enlargement inopportune, and this was not lost on Kinkel. Although it would have undermined Germany's Civilian Power credo to be largely oblivious to the security concerns of its eastern neighbours, which is in fact what Kinkel stood for in 1993, one must also recall that accounting for the security needs of East Central Europe while neglecting those of other states, especially Russia, would have undermined Civilian Power in a similar way. Whereas in 1993 Kinkel's opposition to enlargement was something of an attitude without a policy, his activities from 1995 onwards were textbook diplomacy, especially in terms of his personal commitment and in the use of his office to effect the Nato-Russia Act. Though Kinkel did not embody the role conflicts of German foreign policy culture in the way Kohl did, it is noteworthy that his *Muscovite* activities after 1994 went hand in hand with a principally *Warshaviste* position. He consciously enacted a role that was counterbalanced. Despite the decision-making mumbo-jumbo of 1993–94, he was part of a larger play whose name was Civilian Power.

Out of all three decision makers, Volker Rühe was the one who took the most extreme positions, and who repeatedly risked his political career in order to attain particular policy objectives. He was the first to demand a clearer perspective for the eastern enlargement of the EU. His proposal for Nato enlargement 16 months after the collapse of the Soviet Union did have something revolutionary. That Nato enlargement was put on the agenda and was kept there despite considerable opposition from all sides was a triumphant achievement of Rühe's. Though Rühe assumed the most extreme positions, however, he was also the person whose positions needed to be balanced for the maintenance of the overall Civilian Power consensus. The personified *Warshaviste* had done little conceptual work balancing proposals for Nato enlargement with concerns for Russia and more importantly, for those countries in Eastern Europe that would stand no chance of Nato accession. The charge that German Civilian Power was applied with regional discrimination is a charge that might be levelled at Volker Rühe, although it might also be levelled at the Chancellor, whose position on EU enlargement was focused on only those three countries that were closest to Germany.

This leads to the observation that the Civilian Power act of Germany's key personnel was in part a result of an embodied foreign policy culture and in part a result of a division of labour that kept this foreign policy culture intact. This makes the questions of what would happen after Kohl all the more relevant. If the key player in Germany's foreign policy-making process, the Chancellor, had embodied Civilian Power values by single-handedly dominating EU enlargement and by effecting a consensus on Nato enlargement, one wonders how German foreign policy would develop under a Chancellor who was either weaker or more inexperienced or opposed to some of the principles Kohl had stood for. The new SPD/Green coalition that assumed office in October 1998 had pledged continuity in foreign policy as an integral part of its electoral platform. Although the electoral calculation that Kohl enjoyed considerable competence in foreign policy matters and that it was therefore hard to score points against him in this field most probably contributed to this decision, the pledge for continuity also illustrates that the key principles of German foreign policy culture were covered by a domestic consensus. How the pledge for continuity would develop would show in the first six months of 1999, when the new Schröder government was to assume the concomitant presidencies of the G8, the WEU and the European Union, and was charged in the latter with presiding over the conclusion of the Agenda 2000.

The solution of the Agenda 2000, and in particular the German contributions to the EU budget, assumed the greatest significance and the greatest public interest. The new Chancellor concentrated on the budgetary issue in particular. Only weeks after coming into office, Schröder made a number of public appearances that led to a questioning of the new government's commitment to enlargement. At the European Council's meeting in Pörtschach in October, he stated that enlargement would be 'more complicated than many assume', which on the face of things seemed suitably non-committal but led to considerable insecurity in some applicant states.[2] Suddenly, the pledge of continuity, the commitment to enlargement in the coalition agreement between the SPD and the Greens and in the programme for the German EU Presidency seemed to slide into insignificance.[3] Frustrated with the intransigence of its EU partners over policy reform and the budgetary question, the tunes from Bonn now became increasingly shrill. At the end of November 1998, Schröder warned against setting deadlines for enlargement, clarifying at the same time that Germany would not be the 'paymaster' of the EU.[4] Only days later this had turned into a formal conjunction. Enlargement would only happen, Joschka Fischer said in the Bundestag, if German net contributions to the EU budget were reduced. Germany sought a compromise, he said, but there were limits to the price it would pay.[5]

These statements were highly significant. Above all, of course, they testified to the fact that Germany's negotiating position in the Agenda 2000 was as intricate under the new government as it had been under the old. Günther Verheugen, the new Junior Minister in the Foreign Ministry, correctly asserted that the expectations from a German EC or EU Presidency had never been as high.[6] Since the German proposals for the introduction of national co-financing in the Common Agricultural Policy had little chance of success due to French opposition, the key factors in deciding budgetary flows were the Structural and Cohesion Funds. As we have seen, Germany was hostage to the claims of the southern states in these areas. The difference between the negotiating stance of the Kohl government and the announcements of the Schröder government towards the end of the year was therefore simply this: whereas the Kohl government had occupied different positions that were as unrelated to one another as they were contradictory, the Schröder government now proposed a package deal. The emphasis in this package deal was on budgetary reform: enlargement would be a consequence of financial preconditions. Using a distinction originally put forward by Jeffrey Anderson, we may conclude that the Schröder government had elevated a *regulative* question to become its key aim, and had thus subjected the *constitutive* significance of enlargement to second-rank status.[7] The milieu-oriented objectives of Civilian Power were forsaken for short-term political aims. This was a significant turn away not only from the strategies of the Kohl government, but also from the principles of German foreign policy culture.

This was not lost on Germany's East Central European neighbours. An established political commentator sympathetic to the Polish government wrote an article with the headline 'Germany is turning away from Poland', in which he argued that 'we can now safely state that there is no continuity in [German] European policy.'[8] Though with hindsight this fear appears immature, it seemed at the time as though the Schröder government was gambling away the political capital that its predecessors had built up with such difficulty. To be sure, the negative reaction in Poland was not shared by other East Central European countries, certainly not by Hungary and Slovakia, where the September elections had seen the end of the Meciar government and a renewed turning to the Euro-Atlantic institutions under the government of Mikulas Dzurinda. In the Czech Republic, the delight over the removal of the CSU from the levers of power at the federal level resulted in largely positive expectations from the Schröder government.[9] It is also true that not all political commentators and government officials in

Poland shared the negative view of the new government. One of the leading writers of the new generation, for instance, called for more composure in the Polish stance.[10]

Finally, the Schröder government's stance on the solution of the Agenda 2000 shifted. Within Germany, criticism of the linkage between enlargement and a reduction of Germany's budgetary contributions had fallen thick as autumn leaves.[11] The government seemed to have realized that with its drastic claims it had bitten off a larger piece than it could chew. Moreover, the incumbent of the EU Presidency is traditionally seen as a mediator and negotiator, and the Schröder government thus found itself in a position that did not allow for the poignant pursuit of more narrowly defined national interests. The turn in the German position was exemplified by Joschka Fischer earlier than by other members of the government, including the Chancellor. In his inaugural speech at the European Parliament Fischer expressed the new government's stance on enlargement more powerfully than ever before. The 'events of 1989–90 have already decided the "if" question of Eastern enlargement,' he said, 'only the "how" and the "when" must be identified and decided upon.'[12] His account of the logic of eastern enlargement was deeply rooted in Germany's foreign policy culture and could have come from any politician of the Kohl government: 'Prosperity, peace and stability for the whole of Europe can only be guaranteed in the long-term through the accession of the Central and Eastern European partners.' Repeating Germany's moral engagement in the way Klaus Kinkel and Volker Rühe had done over the previous eight years, he said: 'In Germany we have not forgotten the invaluable contribution of the peoples of Central and Eastern Europe in ending the division of Germany and Europe.' And as a conclusion: 'Germany remains a strong advocate of the early eastern enlargement of the European Union.'

These words were important. They calmed fears in other member states, as well as in East Central Europe, about the new government's pragmatism and assertion of more narrow national interests, which would turn a blind eye to the *constitutive* dimension of European politics in general, and of the enlargement process in particular. It is true that the negotiating stance of the new government was especially difficult because the Agenda 2000 had now moved from the stage of preliminary discussion to the stage of concrete decision. The abstract contradictions of the old government were a luxury whose time had passed; they now had to be resolved, and this was expected to make Germany unpopular. Perhaps the members of the new government did not realize how their every word was going to be scrutinized; they certainly did not anticipate

how difficult it would be to translate tough rhetoric into actually beneficial results. We can assume that the old government would not have
toyed with subjecting the *constitutive* dimension of enlargement to the
regulative dimension of the budgetary question. Yet in the end the new
government kept the hierarchy of *constitutive* and *regulative* aspects
intact. Two weeks after Poland, the Czech Republic and Hungary had
become Nato members, a special European Council in Berlin resolved
the Agenda 2000 issues. The new government's negotiating skills were
widely praised, and the summit was seen as a tremendous success for
Schröder and Fischer. With modest reforms in the structural and agricultural polices of the EU, the key outcome in this context was a largely
unchanged budgetary position for Germany. The Berlin summit not
only established the budgetary details for the period until 2006, it also
set aside special funds for the pre-accession aid, and then accession, of
potential new members. Not all commentators hailed these results as a
success. On the contrary, the unwillingness to enter into large-scale
reform was widely interpreted as indicative of the European Union's
weakness. Towards the end of the reform debate, Claus Giering noted,
nobody had asked why particular policies actually existed and what role
these should play for the future European Union.[13] Instead, the emphasis lay on incremental change in order to rescue the entire package.
Nevertheless, with the budgetary details in place, the road for enlargement was now finally clear. Again, German European policy had
deemed it fit to subordinate its *regulative* interests to the idea of progress
in the integration project.

Presenting the results of the Berlin summit to the Bundestag on the
day after the summit, Joschka Fischer said: 'In the decisive moment the
question was whether the Chancellor should represent national interests – in the sense of the short-term and therefore in a sense that is
misguided – or whether our national interests in the sense of European
unification should take first place.'[14] And he added: 'I realised properly
for the first time last night that this Europe will fly apart hell for leather
if our country does not exercise its leadership function.' These sentences
sum up much of what German foreign policy culture had stood for ever
since the 1950s, and indicates that the chorus of German Civilian Power
after 1990 outreached the voice of Helmut Kohl. The ideas and convictions that tied Kohl and Fischer to one another were strongly indicative
of the beliefs and values that bound them to the polity of which they
were part. Of course, Kohl had not only inherited but also shaped
Germany's foreign policy culture. And in the same way that Kohl, Kinkel
and Rühe had shaped Germany's foreign policy culture, the new gov-

ernment would now have the chance to impress its own designs upon it. Yet considering the two questions at the heart of this book – about the continuity of German foreign policy after unification, and about the extent to which the old Euro-Atlantic institutions would give security and stability to post-Cold War Europe – one cannot but diagnose overwhelming continuity between the Kohl and Schroder governments.

Notes

Introduction

1 Hubert Vedrine, *Les Mondes de François Mitterrand* (Paris: Fayard, 1996), p. 449.
2 Rainer Zitelman, Karlheinz Weißmann and Peter Großheim (eds), *Westbindung. Risiken und Chancen für Deutschland* (Berlin: Propyläen, 1993) for those who hoped; and Georges Valance, *France-Allemagne. Le retour de Bismarck* (Paris: Flammarion, 1990) for those who feared. In a more moderate manner see Arnulf Baring, *Deutschland, was nun?* (Berlin: Siedler, 1991) and Gregor Schöllgen, *Angst vor der Macht. Die Deutschen und ihre Außenpolitik* (Berlin: Ullstein, 1993) for the hopers, and Andrei Markovits and Simon Reich, 'Should Europe fear the Germans?', *German Politics and Society*, 23 (1991) for those who expressed concern.
3 The original article was Hanns W. Maull, 'Germany and Japan: the new Civilian Powers', *Foreign Affairs*, 69/5 (1990); see also Hanns W. Maull, 'Zivilmacht Bundesrepublik Deutschland', *Europa-Archiv*, 10 (1992); Hanns W. Maull, 'Zivilmacht: Die Konzeption und ihre sicherheitspolitische Relevanz', in W. Heydrich et al. (eds), *Sicherheitspolitik Deutschlands: Neue Konstellationen, Risiken, Instrumente* (Baden-Baden: Nomos, 1993); Hanns W. Maull, 'Civilian Power: the concept and its relevance for security issues', in Lidija Babic and Bo Huldt (eds), *Mapping the Unknown: Towards a New World Order* (Stockholm: Swedish Institute for International Affairs, 1993); Hanns W. Maull and Knut Kirste, 'Zivilmacht und Rollentheorie', *Zeitschrift für Internationale Beziehungen*, 3/2 (1996).
4 Volker Rittberger and Frank Schimmelfennig, for instance, refer to a 'civil' or 'civilizing' state as primarily idealistic: 'German foreign policy after reunification; on the applicability of theoretical models of foreign policy', Working Paper, Centre for German and European Studies, Georgetown University, 1997.
5 Taken from the Polish version of Warsaw, Warszawa. The 'sz' is pronounced like an English 'sh'.

1   What Is Civilian Power?

1 Hanns W. Maull and Knut Kirste, 'Zivilmacht und Rollentheorie', *Zeitschrift für Internationale Beziehungen*, 3/2 (1996).

2 Patricia Davis and Peter Dombrowski, 'Appetite of the wolf', *German Politics* , 6/1 (1997), p. 3. For the concept of the trading state see Richard Rosecrance, *The Rise of the Trading State* (New York: Basic Books, 1986).
3 Hans-Peter Schwarz, *Die Zentralmacht Europas, Deutschlands Rückkehr auf die Weltbühne* (Berlin: Siedler, 1994), p. 177.
4 Norbert Elias, *The Civilizing Process* (Oxford: Blackwell, 1994).
5 Elias, *The Civilizing Process*, p. 451.
6 Hanns W. Maull, 'Civilian Power: the concept and its relevance for security issues', in Lidija Babic and B. Huldt (eds), *Mapping the Unknown: Towards a New World Order* (Stockholm: Swedish Institute for International Affairs, (1993), p. 20.
7 Maull, 'Civilian Power: the concept and its relevance for security issues', p. 23.
8 Maull and Kirste, 'Zivilmacht und Rollentheorie', p. 303.
9 Maull and Kirste, 'Zivilmacht und Rollentheorie', p. 303.
10 J. A. Hobson, *Richard Cobden: The International Man* (London: T. Fisher Unwin, 1918), p. 391.
11 See, for instance, Immanuel Kant, *Perpetual Peace* (Westwood Village, LA: US Library Association, 1932), p. 48. Thomas Paine, *The Writings of Thomas Paine* (London: G. P. Putnam, 1894), vol. 2, p. 456.
12 Cobden, cited in William Harbutt Dawson, *Richard Cobden and Foreign Policy* (London: Allen & Unwin, 1926).
13 Maull and Kirste, 'Zivilmacht und Rollentheorie', p. 302.
14 Cited in Dawson, *Richard Cobden*, p. 104.
15 Peter Wilson, 'Leonard Woolf and international government', in David Long and Peter Wilson (eds), *Thinkers of the Twenty Years Crisis* (Oxford: Clarendon Press, 1995).
16 J. A. Hobson, *Towards International Government* (London: Allen & Unwin, 1916).
17 Norman Angell, *The Great Illusion* (London: Heinemann, 1933), p. 127.
18 Robert O. Keohane and Joseph S. Nye, *Power and Interdependence* (Boston: Little, Brown, 1977).
19 Michael Howard, *War and the Liberal Conscience* (London: Temple Smith, 1978), p. 57.
20 Hobson, *Towards International Government*, p. 11.
21 J. A. Hobson, *Problems of a New World* (London: Allen & Unwin, 1921), p. 233.
22 Maull, 'Civilian Power: the concept and its relevance for security issues', p. 23.
23 Maull and Kirste, 'Zivilmacht und Rollentheorie', p. 303.
24 Alexander Wendt, 'Anarchy is what states make of it: the social construction of power politics', *International Organisation*, 46/2 (1992); Alexander Wendt, 'Collective identity formation and the international state', *American Political Science Review*, 88/2 (1994).
25 Karl W. Deutsch (ed.), *Political Community and the North Atlantic Area* (Princeton, NJ: Princeton University Press, 1957), p. 5.
26 Thomas Risse-Kappen, *Co-operation Among Democracies* (Princeton, NJ: Princeton University Press, 1995).

27 For a critical evaluation see the different contributions to Michel E. Brown, Sean M. Lynn-Jones and Steven E. Miller (eds), *Debating the Democratic Peace* (Cambridge: MA: MIT Press, 1996).

28 Emmanuel Adler and Michael Barnett, *Security Communities* (Cambridge: Cambridge University Press, 1999), p. 41.

29 Maull, 'Civilian Power: the concept and its relevance for security issues', p. 20.

30 Steven Lukes, *Power: A Radical View* (London: Macmillan, now Palgrave, 1974), p. 21.

31 Joseph S. Nye, 'Soft power', *Foreign Policy*, 80 (1990), pp. 166–7.

32 The classical realist critique was made by E. H. Carr, *The Twenty Years Crisis, 1919–39* (London: Macmillan (now Palgrave), 1948). For the critique of constructivism see Hans-Martin Jäger below.

33 Hans-Martin Jäger, 'Konstruktionsfehler des Konstruktivismus in den Internationalen Beziehungen', *Zeitschrift für Internationale Beziehungen*, 3/2 (1996), pp. 326–7.

34 This refers to Kenneth Waltz, *Theory of International Politics* (Reading, MA: Addison-Wesley, 1979).

35 For an example of this view see John J. Mearsheimer, 'Back to the future: instability in Europe after the Cold War', *International Security*, 15/1 (1990).

36 Mearsheimer, 'Back to the Future', p. 5.

37 Adrian Hyde-Price, *European Security beyond the Cold War* (London: Royal Institute for International Affairs, 1991), p. 97.

38 See Hoffmann's contribution to Stanley Hoffmann, Robert Keohane and John J. Mearsheimer, 'Correspondence', *International Security*, 15/2 (1990), p. 192.

39 Hans J. Morgenthau, *Politics among Nations*, brief edn (New York: McGraw-Hill, 1993). More recently, realist scholars have turned against neorealism precisely because it has been unable conceptually to account for the significance of institutions. For an attempt to do so see Randall L. Schweller and David Priess, 'A tale of two realisms: expanding the institutions debate', *Mershon International Studies Review*, 41/1 (1997).

40 Hans J. Morgenthau, *Politics among Nations*, p. 201.

41 Morgenthau, *Politics among Nations*, p. 197.

42 Keohane and Nye, *Power and Interdependence*; see also the neoliberal authors in David A. Baldwin (ed.), *Neorealism and Neoliberalism* (New York: Columbia University Press, 1993).

43 Stephen D. Krasner (ed.), *International Regimes* (Ithaca, NY: Cornell University Press, 1983); Volker Rittberger (ed.), *Regime Theory and International Relations* (Oxford: Clarendon Press, 1995).

44 For Keohane, for instance, nation state sovereignty is a persistent feature of interstate cooperation; see Robert O. Keohane, *After Hegemony, Cooperation and Discord in the World Political Economy* (Princeton, NJ: Princeton University Press, 1984), p. 62.

45 For the rationalist liberal approach to regimes see Keohane, *After Hegemony*, p. 14. For the discussion of the extent to which the EU is now a state, and how it should be studied, see Simon Hix, 'The study of the European Community: the challenge to comparative politics', *West European Politics*, 17/1

(1994), and Andrew Hurrell and Anand Menon, 'Politics like any other? Comparative politics, international relations and the study of the EU', *West European Politics*, 19/2 (1996).

46 Graham Allison, *The Essence of Decision* (Boston: Little, Brown, 1971).

47 William Wallace, 'Old states and new circumstances: the international predicament for Britain, France and West Germany', in William Wallace and William E. Paterson (eds), *Foreign Policy Making in Western Europe* (Farnborough: Saxon House, 1978), p. 48.

48 See the literature survey by Margot Light and Christopher Hill, 'Foreign policy analysis', in Margot Light and A. J. R. Groom (eds), *International Relations* (London: Pinter, 1985); see also the contributions to Michael Clarke and Brian White (eds), *Understanding Foreign Policy* (Aldershot: Edward Elgar, 1989), none of which include cultural variables. The same is true even for many authors in the so-called 'second-generation': see for instance most contributions to Laura Neack, Jeanne Hey and Patrick J. Haney (eds), *Foreign Policy Analysis – Continuity and Change in Its Second Generation* (Englewood Cliffs, NJ: Prentice Hall, 1995).

49 The concept of a foreign policy culture is derived from the political culture studies that emerged in postwar American political science. See Lucian W. Pye and Sidney Verba (eds), *Political Culture and Political Development* (Princeton, NJ: Princeton University Press, 1965); Gabriel A. Almond and Sidney Verba, *The Civic Culture: Political Attitudes and Democracy in Five Nations* (Princeton, NJ: Princeton University Press, 1963); Lucian W. Pye, 'Political culture', in David L. Sills (ed.), *International Encyclopedia of the Social Sciences*, 1st edn (Basingstoke: Macmillan, now Palgrave, 1968), Vol. 12.

50 The first part of this definition takes important cues from Peter Katzenstein and Thomas Berger. See Peter J. Katzenstein, 'Introduction: alternative perspectives on national security', and Thomas U. Berger, 'Norms, identity and national security in Germany and Japan', in Peter J. Katzenstein (ed.), *The Culture of National Security* (New York: Columbia University Press, 1996).

51 For the definition of 'academic metaphor for self-in-context' see Thomas F. Fitzgerald, *Metaphors of Identity* (Albany, NY: State University of New York Press, 1993), p. 3.

52 Peter J. Katzenstein, 'Introduction', in Katzenstein (ed.), *The Culture of National Security*, p. 6.

53 Friedrich Kratochwil, 'Is the ship of culture at sea or returning?', in Yosef Lapid and Friedrich Kratochwil (eds), *The Return of Culture and Identity in IR Theory* (Boulder, CO: Lynne Rienner, 1996), p. 206.

54 K. J. Holsti, 'Toward a theory of foreign policy: making the case for role analysis', in Stephen G. Walker (ed.), *Role Theory and Foreign Policy Analysis*, 1st edn (Durham, NC: Duke University Press, 1987), p. 7.

55 Theodore R. Sarbin and Vernon L. Allen, 'Role theory', in Gardner Lindzey and Elliot Aronson (eds), *The Handbook of Social Psychology* (Reading, MA: Addison-Wesley, 1968), p. 489.

56 See Rainer Zitelman, Karlheinz Weißmann and Peter Großheim (eds), *Westbindung. Risiken und Chancen für Deutschland* (Berlin: Propyläen, 1993); more related to German identity and less on foreign policy is Heimo Schwilk and Ulrich Schacht (eds), *Die selbstbewußte Nation* (Berlin: Ullstein, 1994). For a

discussion of these see Peter Pulzer, 'Nation-state and national sovereignty', *Bulletin of the German Historical Institute*, London, November 1995.

57   For a view of this before unification, see Hans-Peter Schwarz (ed.), *Die gezähmten Deutschen. Von der Machtbessenheit zur Machtvergessenheit* (Stuttgart: Deutsche Verlags-Anstalt, 1985).

58   On the same argument after 1990, see for instance Gregor Schöllgen, *Angst vor der Macht. Die Deutschen und ihre Außenpolitik* (Berlin: Ullstein, 1993); also most authors in Arnulf Baring's volume: *Germany's New Position in Europe* (Oxford: Berg, 1994).

59   William E. Paterson, 'Helmut Kohl, "The Vision Thing" and escaping the semi-sovereignty trap', in Clay Clemens and William E. Paterson (eds), *The Kohl Chancellorship* (London: Frank Cass, 1998), pp. 31–2

2   Why is Germany a Civilian Power?

1   Lothar Gall, 'The Deutsche Bank from its foundation to the Great War, 1870–1914', in Lothar Gall et al. (eds), *The Deutsche Bank, 1870–1995* (London: Weidenfeld & Nicolson, 1995), p. 70.

2   Cited in Gall, 'The Deutsche Bank', p. 75.

3   Fritz Fischer, *Griff nach der Weltmacht: Die Kriegszielpolitik des kaiserlichen Deutschland 1914/18* (Düsseldorf: Droste, 1961), pp. 107–13.

4   Jonathan Wright, 'Gustav Stresemann: liberal or realist?', in T. G. Otte and Constantine A. Pagedas (eds), *Personalities, War and Diplomacy* (London: Frank Cass, 1998), p. 87–8.

5   Peter Krüger, *Die Außenpolitik von Weimar* (Darmstadt: Wissenschaftliche Buchgesellschaft, 1985).

6   For Stresemann's troubles to make the Treaty of Locarno acceptable to the domestic political scene, especially the DNVP, see Henry Ashby Turner, *Stresemann and the Politics of the Weimar Republic* (Westport, CT: Greenwood, 1963), pp. 182–220.

7   Wright, 'Gustav Stresemann', p. 96.

8   Michael Stürmer, *Das Ruhelose Reich, Deutschland 1866–1918*, special edn (Berlin: Siedler, 1994), p. 14.

9   See Peter Pulzer, *Germany 1871–1945. Politics, State Formation, and War* (Oxford: Oxford University Press, 1997), p. 7.

10   Volker Berghahn, 'West German reconstruction and American industrial culture 1945–1960', in Reiner Pommerin (ed.), *The American Impact on Postwar Germany* (Providence, RI and Oxford: Berghahn, 1995), p. 72.

11   Quoted in Berghahn, 'West German reconstruction', p. 71.

12   Peter Pulzer, *German Politics 1945–1995* (Oxford: Oxford University Press, 1995), p. 64.

13   Peter Katzenstein, *Policy and Politics in West Germany: The Growth of a Semi-Sovereign State* (Philadelphia: Temple University Press, 1987).

14   Richard Rosecrance, *The Rise of the Trading State* (New York: Basic Books, 1986).

15   Wolfram Hanrieder, *Germany, America, Europe* (New Haven, CT and London: Yale University Press, 1989), p. ix.

16   Andrei S. Markovits and Simon Reich, *The German Predicament. Memory and Power in the New Europe* (Ithaca and London: Cornell University Press, 1997), p. 2.
17   Compare for instance Jürgen Habermas, 'Eine Art Schadensabwicklung', in Anon. (ed.), *Historikerstreit* (Berlin: Piper, 1987), p. 75.
18   Hanrieder, *Germany, America, Europe*, p. 149.
19   A key argument in Timothy Garton Ash, *In Europe's Name: Germany and the Divided Continent* (London: Vintage, 1993).
20   See Chapter 6 in Garton Ash, *In Europe's Name*.

3   Bilateral Relations

1   For an incisive discussion of this see Andrei S. Markovits and Simon Reich, *The German Predicament. Memory and Power in the New Europe* (Ithaca and London: Cornell University Press, 1997), pp. 108–19.
2   Rainer Eisfeld, 'Mitteleuropa in historical and contemporary perspective', *German Politics and Society*, 28 (1993).
3   Peter M. R. Stirk, 'The idea of Mitteleuropa', in Peter M. R. Stirk (ed.), *Mitteleuropa. History and Prospects* (Edinburgh: Edinburgh University Press, 1994), p. 2.
4   Friedrich Naumann, *Mitteleuropa* (Berlin: Georg Reimer, 1915).
5   Peter M. R. Stirk, 'Ideas of economic integration in interwar Mitteleuropa', in Stirk (ed.), *Mitteleuropa*, p. 103.
6   György Konrád, *Antipolitics. An Essay* (London: Quartet Books, 1984). Iver B. Neumann, 'Russia as Central Europe's constituting other', *East European Politics and Societies*, 7/2 (1993); Timothy Garton Ash, 'Does Central Europe exist?', in Timothy Garton Ash, *The Uses of Adversity* (Cambridge: Granta, 1989).
7   Peter Bender, 'Mitteleuropa – Mode, Modell oder Motiv?', in Dietrich Spangenberger (ed.), *Die Blockierte Vergangenheit* (Berlin: Argon, 1987), and Peter Glotz, 'Deutsch-Böhmische Kleinigkeiten oder: Abgerissene Gedanken über Mitteleuropa', *Neue Gesellschaft – Frankfurter Hefte*, 7 (1986).
8   Janusz Reiter, 'Die deutsche Entwicklung aus polnischer Sicht', speech at the Friedrich-Ebert-Foundation, Bonn, 29 January 1991.
9   Helmut Kohl, *Ich wollte Deutschlands Einheit* (Berlin: Propyläen, 1996), pp. 66–75; Hans-Dietrich Genscher, *Erinnerungen* (Munich: Goldmann, 1997), pp. 637–41.
10   Kohl, *Deutschlands Einheit*, p. 74
11   Kohl, *Deutschlands Einheit*, p. 74
12   For the general expression of gratitude see, for instance, Kohl's declaration on 10 September, in response to the Hungarian decision to open the border 'Dank an Ungarn für Menschlichkeit und Solidarität', in Helmut Kohl, *Bilanzen und Perspektiven, Regierungspolitik 1989–1991* (Bergisch Gladbach: Gustav Lübbe, 1992), pp. 165–6. For a discussion of the treaty see Wolf Oschlies, *Die Nachbarschaftsverträge der Bundesrepublik Deutschland mit Ungarn und der Tschechoslowakei* (Cologne: Bundesinstitut für Ostwissenschaftliche und Internationale Studien, 1993), p. 5.

13 Presented in a parliamentary debate on the budget as 'Neue Chancen und neue Herausforderungen in der Deutschland- und Europapolitik', in Kohl, *Bilanzen und Perspektiven*, pp. 296–322.

14 Interview with Krzysztof Skubiszewski, Warsaw, 14 August 1997.

15 Kohl's speech in the Bundestag 'Aufbruch zu Freiheit und Selbstbestimmung', *Bilanzen und Perspektiven*, p. 234.

16 See points eight and seven in 'Das Zehn-Punkte-Programm', in Kohl, *Bilanzen und Perspektiven*, pp. 296–322.

17 See, for instance, Dieter Bingen, *Die Polenpolitik der Bonner Republik von Adenauer bis Kohl, 1949–1991* (Baden-Baden: Nomos, 1998), pp. 161–80.

18 'Aufbruch zu Freiheit und Selbstbestimmung', p. 234.

19 In 'Der Verfassungsrechtliche Weg zur deutschen Wiedervereinigung und die völkerrechtliche Garantie der polnischen Westgrenze', in Kohl, *Bilanzen und Perspektiven*, p. 438.

20 'Die deutsch-deutsche Währungs-, Wirtschafts-, und Sozialunion im Blick auf eine gesamteuropäische Friedensordnung', in Kohl, *Bilanzen und Perspektiven*, pp. 597–8.

21 Karl Kaiser, *Deutschlands Vereinigung* (Bergisch Gladbach: Bastei Lübbe, 1991), p. 53.

22 For the French version of events see Hubert Vedrine, *Les Mondes de François Mitterrand*, (Paris: Fayard, 1996), pp. 433–7.

23 For an account of his heated phone call to Mitterrand see Kohl, *Deutschlands Einheit*, pp. 324–7. Also Karl-Heinz Bender, *Mitterrand und die Deutschen* (Bonn: Bouvier, 1995), pp. 79–84.

24 Philip Zelikow and Condoleezza Rice, *Germany Unified and Europe Transformed* (Cambridge, MA, Harvard University Press, 1995), p. 222.

25 See, for instance, Artur Hajnicz, *Polens Wende und Deutschlands Vereinigung* (Paderborn: Schöningh, 1995); Michael Ludwig, *Polen und die deutsche Frage* (Bonn: Forschungsinstitut der Deutschen Gesellschaft für Auswärtige Politik, Arbeitspapiere zur Internationalen Politik 60, 1990).

26 Interview, Tadeusz Mazowiecki, 4 August 1997.

27 Andrzej Szczypiorski, 'Warum in Polen wieder Angst vor Deutschland herrscht', *Universitas*, 45/6 (1990), p. 540.

28 For a discussion see Hajnicz, *Polens Wende*, chapters 1 and 2.

29 See the Preamble and Art. 8 of the treaty.

30 Dieter Korger, *Die Polenpolitik der deutschen Bundesregierung von 1982–1991* (Bonn: Europa Union Verlag, 1993), pp. 81–5.

31 FAZ Länderanalysen Osteuropa (November 1994), pp. 15–16.

32 Roman Herzog, 'Versöhnung und Verständigung, Vertrauen und gute Nachbarschaft', *Bulletin*, 72/3 August 1994, p. 677.

33 In personal conversation, Warsaw.

34 Karl-Rudolf Korte, *Deutschlandpolitik in Helmut Kohls Kanzlerschaft* (Stuttgart: Deutsche Verlags-Anstalt, 1998), pp. 243–64; Clay Clemens, *Reluctant Realists. The Christian Democrats and West German Ostpolitik* (Durham, NC: Duke University Press, 1989).

35 Ansprache des Polnischen Außenministers, *Bulletin*, no. 35, 4 May 1995, pp. 295–302.

36 'Knallhart im Ton, dialogbereit in der Sache', *Kölner Stadtanzeiger*, 8 July 1998.

37 There were of course exceptions, for instance in the stance taken by the Ackermann Gemeinde. See Ferdinand Seibt, *Deutschland und die Tschechen*, 4th edn (Munich/Zürich: Piper, 1998), pp. 359–70.
38 'Das ist für uns zwingend', *Sonntag Aktuell*, 5 July 1998.
39 'Knallhart im Ton, dialogbereit in der Sache', *Kölner Stadtanzeiger*, 8 July 1998.
40 'Vertriebene, Aussiedler und deutsche Minderheiten sind eine Brücke zwischen den Deutschen und ihren östlichen Nachbarn', Deutscher Bundestag, *Drucksache*, 13/10845. All quotes in this paragraph are from this source. Outsettlers were those people of German origin who had remained in Poland after the war, and who left for the Federal Republic in the 1970s and 1980s when emigration restrictions were eased.
41 Janusz Reiter, 'Cas na powazny dialog', *Rzeczpospolita*, 8 July 1998.
42 'Es gibt keine Grenzfrage zwischen Deutschland und Polen', *Frankfurter Allgemeine Zeitung*, 6 July 1998.
43 Korte, *Deutschlandpolitik*, p. 249.
44 Wolf Oschlies, *Ehe Nachbarschaft zur Nähe wird. Der deutsch-tschechoslowakische Nachbarschaftsvertrag in deutscher, tschechischer und slowakischer Sicht* (Cologne: Bundesinstitut für Internationale und Ostwissenschaftliche Studien, 60, 1991).
45 Seibt, *Deutschland und die Tschechen*, p. 353.
46 Oschlies, *Ehe Nachbarschaft zur Nähe wird*, p. 18.
47 Vladimir Handl, 'Czech-German declaration on reconciliation', *German Politics*, 6/2 (1997), p. 150.
48 On Slovakia see for instance Kari Dahl Martinsen, 'Niedergang der Demokratie in der Slowakei', *Osteuropa*, 47/8 (1997).
49 Vaclav Havel, 'Czechs and Germans on the way to good neighbourship', *Perspectives*, 4 (1995), p. 7–9.
50 Vladimir Handl, 'Die deutsch-tschechische Erklärung von 1997', *Welttrends*, 19 (1998), p. 11.
51 Handl, 'Die deutsch-tschechische Erklärung von 1997' p. 14.
52 Peter Brod, 'Neuer Spuk um altes Gespenst', *Süddeutsche Zeitung*, 8 February 1996.
53 Interview with Christian Schmidt, Bonn, September 1997.
54 On Kohl's success with the CDU see Clay Clemens, 'The Chancellor as party manager. Helmut Kohl, the CDU, and governance in Germany', *West European Politics*, 17/4 (1994).
55 Ralf Dahrendorf, *Society and Democracy in Germany* (London: Weidenfeld & Nicolson, 1967), pp. 197–216.
56 Torsten Krauel, 'Die Deutschen – zu sehr mit sich selbst beschäftigt?', *Eicholz-Brief*, 33/4 (1996), p. 63.

4 Germany and EU Enlargement

1 Phare stands for 'Pologne et Hongrie: Actions pour la Reconversion Économique'. The G24 countries comprise the EC12, the Efta countries, the United States, Canada, Japan, Turkey, Australia and New Zealand.
2 Pierre Favier and Michel Martin-Roland, *La décennie Mitterrand*, vol. 3, *Les défis* (Paris: Points – éditions du Seuil, 1996), pp. 190–3.

3   For an early mention see point seven (p. 318) of the ten-point plan, in Helmut Kohl, 'Das Zehn-Punkte-Programm' in Kohl, *Bilanzen und Perspektiven, Regierungspolitik 1989–1991* (Bergisch Gladbach: Gustave Lübbe, 1992), pp. 296–322.

4   'Ein gemeinsames Werk der Verständigung, des Friedens und der Versöhnung. Das wiedervereinigte Deutschland in weltpolitischer Verantwortung', in Kohl, *Bilanzen und Perspektiven*, p. 687.

5   See Helmut Kohl's contribution to the *Handelsblatt*, 31 October 1991: 'Die innere Einheit stärken, die europäische Einigung vollenden', in Kohl, *Bilanzen und Perspektiven*, p. 740.

6   In 'Koalition der Mitte: Für eine Politik der Erneuerung' in Helmut Kohl, *Reden 1982–1984* (Bonn: Presse- und Informationsamt der Bundesregierung, 1984), p. 30.

7   In 'Programm der Erneuerung: Freiheit, Mitmenschlichkeit, Verantwortung' in the Bundestag on 4 May 1983, in Kohl, *Reden 1982–1984*, p. 149.

8   In 'Deutschlands Einheit vollenden' in Kohl, *Bilanzen und Perspektiven*, p. 789.

9   'Deutschlands Einheit vollenden', in Kohl, *Bilanzen und Perspektiven*, pp. 790–4.

10 'Solidarität und Bereitschaft zur Verantwortung. Die Rolle Deutschlands in Europa' on 13 March 1991, in Kohl, *Bilanzen und Perspektiven*, p. 818.

11 Margaret Thatcher, cited in *The Times*, 6 August 1990.

12 Editorial, *The Times*, 6 August 1990.

13 William E. Paterson, 'Helmut Kohl, "The Vision Thing" and escaping the semi-sovereignty trap', in Clay Clemens and William E. Paterson (eds), *The Kohl Chancellorship* (London: Frank Cass, 1998), pp. 31–2.

14 Thus, despite trade restrictions, agricultural products constituted 22 per cent of Polish exports to the EC in 1990; see Jan Mulewicz, 'Complex bargaining with a difficult partner – Poland's experiences with the Community', in Barbara Lippert and Heinrich Schneider (eds), *Monitoring Association and Beyond* (Bonn: Europa Union Verlag, 1995), p. 190. On the politics of EC protectionism see Alan Mayhew, *Recreating Europe. The European Union's Policy towards Central and Eastern Europe* (Cambridge: Cambridge University Press, 1998), pp. 90–3.

15 Mayhew, *Recreating Europe*, pp. 92–9.

16 In the whole 1089 pages of his memoirs, for instance, Hans-Dietrich Genscher devotes only one sentence to the Europe Agreements. Hans-Dietrich Genscher, *Erinnerungen*, (Munich: Goldmann, 1997), p. 993.

17 Ulrich Sedelmeier, 'The European Union's association policy towards Central and Eastern Europe', Sussex European Institute Discussion Paper, 1994.

18 Edith Heller, 'Polen fühlen sich "wie Albaner" behandelt', *Süddeutsche Zeitung*, 12 August 1991.

19 According to Ulf Ellemann-Jensen, then Denmark's foreign minister. Quoted in Charles Grant, *Delors – Inside the House that Jacques Built* (London: Nicholas Brealey, 1994), p. 158.

20 See the conflicting views on the significance of the Moscow Coup in Jan Mulewicz, 'Complex bargaining', p. 190, and Barbara Lippert, 'Shaping and evaluating the Europe Agreements – the community side', both in Lippert and Schneider (eds), *Monitoring Association and Beyond*, p. 229.

21 Interview, Economics Ministry, Bonn, 9 December, 1997.
22 The seminal study on West German European policy is Simon Bulmer and William E. Paterson, *The Federal Republic and the European Community* (London: Allen & Unwin, 1987).
23 Interview, Federal Economics Ministry, Bonn, 15 September 1997.
24 Eckart Gaddum, *Die deutsche Europapolitik in den 80er Jahren. Interessen, Konflikte und Entscheidungen der Regierung Kohl* (Paderborn: Schöningh, 1994), chapter 4. Also Keith Middlemas, *Orchestrating Europe. The Informal Politics of European Union 1973–1995* (London: Fontana, 1995), p. 107.
25 Interview, Federal Economics Ministry, Bonn, 15 September 1997.
26 Ulrich Sedelmeier, 'The European Union's association policy towards Central and Eastern Europe', Sussex European Institute Discussion Paper, p. 14.
27 Helmut Kohl, in *Protokoll des 3. Parteitages der CDU Deutschlands*, 26–28 October 1992, Düsseldorf.
28 Michael Mertes and Norbert Prill, 'Der verhängnisvolle Irrtum eines Entweder-Oder. Eine Vision für Europa', *Frankfurter Allgemeine Zeitung*, 19 July 1989.
29 See Barbara Lippert, 'EC-Ostpolitik revisited', in Barbara Lippert and Heinrich Schneider (eds), *Monitoring Association and Beyond* (Bonn: Europa Union Verlag, 1995), p. 60.
30 Heinz Kramer, 'The European Community's response to the "New Eastern Europe"', *Journal of Common Market Studies*, 31/2 (1993).
31 In *Protokoll des 3. Parteitages der CDU Deutschlands*, 26–28 October 1992, Düsseldorf.
32 William Pfaff, 'Keeping the East Europeans out', *New York Review of Books*, 38/17 (1991), p. 67.
33 Timothy Garton Ash, Michael Mertes and Dominique Moïsi, 'Let the East Europeans in!', *New York Review of Books*, 38/17 (1991), p. 19.
34 It would be quite impossible to list all the different contributions to this debate here. Instead a number of review articles, which were found particularly useful, can be pointed out. See Gunther Hellmann, 'Goodbye Bismarck? The foreign policy of contemporary Germany', *Mershon International Studies Review*, 40/1 (1996); Ingo Peters, 'Vom "Scheinzwerg" zum "Scheinriesen" – deutsche Außenpolitik in der Analyse', *Zeitschrift für Internationale Beziehungen*, 4/2 (1997); Peter Pulzer, 'Nation-state and national sovereignty', *Bulletin of the German Historical Institute*, London, November 1995.
35 Günther Nonnenmacher, 'Deutsche Interessen', *Frankfurter Allgemeine Zeitung*, 25 March 1993.
36 Penny Henson and Nisha Malhan, 'Endeavours to Export a Migration Crisis', *German Politics* , 4/3 (1995), p. 132.
37 In *Protokoll des 3. Parteitages der CDU Deutschlands*, 26–28 October 1992, Düsseldorf.
38 'Memorandum of the Governments of the Czech and Slovak Federal Republic, the Republic of Hungary and the Republic of Poland on strengthening their integration with the European Communities and on the perspective of accession', Prague, Budapest, Warsaw, September 1992; cited in Jose Ignacio Torreblanca Paya, *The European Community and Central and Eastern Europe (1989–1993): Foreign Policy and Decision-Making* (Madrid: Instituto Juan March de Eastudieos e Investigaciones, 1997), pp. 476–7. See also 'Gemeinsame

Erklärung der Außenminister der Europäischen Gemeinschaft und der Visegrad-Länder anläßlich ihres Treffens in Luxemburg am 5. Oktober 1992', *Europa-Archiv*, 21 (1992), pp. D 606–608.

39   Valerie Bunce, 'The Visegrad Group', in Peter J. Katzenstein (ed.), *Mitteleuropa: Between Europe and Germany* (Oxford: Berg, 1997).

40   Genscher, *Erinnerungen*, p. 894.

41   Genscher, *Erinnerungen*, p. 895.

42   Interview with Bronislaw Geremek, Warsaw, 5 August 1997.

43   Figures obtained from the OECD, *Aid and Other Resource Flows to the Central and Eastern European Countries and the Independent States of the Former Soviet Union (1990–1994)*, Paris, 1996.

44   'Deklaration von Weimar', *Bulletin*, no. 92, 3 September 1991, pp. 734–5.

45   'Gemeinsame Erklärung der Außenminister von Deutschland, Frankreich und Polen', *Bulletin*, no. 100, 18 November 1993, pp. 1122–3.

46   Interview, Bronislaw Geremek, Warsaw, 5 August 1997.

47   Interview, Andrzej Olechowski, Warsaw, 19 August 1997. For the proposal of associated WEU membership see 'Gemeinsame Erklärung der Außenminister von Deutschland, Frankreich und Polen', *Bulletin*, no. 100, 18 November 1993, pp. 1122–3; also Kinkel's declaration on the occasion of the WEU Council in May 1994, where association was offered to East Central Europe, in *Bulletin*, no. 46, 20 May 1994, p. 409–12.

48   'Bonn und Paris sagen Hilfe zu', *Süddeutsche Zeitung*, 26 September 1994.

49   Interview, British official, Oxford, 15 February 1996.

50   'Europäischer Rat in Edinburgh, Schlußfolgerungen des Vorsitzes.' *Bulletin*, no. 140, 28 December 1992, p. 1299.

51   Sedelmeier, 'The European Union's association policy' pp. 24–5.

52   'Genscher: Alle europäischen Staaten in die EG', dpa [deutsche presse agentur] press release, 14 March 1992.

53   Interview, Krzysztof Skubiszewski, Warsaw, 14 August 1997.

54   'Kohl will Osteuropäer als Gäste beim nächsten EG-Gipfel', *General-Anzeiger*, 28 May 1993.

55   Horst Teltschik, *329 Tage* (Munich: Goldmann, 1991), p. 369; Favier and Martin-Roland, *La décennie Mitterrand*, pp. 190–3.

56   Daniel Vernet, 'M. Kinkel propose un programme commun pour les présidences allemande et française de la communauté', *Le Monde*, 25 April 1994.

57   'Polen und Ungarn drängen in die Europäische Union', *Frankfurter Rundschau*, 8 March 1994.

58   'Kohl und Balladur für jährliche Treffen mit EU-Kandidaten', dpa press release, 26 May 1994.

59   'Osterweiterung der EU befürwortet. Kinkel verspricht Albanien, Bulgarien und Ungarn Unterstützung', *Frankfurter Allgemeine Zeitung*, 18 April 1994.

60   One cannot, for economy of argument, distinguish at this juncture between the differences that exist among concepts of flexibilization. See Claus Giering, 'Vertiefung durch Differenzierung', *integration*, 20/2 (1997), p. 76; Josef Janning, 'Dynamik in der Zwangsjacke', *integration*, 20/4 (1997).

61   CDU/CSU Fraktion des Deutschen Bundestages, Überlegungen zur Europäischen Politik, 1 September 1994. Schäuble was the head of the CDU/CSU's Bundestag caucus, Lamers its foreign policy spokesman.

62 Überlegungen zur Europäischen Politik, p. 8.
63 Überlegungen zur Europäischen Politik, p. 3.
64 Gunther Hellmann, 'Eine Flucht nach vorn ohne Ende?', *Aus Politik und Zeitgeschichte*, 30/95 (1995), pp. 23–4.
65 'Deutsche Außenpolitik in einer neuen Weltlage', *Bulletin*, no. 76, 29 August 1994, p. 714.
66 Kohl's speech in Paris, *Bulletin*, no. 11, 27 January 1988, p. 81.
67 Michael Mertes and Norbert Prill, 'Der verhängnisvolle Irrtum eines Entwe-der-Oder', *Frankfurter Allgemeine Zeitung*, 19 July 1989.
68 Interview, CDU/CSU Bundestagsfraktion, 16 September 1997. Confirmed by Karl Lamers, 'A German Agenda for the European Union', speech delivered on 17 November 1994, p. 1.
69 Konrad Schuller, 'Zuerst freundlich, dann kritisch. Kern-Europa aus östlicher Sicht', *Frankfurter Allgemeine Zeitung*, 7 October 1994.
70 Interview, Bronislaw Geremek, Warsaw, 5 August 1997. For similar proposals also interpreted as 'second-class membership' in East Central Europe see Rudolf Seiters, 'Der Europa-Zug und die Fahrgäste aus dem Osten', *Die Welt*, 26 June 1996; Hans-Gert Pöttering, 'Plädoyer für eine neue Erweiterungsstrategie der Europäischen Union, *Europäische Zeitung*, no. 8, July/August 1997.
71 On classes see Hans-Ulrich Klose, 'Vorbild, nicht Vormacht', *Bild-Zeitung*, 7 September 1994. On the idea that this would destroy the EU, see Heidemarie Wieczorek-Zeul, 'CDU/CSU-Papier zu "Kerneuropa" sofort zurückziehen', *Presseservice der SPD*, 12 September 1994. On credibility and reliability, and the embarrassment to Kinkel, see *Presseservice der SPD*, 5 and 14 September.
72 *Presseservice der SPD*, 5 September 1994.
73 'Koalitionsvereinbarung', 11 November 1994, p. 45.
74 Of course 'the treaty' refers to the Treaty on European Union negotiated at Maastricht, the revision of which was the task of the 1996/97 IGC. 'Gemeinsamer Brief des deutschen Bundeskanzlers und des französischen Staatspräsidenten an den Vorsitzenden des Europäischen Rates vom 6. 12. 1995' (excerpts), in Mathias Jopp and Otto Schmuck, *Die Reform der Europäischen Union* (Bonn: Europa Union Verlag, 1996), pp. 115–17. See also Hervé de Charette and Klaus Kinkel, 'Unsere Vorstellung von Europa', *Bulletin*, no. 27, 3 April 1996, pp. 273–4.
75 Karl Lamers, 'A German Agenda for the European Union', speech delivered at a Federal Trust/Konrad Adenauer Foundation conference, 17 November 1994, p. 4.
76 Josef Janning, 'Am Ende der Regierbarkeit? Gefährliche Folgen der Erweiterung der Europäischen Union', *Europa-Archiv*, 22 (1993).
77 Josef Janning, 'Bundesrepublik Deutschland', in Werner Weidenfeld and Wolfgang Wessels (eds), *Jahrbuch der Europäischen Integration 1994/95* (Bonn: Europa Union Verlag, 1995). For German positions in the IGC see Werner Hoyer, 'Perspektiven für die Regierungskonferenz 1996 und die europapolitische Agenda', *integration*, 18/4 (1995).
78 Klaus Kinkel, 'Die Europäische Union vor der Runderneuerung', Pressereferat Auswärtiges Amt, 21 February 1995.
79 The Schengen Agreement, concluded in 1985, envisaged the abolition of border controls between signatory states.

80 See also the successor documents to the Schäuble-Lamers paper issued by the CDU/CSU parliamentary caucus: 'Die Europäische Union außen- und sicherheitspolitisch handlungsfähiger machen', 13 June 1995; and 'Schäuble und Lamers: EU braucht konkrete Reformschritte', 28 March 1996.

81 Karl Lamers, 'Facing the IGC '96', speech at the Royal Institute for International Affairs, Brussels, 19 October 1995.

82 Karl Lamers, speech at the Hessische Stiftung für Frieden- und Konfliktforschung (HSFK), 31 October 1995, p. 3.

83 See Lamers quote at HSFK, 31 October 1995, p. 3.

84 Charles Grant, *Delors*, Chapter 4.

85 For an account of the following developments see David Marsh, *Germany and Europe. The Crisis of Unity* (London: Mandarin, 1995), pp. 155–64.

86 Ulrike Guèrot, 'Die französische Perzeption der deutschen Europapolitik im Bereich der Wirtschafts- und Währungsunion', in Werner Weidenfeld (ed.), *Deutsche Europapolitik* (Bonn: Europa Union, 1998), p. 393.

87 This could be an endless list. See, for instance, Rudolf Augstein, 'Maastricht – eine Fehlrechnung?', *Der Spiegel*, no. 21, 1995.

88 Guèrot, 'Die französische Perzeption', p. 134.

89 See, for instance, Lionel Barber, 'Enlargement may test EU's treaty', *Financial Times*, 19 June 1997.

90 On Helmut Kohl's preference for Poland, Hungary and the Czech Republic see, for instance, Lionel Barber, 'Enlargement may test EU's treaty', *Financial Times*, 19 June 1997; 'Leaders hope to agree on "Euro" currency', *Financial Times*, 15 December 1995; and Lionel Barber and David White, 'Kohl summit success on enlargement', *Financial Times*, 18 December 1995.

91 'See 'Europäischer Rat in Lissabon – Schlußfolgerungen des Vorsitzes', *Bulletin*, no. 71, 1 July 1992, p. 673.

92 Joachim Schild, 'Deutschland, Frankreich und die EFTA- Erweiterung der Europäischen Union', in Axel Sauder and Joachim Schild (eds), *Handeln für Europa* (Opladen: Leske und Budrich, 1995).

93 Karl Lamers, 'Deutschlands außenpolitische Verantwortung und seine Interessen', paper delivered at the 'Klausurtagung des Geschäftsführenden Fraktionsvorstandes der CDU/CSU', Berlin, 23/24 August 1993.

94 The 'double majority' refers to a system whereby a majority of states and a majority of the EU's population would have to back a decision in the Council; it is therefore another way of proposing a reweighting of votes in favour of large member states.

95 Karl Lamers, 'Deutschlands außenpolitische Verantwortung und seine Interessen', p. 12.

96 Helen Wallace, 'Vereinigtes Königreich', in Werner Weidenfeld and Wolfgang Wessels (eds), *Jahrbuch der europäischen Integration* (Bonn: Europa Union Verlag, 1994), p. 367.

97 Josef Janning, 'Bundesrepublik Deutschland', in Weidenfeld and Wessels (eds), *Jahrbuch der europäischen Integration*, p. 310.

98 'Schweden und Finnland mit Europa einig', *Frankfurter Allgemeine Zeitung*, 2 March 1994; Klaus-Peter Schmid, 'Der Beitritt als Basar', *Die Zeit*, 4 March 1994.

99 In 'Regierungserklärung vom 10. März 1994', *Das Parlament*, no. 11, 18 March 1994.

100 Helmut Kohl, Bundestag declaration entitled 'Aktuelle Fragen der Europapolitik', *Bulletin*, no. 51, 31 May 1997, p. 477.

101 'London fördert die Auflösung', *Frankfurter Allgemeine Zeitung*, 17 March 1994.

102 Simon Bulmer, Charlie Jeffery and William E. Paterson, 'Deutschlands Europäische Diplomatie', in Weidenfeld (ed.), *Deutsche Europapolitik*, p. 52. See also Kinkel's and Juppé's article 'Deutschland und Frankreich bleiben der Motor der europäischen Integration', *Frankfurter Allgemeine Zeitung*, 12 January 1995.

103 Representative of many see Klaus Manfrass, 'Das deutsch-französische Verhältnis nach der historischen Zäsur des Jahres 1989', *Aus Politik und Zeitgeschichte*, 30/95 (1995), p. 17.

104 Kohl's phrase was cautiously drafted. See 'Offizieller Besuch des Bundeskanzlers in der Republik Polen. Rede vor Sejm und Senat', *Bulletin*, no. 57, 14 July 1995, p. 572. Françoise de la Serre and Christian Lequesne, 'Frankreich', in Werner Weidenfeld and Wolfgang Wessels (eds), *Jahrbuch der europäischen Integration* (Bonn: Europa Union Verlag, 1997).

105 De La Serre and Lequesne, 'Frankreich', p. 332.

106 De La Serre and Lequesne, 'Frankreich', p. 333.

107 Peter Hort, 'Die deutsche Europapolitik wird ''britischer'' ', *Frankfurter Allgemeine Zeitung*, 4 November 1997.

108 Karl Lamers, cited in 'Meinungsunterschiede in der Wirtschaftspolitik', *Frankfurter Allgemeine Zeitung*, 4 November 1997.

109 'Außenminister Vedrine sieht Europa an einer ''Wegscheide'' ', *Handelsblatt*, 4 December 1997.

110 Michael Stabenow, 'Auf der Suche nach gemeinsamen Grundlagen der Europapolitik', *Frankfurter Allgemeine Zeitung*, 3 November 1997.

111 As an introduction, see Roland Sturm, 'Die Reform der Agrar- und Strukturpolitik', in Werner Weidenfeld (ed.), *Europa öffnen* (Gütersloh: Verlag Bertelsmann Stiftung, 1997).

112 Peter Katzenstein, *Tamed Power. Germany in Europe* (Ithaca, NY and London: Cornell University Press, 1997), p. 28.

113 Jochen Borchert, 'Perspektiven der Agrarpolitik', *Bulletin*, no. 46, 6 June 1997, p. 487.

114 'Brüssels Agenda 2000 stößt auf erste Einwände', *Handelsblatt*, 19 July 1997.

115 The author encountered this view in the numerous background interviews held in the Foreign Ministry and in the governing parties.

116 Ingo Kolboom, 'Stabilität ist ein kostbares Gut', *Christ und Welt – Rheinischer Merkur*, 11 October 1991.

5   Germany and Nato Enlargement

1 Hanns W. Maull and Knut Kirste, 'Zivilmacht und Rollentheorie', *Zeitschrift für Internationale Beziehungen*, 3/2 (1996), p. 303; for a discussion of the problems with this broad definition see Henning Tewes, 'Das Zivilmachtkonzept in der Theorie der Internationalen Beziehungen', *Zeitschrift für Internationale Beziehungen*, 4/2 (1997).

2 Helmut Kohl, 'Die deutsche Außenpolitik', in Kohl, *Reden 1982–1984* (Bonn: Presse- und Informationsamt der Bundesregierung, 1984), p. 379 (italics removed from the original).

3 Helmut Kohl, 'Die deutsche Außenpolitik', p. 381.

4 For an overview of American diplomacy towards Germany and the end of the Cold War see Joseph S. Nye and Robert O. Keohane, 'The United States and international institutions in Europe after the Cold War', in Joseph S. Nye, Robert O. Keohane and Stanley Hoffmann (eds), *After the Cold War* (Cambridge, MA: Harvard University Press, 1993).

5 Philip Zelikow and Condoleezza Rice, *Germany Unified and Europe Transformed* (Cambridge, MA: Harvard University Press, 1995), pp. 131–44.

6 Manfred Knapp, 'Europäische Sicherheit und die Osterweiterung der NATO aus der Sicht der USA', in August Pradetto (ed.), *Ostmitteleuropa, Rußland und die Osterweiterung der NATO* (Opladen: Westdeutscher Verlag, 1997), p. 263.

7 Genscher offers an incomplete discussion of the debate surrounding the speech. See Hans-Dietrich Genscher, *Erinnerungen*, (Munich: Goldmann, 1997), pp. 709–15.

8 Genscher, cited in Zelikow and Rice, *Germany Unified*, p. 175. See also Richard Kiessler and Frank Elbe, *Der diplomatische Weg zur deutschen Einheit* (Baden-Baden: Suhrkamp, 1996), pp. 77–85.

9 Cited in Zelikow and Rice, *Germany Unified*, p. 204.

10 'Botschaft an alle Deutschen', in Kohl, *Bilanzen und Perspektiven*, p. 413.

11 For a discussion of the significance of arms reductions for the diplomacy of the end of the Cold War see Michael Beschloss and Strobe Talbott, *Auf Höchster Ebene. Das Ende des Kalten Krieges und die Geheimdiplomatie der Supermächte 1988–1991* (Düsseldorf: Econ, 1994).

12 Adrian Hyde-Price, 'Uncertainties of security policy', in Gordon Smith et al. (eds), *Developments in German Politics* (London: Macmillan, now Palgrave, 1992), p. 163.

13 Friedbert Pflüger in Deutscher Bundestag, *Drucksachen*, 13/184, 26 June 1997, p. 16623.

14 This is not the case for the deployment of Bundeswehr troops in out-of-area missions. For a discussion of the overall consensus see Gunther Hellmann, ' "Machtbalance und Vormachtdenken sind überholt": Zum außenpolitischen Diskurs im vereinigten Deutschland', in Monika Oledick-Krakau (ed.), *Außenpolitischer Wandel in theoretischer und vergleichender Sicht* (Baden-Baden: Nomos, 1998).

15 Wolfram Hanrieder, *Deutschland, Europa, Amerika*, 2nd revised and expanded edn (Paderborn: Schöningh, 1995), p. 449.

16 An unpronounceable acronym often pronounced as 'Naksy'.

17 The term 'council' is used when the North Atlantic Council meets at the level of foreign ministers. When it meets at the level of heads of government, the term 'summit' is used.

18 'Kleine Sensation am Rande', *Christ und Welt – Rheinischer Merkur*, 8 December 1995.

19 Ralf Roloff, *Auf dem Weg zur Neuordnung Europas* (Vierow bei Greifswald: SH-Verlag, 1995).

20 Interview, Krzysztof Skubiszewski, Warsaw, 14 August 1997.

21 Helmut Kohl, 'Grundlagen und Leitlinien für eine gemeinsame europäische Zukunft', *Bulletin*, no. 26, 5 March 1992, p. 256.

22 Ottfried Hennig, 'Prinzipien deutscher Politik und europäischer Partnerschaft', *Bulletin*, no. 7, 16 January 1992, p. 46.

23 Hans-Dietrich Genscher, 'Perspektiven gemeinsamer Politik und kooperativer Sicherheit in Europa', *Bulletin*, no. 81, 12 July 1991, p. 655.

24 This hope was no passing fancy. For an early elaboration see Kohl, 'Die deutsche Außenpolitik', in *Reden 1982–1984*, p. 383.

25 Desmond Dinan, *Ever Closer Union?* (London: Macmillan, now Palgrave, 1994), pp. 471–3; Charles Grant, *Delors – Inside the House that Jacques Built.* (London: Nicholas Brealey, 1994), pp. 185–90; Keith Middlemas, *Orchestrating Europe. The Informal Politics of European Union 1973–1995* (London: Fontana, 1995), pp. 184–93.

26 For a comprehensive discussion of the differences and similarities in the security policies of East Central European countries see the contributions to August Pradetto (ed.), *Ostmitteleuropa, Rußland und die Osterweiterung der NATO* (Opladen: Westdeutscher Verlag, 1996).

27 Cited in Winfried Münster, 'Havel huldigt dem Atlantischen Bündnis', *Süddeutsche Zeitung*, 22 March 1992.

28 Interview, Jan Parys, Warsaw, 14 July 1997.

29 Edith Heller, 'Polen möchte Schutz der NATO', *Frankfurter Rundschau*, 14 March 1992.

30 Rüdiger Moniac, 'Polen sucht Schutz vor Unruhe im Osten', *Die Welt*, 25 March 1992.

31 Interview, Janusz Onyszkiewicz, Warsaw, 22 July 1997; see also 'Mitgliedschaft in der Nato polnische Verteidigungsdoktrin', *Frankfurter Allgemeine Zeitung*, 1 August 1992.

32 Rüdiger Moniac, 'Polen sucht Schutz vor Unruhe im Osten', *Die Welt*, 25 March 1992.

33 Geremek's speech is reprinted in Roland Freudenstein (ed.), *VII. Deutsch-Polnisches Forum:* (Bonn: Europa-Union Verlag, 1993), p. 53.

34 For instance in Jörg Schönbohm's speech, reprinted in Freudenstein (ed.), *VII. Deutsch-Polnisches Forum*, p. 49.

35 For a juxtaposition of Nato and the Warsaw Pact see John Lewis Gaddis, *We Now Know. Rethinking Cold War History* (Oxford: Oxford University Press, 1997), chapter 7; for the effect the weaker European states had on American decision making in Nato, see Thomas Risse-Kappen, *Co-operation Among Democracies* (Princeton, NJ: Princeton University Press, 1995).

36 Pàl Dunay, 'Theological debates on NATO in Hungary', *Foreign Policy* (Hungarian version), 3/special issue (1997).

37 Both Verheugen and Irmer are cited in Deutscher Bundestag, *Drucksachen*, 13/184, 26 June 1997, p. 16629.

38 See, for instance, Philip H. Gordon, *France, Germany, and the Western Alliance* (Oxford: Westview, 1995), pp. 46–53.

39 Michael Mandelbaum, *The Dawn of Peace in Europe* (New York: Twentieth Century Fund Press, 1996).

40 For a cautious elaboration of this argument see Helmut Kohl, 'Bündnis- und Einsatzfähigkeit der Bundeswehr bleiben gewährleistet', *Bulletin*, no. 58, 2 July 1993, pp. 609–12.

41   Volker Rühe, 'Gestaltung euro-atlantischer Politik – eine "Grand Strategy" für unsere Zeit', *Bulletin*, no. 27, 1 April 1993, pp. 229–33. Rühe had mentioned the possibility of Nato enlargement in previous speeches, but had not been as explicit. The London speech was therefore seen as pathbreaking. See also Volker Rühe 'Die Bundeswehr im europäischen Einigungsprozeß', *Bulletin*, no. 18, 19 February 1993, pp. 145–7.

42   In the 1990s, preventive, precautionary diplomacy posed fewer problems for German security policy than military intervention in crisis situations. Hanrieder, *Deutschland, Europa, Amerika*, pp. 124–5.

43   Rühe, 'Gestaltung euro-atlantischer Politik', p. 231.

44   For the academic argument see Daniel N. Nelson, 'Democracy, markets, and security in Eastern Europe', *Survival*, 35/2 (1993).

45   Rühe, 'Gestaltung euro-atlantischer Politik', p. 232. The stabilization of East Central Europe had long been a preoccupation of Rühe's. See the speeches on EU enlargement cited in Chapter 3. See also, for instance, his 'Verantwortung Deutschlands in der internationalen Völkergemeinschaft', *Bulletin*, no. 6, 18 January 1997, pp. 41–4.

46   Rühe, 'Gestaltung euro-atlantischer Politik', p. 232.

47   Interview, Bronislaw Geremek, Warsaw, 5 August 1997.

48   Helmut Kohl, 'Die Sicherheitsinteressen Deutschlands', *Bulletin*, no. 13, 10 February 1993, p. 103.

49   Helmut Kohl, 'Bündnis- und Einsatzfähigkeit der Bundeswehr bleiben gewährleistet'.

50   'Auf der Suche nach einem Mittelweg', *Frankfurter Allgemeine Zeitung*, 6 March 1993.

51   Volker Rühe, 'Die NATO als Fundament der Sicherheitsarchitektur der Zukunft', *Bulletin*, no. 46, 2 June 1993, p. 494.

52   Françoise Manfrass-Sirjacques, 'Frankreichs Position zur NATO-Osterweiterung', in August Pradetto (ed.), *Ostmitteleuropa, Rußland und die Osterweiterung der NATO* (Opladen: Westdeutscher Verlag, 1996). Gordon, *France, Germany, and the Western Alliance*.

53   Trevor Taylor, 'Großbritannien und die Erweiterung der NATO', in Pradetto (ed.), *Ostmitteleuropa, Rußland und die Osterweiterung der NATO*.

54   Manfred Knapp, 'Europäische Sicherheit und die Osterweiterung der NATO aus der Sicht der USA', in Pradetto (ed.), *Ostmitteleuropa, Rußland und die Osterweiterung der NATO*.

55   'Wir handeln "out of area" und sind sehr wohl "in business"', reprinted in Manfred Wörner, *Für Frieden in Freiheit* (Berlin: edition q, 1995), p. 289. For an example of how Rühe played on Wörner's support see Rühe's speech, 'Deutsche Sicherheitspolitik vor neuen Aufgaben', *Bulletin*, no. 83, 8 October 1993, p. 952.

56   Uwe Nerlich, 'Neue Sicherheitsfunktionen der NATO', *Europa-Archiv*, 23 (1993), p. 670.

57   'Polen fordert Zeitplan für NATO-Beitritt', *Frankfurter Allgemeine Zeitung*, 27 August 1993.

58   'Bedenken Jelzins gegen eine Ausweitung der NATO nach Osten', *Frankfurter Allgemeine Zeitung*, 2 October 1993.

59   For a discussion of what follows see Nick Williams, 'Partnership for Peace: permanent fixture or declining asset?', *Survival*, 38/1 (1996).

60 For details on Partnership for Peace see Anon., *NATO-Handbuch* (Brussels: NATO Presse- und Informationsdienst, 1995), pp. 55–64.

61 See also his 'Polen und die Nordatlantische Allianz', *Frankfurter Rundschau*, 3 January 1994. The members of the Clinton Administration were Madeleine Albright, Ambassador to the United Nations, and Jon Shalikashvili, Chairman of the Joint Chiefs of Staff.

62 Stefan Kornelius, 'Die NATO verordnet sich eine lange Denkpause – In der Debatte um die Osterweiterung mußte Volker Rühe vorerst zurückstecken', *Süddeutsche Zeitung*, 23 October 1993.

63 Karl Lamers, 'Suche nach einer neuen Balance', *Deutsches Allgemeines Sonntagsblatt*, 24 September 1993.

64 'Minister Rühe nennt die alte NATO überholt', *General-Anzeiger*, 29 September 1993.

65 'Deutsches Doppel', *Focus*, no. 41, 11 October 1993, p. 30.

66 Herbert Kremp, 'Rückkehr zum Realismus', *Die Welt*, 6 October 1993.

67 Interview, Foreign Ministry, Bonn, 1 September 1997.

68 Interview, Foreign Ministry, Bonn, 11 September 1997.

69 Herbert Kremp, 'Rückkehr zum Realismus', *Die Welt*, 6 October 1993.

70 'Kohl lehnt größere NATO ab', *Frankfurter Rundschau*, 2 December 1993.

71 Interview, CDU Bundestag Caucus, Bonn, 3 September 1997.

72 'Rühe warnt vor "Vetorecht" für Rußland', *Frankfurter Allgemeine Zeitung*, 9 December 1993.

73 Kurt Kister, 'Washingtoner Absage an Rühe und Wörner', *Süddeutsche Zeitung*, 18 December 1993.

74 'Rüttgers: Gefahr im Verzug', *Frankfurter Allgemeine Zeitung*, 22 December 1993. In January, Heiner Geißler, former CDU general secretary, and Wolfgang Schäuble, the CDU/CSU parliamentary leader, also argued in favour of Nato enlargement with reference to the Duma elections. See dpa press release, 'NATO/Beitritt' (Zweite Zusammenfassung), 8 January 1994.

75 'Für die Osterweiterung der Nato', in Friedbert Pflüger, *Die Zukunft des Ostens liegt im Westen* (Düsseldorf and Vienna: econ, 1994), pp. 113–14, see also Friedbert Pflüger, 'Polen – unser Frankreich im Osten', in Wolfgang Schäuble and Rudolf Seiters (eds.), *Außenpolitik im 21. Jahrhundert. Die Thesen der jungen Außenpolitiker* (Bonn: Bouvier, 1996).

76 We thus have a slightly different interpretation here than Reinhard Wolf, 'The doubtful mover: Germany and NATO expansion', in David J. Haglund (ed.), *Will NATO go East?* (Belfast: Queens University, Centre for International Relations, 1996).

77 'Die Lava läuft noch', *Der Spiegel*, vol. 51, 20 December 1993, p. 18–20.

78 'Jelzin warnt abermals vor einer Erweiterung der atlantischen Allianz nach Osten', *Frankfurter Allgemeine Zeitung*, 6 January 1994.

79 Jiri Dienstbier, 'Die NATO-Partnerschaft für den Frieden darf kein Ersatzzuckerl sein', *Frankfurter Rundschau*, 6 January 1994.

80 Clinton is cited in 'Jelzin warnt abermals vor einer Erweiterung der atlantischen Allianz nach Osten', *Frankfurter Allgemeine Zeitung*, 6 January 1994.

81 Claus Gennrich, 'Kohl: Die NATO muß die Sicherheitsbedürfnisse der östlichen Nachbarn sehr ernst nehmen', *Frankfurter Allgemeine Zeitung*, 8 January 1994.

82 'Die "Partnerschaft für den Frieden" im Wortlaut', dpa press release, 10 January 1994.

83   'Wehrübung mit Polen noch in diesem Jahr', *Frankfurter Allgemeine Zeitung*, 28 January 1994.
84   Wolfgang Pailer, *Stanisław Stomma. Nestor der deutsch- polnischen Aussöhnung* (Bonn: Bouvier, 1995), p. 157.
85   For a discussion see Sven Berhard Gareis, 'Gemeinsam für Stabilität in Europa', *Welttrends*, 13 (1996). Much of what follows is taken from a bro- chure of the Defence Ministry: 'Ko-operation – ein entscheidender Faktor für Stabilität und Frieden in Europa', Bundesministerium der Verteidigung, Referat Öffentlichkeitsarbeit, May 1997. The author is grateful to two offi- cials in the ministry who took the time to explain the details and answer his questions.
86   Documents obtained from the Defence Ministry.
87   Helmut Kohl, 'Erklärung der Bundesregierung zum NATO-Gipfel in Brüssel, *Bulletin*, no. 3, 17 January 1994, pp. 17–18.
88   To underline that this consensus had now been established see also Kohl's speech in Munich two weeks afterwards: 'Europäische Sicherheit und die Rolle Deutschlands', *Bulletin*, no. 15, 16 February 1994, pp. 131–7.
89   Interview, Foreign Ministry, Bonn, 19 September 1997.
90   'Deutschlands Verantwortung in und für Europa', *Bulletin*, no. 47, 24 May 1994, p. 422, see also 'Europäische Sicherheit und die Zukunft der Bundes- wehr', *Bulletin*, no. 28, 28 March 1994, p. 254.
91   See, for instance, 'Zukunftssicherung durch europäisch-atlantische Partnerschaft', *Bulletin*, no. 36, 26 April 1994, pp. 322–4; 'Rolle der Nato als europäischer Stabilitätsanker', *Bulletin*, no. 58, 16 June 1994, pp. 545–6.
92   'Rühe: Polen noch in diesem Jahrzehnt NATO-Mitglied', dpa press release, 18 July 1994.
93   'Die NATO muß Namen nennen', *Süddeutsche Zeitung*, 1 October 1994.
94   'Kinkel und Rühe uneins über Nato- Erweiterung', *Frankfurter Allgemeine Zeitung*, 7 October 1994. 'Außenminister Kinkel geht auf Distanz zu Rühe. Gegen rasche Erweiterung der NATO nach Osten', *Süddeutsche Zeitung*, 7 October 1994.
95   Koalitionsvereinbarung, 11 November 1994.
96   'Perry fordert zur Unterstützung Jelzins auf', *Frankfurter Allgemeine Zeitung*, 7 February 1994.
97   'NATO-Mitgliedschaft der Reformstaaten nur Frage der Zeit', *Süddeutsche Zeitung*, 8 July 1994.
98   'Kosyrev unterschreibt die Vereinbarungen über Partnerschaft für den Frie- den nicht', *Frankfurter Allgemeine Zeitung*, 2 December 1994.
99   It is remarkable how profoundly Holbrooke shaped European security affairs within a period of two and a half years. There is little material about his involvement, though some written by himself. See Richard Hol- brooke, 'America, a European power', *Foreign Affairs*, 74/2 (1995).
100 Stephen F. Szabo, 'Ein Projekt "Made in Germany"', *Frankfurter Allgemeine Zeitung*, 24 July 1997.
101 James M. Goldgeier, 'NATO expansion: the anatomy of a decision', *Washington Quarterly*, 21/2 (1997).
102 Karsten D. Voigt, 'Die wichtigste Aufgabe einer neuen Ostpolitik: Die Ver- westlichung Osteuropas', manuscript, 4 February 1992 (obtained from Mr Voigt's office).

103 Bahr presented his views in a number of newspaper articles. As a good summary see his *Deutsche Interessen* (Munich: Blessing, 1998).

104 'Brett vor dem Kopf – Ein linkes Flügel-Bündnis unterläuft Rudolf Scharpings außenpolitische Kurskorrektur', *Focus*, no. 49, 2 December 1996, pp. 41–2.

105 Interview, Karsten Voigt, Bonn, 22 September 1997.

106 Interview, Karsten Voigt, Bonn, 22 September 1997.

107 Interview with Günther Verheugen, Bonn, 8 December 1997.

108 Deutscher Bundestag, *Drucksachen*, 13/224, Bonn, 26 March 1998, p. 20453.

109 Two SPD deputies, six from the Greens and the entire PDS caucus objected; one CDU deputy and four SPD deputies abstained, the other abstentions came from the Greens. Deutscher Bundestag, *Drucksachen*, 13/224, Bonn, 26 March 1998, p. 20461.

110 Stefan Kornelius, 'Schickt den Russen eine klare Botschaft', *Süddeutsche Zeitung*, 25 January 1995.

111 'Rühe spricht erstmals von einem Vertrag der NATO mit Rußland', *Frankfurter Allgemeine Zeitung*, 16 February 1995.

112 'Gratschow droht der Nato', *Die Welt*, 4 April 1995; 'Kinkel nennt Drohungen Gratschows und Lebeds äußerst unklug', *Frankfurter Allgemeine Zeitung*, 18 April 1995.

113 Selectively, see 'Bundesregierung über angebliche Pläne Washingtons befremdet', *Frankfurter Allgemeine Zeitung* , 9 May 1995; 'Angebot einer NATO-Mitgliedschaft Rußlands in Clintons Brief an Jelzin wohl nicht enthalten', *Frankfurter Allgemeine Zeitung*, 11 May 1995.

114 For Kinkel see 'Washington: Kanzleramt ist Inhalt des Briefes an Jelzin bekannt', *Frankfurter Allgemeine Zeitung*, 12 May 1995; for Hoyer see 'Angebot einer NATO-Mitgliedschaft Rußlands in Clintons Brief an Jelzin wohl nicht enthalten', *Frankfurter Allgemeine Zeitung*, 11 May 1995.

115 'Europäische Sicherheit und die Rolle Deutschlands', *Bulletin*, no. 15, 16 February 1994, p. 136.

116 'Europa und Amerika – neue Partnerschaft für die Zukunft', *Bulletin*, no. 9, 6 February 1995, p. 75.

117 'Eine gerechte und dauerhafte Friedensordnung für ganz Europa', *Bulletin*, no. 12, 16 February 1995, p. 96.

118 Ronald D. Asmus, Richard L. Kugler and F. Stephen Larrabee, 'NATO expansion: the next steps', *Survival*, 37/1 (1995).

119 'Rühe: Ost-Erweiterung der NATO noch vor dem Jahr 2000', *Frankfurter Allgemeine Zeitung*, 30 May 1995.

120 'Junktim mit EU-Mitgliedschaft?', *Frankfurter Allgemeine Zeitung*, 5 July 1995.

121 See 'Offizieller Besuch des Bundeskanzlers in der Republik Polen. Rede vor Sejm und Senat', *Bulletin*, no. 57, 14 July 1995, p. 572.

122 'Die Außenpolitik als Wahlkampfthema', *Frankfurter Allgemeine Zeitung*, 24 October 1996.

123 Klaus Kinkel and Andrej Kozyrev, 'Rußlands Größe wird nicht von der Zahl seiner Soldaten bestimmt', *Frankfurter Allgemeine Zeitung*, 18 February 1994.

124 Anneli Ute Gabanyi, 'Rumäniens Beitrittsstrategie zur NATO', *Osteuropa*, 47/9 (1997).

125 Interview, Foreign Ministry, Bonn, 11 September 1997.

126 Volker Rühe, 'Gestaltung euro-atlantischer Politik'.

127 Interview with Günther Verheugen, Bonn, 8 December 1997.

Conclusion

1 Joschka Fischer, 'Die Schwerpunkte der deutschen Ratspräsidentschaft', *Bulletin*, no. 2, 14 January 1999, pp. 9–12.
2 A point initially raised by Hans-Martin Jäger, 'Konstruktionsfehler des Konstruktivismus in den Internationalen Beziehungen', *Zeitschrift für Internationale Beziehungen*, 3/2 (1996).
3 Gunther Hellmann, 'Die Prekäre Macht. Deutsche Außenpolitik an der Schwelle zum 21. Jahrhundert', in Karl Kaiser and Wolf-Dieter Eberwein (eds), *Deutschlands Neue Außenpolitik* (Munich: Oldenbourg, 1998), vol. 4: Resourcen und Institutionen.
4 Simon Bulmer, Charlie Jeffery and William E. Paterson, 'Deutschlands Europäische Diplomatie', in Werner Weidenfeld (ed.), *Deutsche Europapolitik. Optionen wirksamer Interessenvertretung* (Bonn: Europa Union, 1998).
5 Joseph M. Grieco, 'Anarchy and the limits of co- operation: a realist critique of the newest liberal institutionalism', *International Organisation*, 42/3 (1988).
6 Hanns W. Maull, 'Germany and Japan: the new Civilian Powers', *Foreign Affairs*, 69/5 (1990).
7 Hanns W. Maull and Knut Kirste, 'Zivilmacht und Rollentheorie', *Zeitschrift für Internationale Beziehungen*, 3/2 (1996).

Epilogue

1 Clay Clemens, 'The Chancellor as Party Manager. Helmut Kohl, the CDU, and Governance in Germany', *West European Politics*, 17/4 (1994); Karl-Rudolf Korte, *Deutschlandpolitik in Helmut Kohls Kanzlerschaft* (Stuttgart: Deutsche Verlags-Anstalt, 1998).
2 'Schröder mahnt europäische Koordinierung in Wirtschaftspolitik an', dpa press release, 24 October 1998.
3 See Auswärtiges Amt, 'Ziele und Schwerpunkte der deutschen Präsidentschaft im Rat der Europäischen Union, 1 September 1998, 'Koalitionsvereinbarung zwischen der Sozialdemokratischen Partei Deutschlands und Bündnis 90/ Die Grünen' at http://www.spd.de/aktuell/programmatisches/vertrag.htm
4 Peter Norman, 'Schröder warns on EU enlargement', *Financial Times*, 27 November 1998.
5 'Bundesregierung: Keine EU-Erweiterung ohne Finanzreform', *Frankfurter Allgemeine Zeitung*, 3 December 1998.
6 Günther Verheugen, 'Deutschland und die EU-Ratspräsidentschaft', *integration*, 22/1 (1999), p. 1.
7 Jeffrey J. Anderson, 'Hard interests, soft power, and Germany's changing role in Europe', in Peter J. Katzenstein (ed.), *Tamed Power. Germany in Europe* (Ithaca, NY and London: Cornell University Press, 1997).
8 Marek A. Cichocki, 'Niemcy odwracają się od Polski', *Zycie*, 28 January 1999.
9 Vladimir Handl, 'Die neue deutsche Außenpolitik: Erwartungen aus tschechischer Sicht', *Welttrends*, 21 (1998).
10 Piotr Buras, 'Niemiecka Neuroza?', *Gazeta Wyborcza*, 9 December 1998.

11 From parts of the opposition, interest groups and in published opinion. See, for instance, Ludger Kühnhardt, 'Bonn muß Zeitplan für Osterweiterung einhalten', *Focus*, no. 52, 1998, p. 40.

12 For this and all following quotations until the end of the paragraph see Fischer, 'Die Schwerpunkte der deutschen Ratspräsidentschaft', pp. 9–12.

13 Claus Giering, 'Europa im Wandel. Perspektiven deutscher Europapolitik', *Welttrends*, 21 (1998), p. 20.

14 For this and the following quotation see Deutscher Bundestag, *Plenarprotokoll*, 14/31, 26 March 1999, p. 2586.

Select Bibliography

On international relations theory, Civilian Power and role theory

Adler, Emmanuel and Barnett, Michael, *Security Communities* (Cambridge: Cambridge University Press, 1999).

Almond, Gabriel A. and Verba, Sidney, *The Civic Culture: Political Attitudes and Democracy in Five Nations* (Princeton, NJ: Princeton University Press, 1963).

Angell, Norman, *The Great Illusion* (London: Heinemann, 1933).

Baldwin, David A. (ed.), *Neorealism and Neoliberalism, The Contemporary Debate* (New York: Columbia University Press, 1993).

Brown, Michael E., Lynn-Jones, Sean M. and Miller, Steven E. (eds), *Debating the Democratic Peace* (Cambridge, MA: MIT Press, 1996).

Carr, E. H., *The Twenty Years Crisis, 1919–39* (London: Macmillan, now Palgrave, 1948).

Clarke, Michael and White, Brian (eds), *Understanding Foreign Policy* (Aldershot: Edward Elgar, 1989).

Deutsch, Karl W. (ed.), *Political Community and the North Atlantic Area* (Princeton, NJ: Princeton University Press, 1957).

Dunne, Timothy, 'The social construction of international society', *European Journal of International Relations*, 1/3 (1995).

Elias, Norbert, *The Civilising Process* (Oxford: Blackwell, 1994).

Fitzgerald, Thomas F., *Metaphors of Identity* (Albany, NY: State University of New York Press, 1993).

Fosdick, Raymond B., *Letters on the League of Nations* (Princeton, NJ: Princeton University Press, 1966).

Hobson, J. A., *Towards International Government* (London: Allen & Unwin, 1916).

Hobson, J. A., *Richard Cobden: The International Man* (London: T. Fisher Unwin, 1918).

Howard, Michael, *War and the Liberal Conscience* (London: Temple Smith, 1978).

Jonas, Hans, 'Role theories and socialisation research', in H. J. Helle and S. N. Eisenstadt (eds), *Micro-Sociological Theory* (London: Sage, 1985).

Kant, Immanuel, *Perpetual Peace* (Westwood Village, LA, US Library Association, 1932).

Katzenstein, Peter J. (ed.), *The Culture of National Security* (New York: Columbia University Press, 1996).

Keohane, Robert O., *After Hegemony, Cooperation and Discord in the World Political Economy* (Princeton, NJ: Princeton University Press, 1984).

Lapid, Yosef and Kratochwil, Friedrich (eds), *The Return of Culture and Identity in IR Theory* (Boulder, CO: Lynne Rienner, 1996).

Long, David and Wilson, Peter, *Thinkers of the Twenty Years' Crisis* (Oxford: Clarendon, 1995).

Lukes, Steven, *Power: A Radical View* (London: Macmillan, now Palgrave, 1974).

Maull, Hanns W., 'Germany and Japan: the new Civilian Powers', *Foreign Affairs*, 69/5 (1990).

Maull, Hanns W., 'Zivilmacht Bundesrepublik Deutschland', *Europa-Archiv*, 10 (1992).

Maull, Hanns W., 'Civilian Power: the concept and its relevance for security issues', in Lidija Babic and Bo Huldt (eds), *Mapping the Unknown: Towards a New World Order* (Stockholm: Swedish Institute for International Affairs, 1993).

Maull, Hanns W., 'Zivilmacht: Die Konzeption und ihre sicherheitspolitische Relevanz', in W. Heydich et al. (eds), *Sicherheitspolitik Deutschlands: Neue Konstellationen, Risiken, Instrumente* (Baden-Baden: Nomos, 1993).

Maull, Hanns W. and Gordon, Philip H., 'German foreign policy and the German "National Interest": German and American perspectives', *AICGS Working Papers*, 5 (1993).

Maull, Hanns W. and Kirste, Knut, 'Zivilmacht und Rollentheorie', *Zeitschrift für Internationale Beziehungen*, 3/2 (1996).

Maull, Hanns W. et al., 'Deutsche, amerikanische und japanische Außenpolitikstrategien 1985–1995: Eine vergleichende Untersuchung zu Zivilisierungsprozessen in der Triade', DFG–Forschungsprojekt 'Zivilmächte' (1997). Schlussbericht und Ergebnisse. Deutsche, amerikanische und japanische Außenpolitikstrategien 1985–1995: Eine vergleichende Untersuchung zu Zivilisierungsprozessen in der Triade (gefördert durch die Deutsche Forschungsgemeinschaft (MA 687/4–1 und 2), Trier: Universität Trier), http://www.unitrier.de/uni/fb3/politik/workshop/dfgfinal.pdf (accessed 22 December 2000).

Mearsheimer, John, 'Back to the future: instability in Europe after the Cold War', *International Security*, 15/1 (1990).

Morgenthau, Hans J., *Politics among Nations*, brief edn (New York: McGraw-Hill, 1993).

Neack, Laura, Hey, Jeanne and Haney, Patrick J. (eds.), *Foreign Policy Analysis – Continuity and Change in its Second Generation* (Englewood Cliffs, NJ: Prentice Hall, 1995).

Nye, Joseph S., 'Soft Power', *Foreign Policy*, 80 (1990).

Pye, Lucian W. and Verba, Sidney (eds.), *Political Culture and Political Development* (Princeton, NJ: Princeton University Press, 1965).

Risse-Kappen, Thomas, *Cooperation Among Democracies* (Princeton, NJ: Princeton University Press, 1995).

Rosecrance, Richard, *The Rise of the Trading State* (New York: Basic Books, 1986).

Rosenau, James N., 'Roles and role scenarios in foreign policy', in Stephen G. Walker (ed.), *Role Theory and Foreign Policy Analysis* (Durham, NC: Duke University Press, 1987).

Sarbin, Theodore R. and Allen, Vernon L., 'Role theory', in Gardner Lindzey and Elliot Aronson (eds), *The Handbook of Social Psychology* (Reading, MA: Addison-Wesley, 1968).

Turner, Ralph H., 'Unanswered questions in the convergence between structuralist and interactionist role theories', in H. J. Helle and S. N. Eisenstadt (eds), *Micro-Sociological Theory* (London: Sage, 1985).

Walker, S. G. (ed.), *Role Theory and Foreign Policy Analysis* (Durham, NC: Duke University Press, 1987).

Waltz, Kenneth, *Theory of International Politics* (Reading, MA: Addison-Wesley, 1979).

Wendt, Alexander, 'The agent–structure problem in international relations theory', *International Organisation*, 41/3 (1987).

Wendt, Alexander, 'Anarchy is what states make of it: the social construction of power politics', *International Organisation*, 46/2 (1992).

On the history of German foreign policy

Eisfeld, Rainer, 'Mitteleuropa in historical and contemporary perspective', *German Politics and Society*, 28, Spring (1993).

Fischer, Fritz, *Griff nach der Weltmacht: Die Kriegszielpolitik des kaiserlichen Deutschland 1914/18* (Düsseldorf: Droste, 1961).

Gall, Lothar et al. (eds), *The Deutsche Bank, 1870–1995* (London: Weidenfeld & Nicolson, 1995).

Keynes, John Maynard, *The Economic Consequences of the Peace* (New York: Harcourt, Brace & Howe, 1920).

Krekeler, Norbert, *Revisionsanspruch und geheime Ostpolitik der Weimarer Republik* (Stuttgart: Deutsche Verlags-Anstalt, 1973).

Krüger, Peter, *Die Außenpolitik der Republik von Weimar* (Darmstadt: Wissenschaftliche Buchgesellschaft, 1984).

Naumann, Friedrich, *Mitteleuropa* (Berlin: Georg Reimer, 1915).

Stirk Peter M. R., (ed.), *Mitteleuropa. History and Prospects* (Edinburgh: Edinburgh University Press, 1994).

Turner, Henry Ashby, *Stresemann and the Politics of the Weimar Republic* (Westport, CT: Greenwood, 1963).

On the Federal Republic and its foreign policy

Baring, Arnulf, *Machtwechsel. Die Ära Brandt-Scheel* (Stuttgart: Deutsche Verlags-Anstalt, 1982).

Bingen, Dieter, *Die Polenpolitik der Bonner Republik von Adenauer bis Kohl, 1949–1991* (Baden-Baden: Nomos, 1998).

Clemens, Clay, *Reluctant Realists. The Christian Democrats and West German Ostpolitik* (Durham, NC: Duke University Press, 1989).

Dahrendorf, Ralf, *Society and Democracy in Germany* (London: Weidenfeld & Nicolson, 1967).

Gaddum, Eckart, *Die deutsche Europapolitik in den 80er Jahren. Interessen, Konflikte und Entscheidungen der Regierung Kohl* (Paderborn: Schöningh, 1994).

Garton Ash, Timothy, *In Europe's Name: Germany and the Divided Continent* (London: Vintage, 1993).

Genscher, Hans-Dietrich, *Erinnerungen* (Munich: Goldmann, 1997).

Hacke, Christian, *Die Außenpolitik der Bundesrepublik Deutschland* (Berlin: Ullstein, 1997).

Haftendorn, Helga, 'Außenpolitische Prioritäten und Handlungsspielraum. Ein Paradigma zur Analyse der Außenpolitik der Bundesrepublik Deutschland', *Politische Vierteljahresschrift*, 30/1 (1989).

Hanrieder, Wolfram, *Germany, America, Europe* (New Haven, CT and London: Yale University Press, 1989).

Hrbek, Rudolf and Wessels, Wolfgang (eds), *EG-Mitgliedschaft: Ein nationales Interesse der Bundesrepublik Deutschland?* (Bonn: Europa Union Verlag, 1984).

Katzenstein, Peter, *Policy and Politics in West Germany: The Growth of a Semi-Sovereign State* (Philadelphia: Temple University Press, 1987).

Korte, Karl-Rudolf, *Deutschlandpolitik in Helmut Kohls Kanzlerschaft* (Stuttgart: Deutsche Verlags-Anstalt, 1998).

Pommerin, Reiner (ed.), *The American Impact on Postwar Germany* (Providence, RI,: Berghahn, 1995).

Pulzer, Peter, *German Politics 1945–1995* (Oxford: Oxford University Press, 1995).

Schöllgen, Gregor, *Angst vor der Macht. Die Deutschen und ihre Außenpolitik* (Berlin: Ullstein, 1993).

Schwarz, Hans-Peter, *Die gezähmten Deutschen. Von der Machtvergessenheit zur Machtbessessenheit* (Stuttgart: Deutsche Verlags-Anstalt, 1985).

On German foreign policy after unification

Anderson, Jeffrey J. and Goodman, John B., 'Mars or Minerva? A united Germany in a post-Cold War Europe', in Robert O. Keohane, Joseph S. Nye, and Stanley Hoffmann (eds), *After the Cold War* (Cambridge, MA: Harvard University Press, 1993).

Bahr, Egon, *Deutsche Interessen* (Munich: Blessing, 1998).

Baring, Arnulf, *Deutschland, was nun?* (Berlin: Siedler, 1991).

Baring, Arnulf, *Germany's New Position in Europe* (Oxford and Washington, DC: Berg, 1994).

Deubner, Christian, *Deutsche Europapolitik: Von Maastricht nach Kerneuropa?* (Baden-Baden: Nomos, 1995).

Guèrot, Ulrike, 'Deuschland, Frankreich und die Währungsunion – über Diskussionen und Metadiskussionen', *Frankreich Jahrbuch 1997* (Opladen: Leske und Budrich, 1997).

Hellmann, Gunther, 'Goodbye Bismarck? The foreign policy of contemporary Germany', *Mershon International Studies Review*, 40/1 (1996).

Kaiser, Karl and Eberwein, Wolf-Dieter (eds), *Deutschlands Neue Außenpolitik* (Munich: Oldenbourg, 1998), Vol. 4: Resourcen und Institutionen.

Kaiser, Karl and Maull, Hanns W. (eds), *Deutschland Neue Außenpolitik* (Munich: Oldenbourg, 1994), Vol. 1: Grundlagen.

Kaiser, Karl and Maull, Hanns W. (eds), *Deutschlands Neue Außenpolitik* (Munich: Oldenbourg, 1995), Vol. 2: Herausforderungen.

Katzenstein, Peter, *Tamed Power. Germany in Europe* (Ithaca, NY and London: Cornell University Press, 1997).

Kohl, Helmut, *Ich wollte Deutschlands Einheit* (Berlin: Propyläen, 1996).

Markovits, Andrei and Reich, Simon, 'Should Europe fear the Germans?', *German Politics and Society*, 23 (1991).

Markovits, Andrei and Reich, Simon, *The German Predicament. Memory and Power in the New Europe* (Ithaca and London: Cornell University Press, 1997).

Paterson, William E., 'Beyond semi-sovereignty: the new Germany in the new Europe', *German Politics*, 5/2 (1996).

Paterson, William E., 'Helmut Kohl, "The Vision Thing" and escaping the semi-sovereignty trap', in Clay Clemens and William E. Paterson (eds), *The Kohl Chancellorship* (London: Frank Cass, 1998).

Peters, Ingo, 'Vom "Scheinzwerg" zum "Scheinriesen" – deutsche Außenpolitik in der Analyse', *Zeitschrift für Internationale Beziehungen*, 4/2 (1997).

Pulzer, Peter, 'Nation-state and national sovereignty', *Bulletin of the German Historical Institute*, London, November 1995.

Rittberger, Volker and Schimmelfennig, Frank, 'German foreign policy after re-unification; on the applicability of theoretical models of foreign policy', Working Paper, Centre for German and European Studies, Georgetown University, 1997.

Schwarz, Hans-Peter, *Die Zentralmacht Europas, Deutschlands Rückkehr auf die Weltbühne* (Berlin: Siedler, 1994).

Schwilk, Heimo and Schacht, Ulrich (eds), *Die selbstbewußte Nation* (Berlin: Ullstein, 1994).

Weidenfeld, Werner (ed.), *Deutsche Europapolitik. Optionen wirksamer Interessenvertretung* (Bonn: Europa Union, 1998).

Zitelman, Rainer, Weißmann, Karlheinz and Großheim, Peter (eds), *Westbindung. Risiken und Chancen für Deutschland* (Berlin: Propyläen, 1993).

On European integration and Nato

Asmus, Ronald D., Kugler, Richard L. and Larrabee, F. Stephen, 'NATO expansion: the next steps', *Survival*, 37/1 (1995).

Beschloss, Michael and Talbott, Strobe, *Auf Höchster Ebene. Das Ende des Kalten Krieges und die Geheimdiplomatie der Supermächte 1988–1991* (Düsseldorf: Econ, 1994).

Bofinger, Peter, 'The political economy of the Eastern enlargement of the EU', Discussion Paper 1234, Centre for Economic Policy Research, London, 1995.

Bulmer, Simon and Paterson, William E., *The Federal Republic and the European Community* (London: Allen & Unwin, 1987).

Eyal, Jonathan, 'NATO's enlargement: anatomy of a decision', *International Affairs*, 73/4 (1997).

Fritsch-Bournazel, Renata, *Europa und die deutsche Einheit*, 2nd edn (Stuttgart: Bonn Aktuell, 1993).

Gaddis, John Lewis, *We Now Know. Rethinking Cold War History* (Oxford: Oxford University Press, 1997).

Geißmann, Hans-Joachim, *Sicherheitspolitik in Ostmitteleuropa* (Baden-Baden: Nomos, 1995).

Giering, Claus, 'Vertiefung durch Differenzierung – Flexibilisierungskonzepte in der aktuellen Reformdebatte', *integration*, 20/2 (1997).

Goldgeier, James M., 'NATO expansion: the Anatomy of a Decision', *Washington Quarterly*, 21/1 (1997).

Gordon, Philip H., *France, Germany, and the Western Alliance* (Oxford: Westview, 1995).

Grant, Charles, *Delors – Inside the House that Jacques built* (London: Nicholas Brealey, 1994).

Handl, Vladimir, 'Czech-German declaration on reconciliation', *German Politics*, 6/2 (1997).

Hyde-Price, Adrian, *European Security beyond the Cold War* (London: Royal Institute for International Affairs, 1991).

Hyde-Price, Adrian, *The International Politics of East Central Europe* (Manchester: Manchester University Press, 1996).

Janning, Josef, 'Am Ende der Regierbarkeit? Gefährliche Folgen der Erweiterung der Europäischen Union', *Europa-Archiv*, 22/1993 (1993).

Janning, Josef, 'Dynamik in der Zwangsjacke – Flexibilität in der Europäischen Union nach Amsterdam', *integration*, 20/4 (1997).

Keohane, Robert O., Nye, Joseph S. and Hoffmann, Stanley (eds), *After the Cold War* (Cambridge, MA: Harvard University Press, 1993.

Lippert, Barbara and Becker, Peter, 'Bilanz und Zukunft des Strukturierten Dialogs', *integration*, 20/2 (1997).

Lippert, Barbara and Schneider, Heinrich (eds), *Monitoring Association and Beyond. The European Union and the Visegrad States* (Bonn: Europa Union Verlag, 1995).

McCarthy, Patrick (ed.), *France–Germany, 1983–1993: The struggle to Cooperate* (London: Macmillan, now Palgrave, 1993).

Mandelbaum, Michael, *The Dawn of Peace in Europe* (New York: Twentieth Century Fund Press, 1996).

Maresceau, Marc (ed.), *Enlarging the European Union* (London and New York: Longman, 1997).

Marsh, David, *Germany and Europe. The Crisis of Unity* (London: Mandarin, 1995).

Mayhew, Alan, *Recreating Europe. The European Union's Policy towards Central and Eastern Europe* (Cambridge: Cambridge University Press, 1998).

Middlemas, Keith, *Orchestrating Europe. The Informal Politics of European Union 1973–1995* (London: Fontana, 1995).

Neumann, Iver B., 'Russia as Central Europe's constituting other', *East European Politics and Societies*, 7/2 (1993).

Paya, Jose Ignacio Torreblanca, *The European Community and Central and Eastern Europe 1989–1993: Foreign Policy and Decision-Making* (Madrid: Instituto Juan March de Eastudieos e Investigaciones, 1997).

Valance, Georges, *France-Allemagne. Le retour de Bismarck* (Paris: Flammarion, 1990).

Vedrine, Hubert, *Les Mondes de François Mitterrand* (Paris: Fayard, 1996).

Wolf, Reinhard, 'The doubtful mover: Germany and NATO expansion', in David J. Haglund (ed.), *Will NATO go East?* (Belfast: Queens University, Centre for International Relations, 1996).

Zelikow, Philip and Rice, Condoleezza, *Germany Unified and Europe Transformed* (Cambridge, MA: Harvard University Press, 1995).

Index